# Raising Happiness

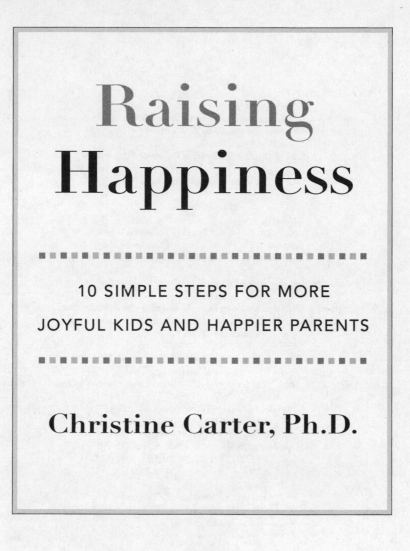

# Raising
# Happiness

## 10 SIMPLE STEPS FOR MORE
## JOYFUL KIDS AND HAPPIER PARENTS

## Christine Carter, Ph.D.

Ballantine Books Trade Paperbacks / New York

2011 Ballantine Books Trade Paperback Edition

Published in the United States by Ballantine Books,
an imprint of The Random House Publishing Group,
a division of Random House, Inc., New York.

BALLANTINE and colophon are registered trademarks of Random House, Inc.

Originally published in hardcover in the United States by Ballantine Books,
an imprint of The Random House Publishing Group, a division of
Random House, Inc., in 2010.

Library of Congress Cataloging-in-Publication Data
Carter, Christine.
Raising happiness : 10 simple steps for more joyful kids and happier parents / Christine Carter.
p.   cm.
Includes bibliographical references and index.
ISBN 978-0-345-51562-9
eBook ISBN 978-0-345-51932-0
1. Happiness in children.   2.  Child rearing.   I. Title.
BF723.H37C37 2010
646.7'8—dc22            2009044711

Printed in the United States of America

www.ballantinebooks.com

6 8 9 7 5

Book design by JoAnne Metsch

*For my parents,*
*Tim and Sylvia Carter,*
*the people who first taught me how important parents*
*and grandparents are for raising happiness.*


*And for my daughters,*
*Fiona and Molly, my muses and the great loves of my life.*

# CONTENTS

■ ■ ■ ■ ■ ■

CONTENTS

■■■■■■

# The Art and Science of Raising Happy Kids

*The most important work you and I will ever do will be within the walls of our own homes.*

—HAROLD B. LEE

Recently I was an observer at a sold-out parent education seminar about the epidemic levels of depression, suicide, and anxiety disorders affecting children. The lecturer asked the audience rhetorically, "What is it that we most want our children to be?" In stunning synchronicity, the audience roared, "*Happy.*"

Of course.

We parents want our children to grow into happy adults—but the trouble is, sometimes we feel as though our children's personalities are already more or less set in genetic stone: "Timmy is my sunny optimist, Ben is my Eeyore, and look—they've been raised in the same house. Clearly I have no control!" a friend recently exclaimed. The good news is that we actually *do* have a lot of influence: parenting practices have a tremendous effect on children's emotional outlook on life. Personality is not predetermined at birth, and neither is happiness. Nearly half—maybe more—of the factors that determine children's happiness can be attributed to the environments in which they are raised. That isn't to say that genetic makeup doesn't play a role; it does. But "it is biologically impossible for a gene to operate independently of its environment," explains Daniel Goleman, an expert on social and emotional intelligence. "Genes are *designed* to be regulated by signals from their immediate surroundings." These signals include, of course, what we do as parents.

So there is a lot that we can do to ensure our children's happiness—

and our own at the same time. In fact, there is a perpetual "buy one, get one free" special: teach your kids the skills they need to be happy, and you'll become happier yourself in the process.

**What does it mean to have a happy childhood?** Happiness, as I conceptualize it, is much more than a mood or a cheerful disposition. Rather, a happy life is one that is full of lots of different types of positive emotions. For example, positive emotions about the past, such as gratitude, forgiveness, and appreciation, are important components of a happy life, as are future-based positive emotions such as optimism, faith, and confidence. The field of sociology has long shown us that people find happiness through their connections to other people. Positive emotions such as love, kindness, and empathy help us make those connections. And present-based positive emotions such as joy and contentment are obvious ingredients in a happy childhood.

Kids become accustomed to different ways of thinking, feeling, and behaving based in large part on what we teach them about the world, their relationships, and our expectations. These habits profoundly influence how happy they are. That's what this book is all about: how to foster the skills, habits, and mind-sets that will set the stage for a wide range of positive emotions in childhood and beyond.

## BASED ON SCIENTIFIC RESEARCH

Everything in this book draws on scientific research related to happiness. Much of this research comes from the new field of "positive psychology." Social scientists used to focus solely on why people and society fall short: what makes depressed people so sad, what constitutes autism, why some cultures are racist and others harbor violent class conflict. Generally speaking, the aim of traditional social science is to understand dysfunction and relieve suffering. But in the last few years, social scientists across disciplines have turned their attention to the reverse: what makes happy people happy, functional families functional? Instead of trying to get something negative back to neutral—to get a depressed person functioning, perhaps—this science is about how parents and children can be happier, no matter where we are starting from.

As a sociologist and the executive director of the Greater Good Science Center at the University of California, Berkeley, I've made it my business to make the psychology, sociology, and neuroscience of raising happy children approachable to real people. That said, this book is also about me and my family. I have two daughters: Molly, age six, and Fiona, age eight. I'm not married to their father, Mike, anymore, but he and I work hard at being a great co-parenting team. My parents (the kids call them Nonie and Dadu) are part of our daily lives. So this book represents the intersection of my brain and my heart: my intellectual training in the social sciences and my very real, sometimes raw, experiences as a mother struggling daily to put the science into practice.

## IT IS NEVER TOO EARLY—OR TOO LATE—TO READ THIS BOOK

*Happiness is a continuous creative activity.*
                    —BABA AMTE

This is not a book targeted to children of a specific age, because children and adults of all ages benefit from practices that are scientifically proven to contribute to human happiness. *Raising Happiness* is about setting up your children to thrive. And you don't have to be a parent to read this book. Think of all the people who care about kids: teachers, grandparents, health-care providers, aunts and uncles, librarians, babysitters . . . the list goes on and on. Some of them spend a lot of time with our children each day. These people also contribute a lot to our kids' happiness skills. This is a book for all of us to read during pregnancy and keep handy through our kids' adolescence.

Why? According to a series of studies commissioned by The Lucile Packard Foundation for Children's Health, only about half of parents rate their children's overall emotional and behavioral health as excellent, and 67 percent worry that their teens are too stressed. But according to the same studies, the well-being of children is more important to adults than just about anything else—health care, the well-being of seniors, the cost of living, terrorism, and the war in Iraq. More than two-thirds of adults say they are "extremely concerned" about the well-being of children, and this concern cuts across gender, income, ethnicity, age, and political affiliation.

We have reason to be concerned: nearly a third of high school students have reported feeling sad or hopeless almost every day for two or more weeks in a row. Persistent sadness and hopelessness are predictors of clinical depression, and depression in youth is linked to anxiety disorders, suicidal behavior, obesity, and deficits in social functioning. Depressed youth are also much more likely to use drugs or alcohol, drop out of school, and engage in promiscuous sexual activities.

**The good news is that happiness is a skill that we can teach our children.** The new science of positive emotions shows that this seemingly crazy idea is, in fact, true. What we say and do with our children is far more important in determining their success and happiness than any God-given talent or innate disposition. For example:

## When Pregnant
Mothers who are anxious or stressed during pregnancy can hardwire their children to be anxious and fearful. Stress can damage unborn babies' nervous systems in a way that affects their ability to calm themselves and focus their attention. The good news: almost no hardwiring is permanent in a baby's brain, so this damage can be consciously reversed.

## In Infancy and Early Childhood
Emotional literacy is a skill that parents and other caregivers can begin teaching children virtually from birth and continuously throughout childhood. Emotional literacy, perhaps the most important skill for growing into a happy and successful adult, is the ability to regulate and understand emotions. Children who can regulate their emotions are better at soothing themselves when they are upset, which means that they experience negative emotions for a shorter period of time. In addition, emotionally literate children understand and relate to people better, form stronger friendships, and do better in school.

## In Adolescence
Parenting practices still matter a lot. Despite the popular notion that most teenagers are tormented and difficult, 70 percent of teenagers are actually happy—but their home and school environments are very different from those of their unhappy counterparts. One recent study shows that parenting moderates genetic vulnerabilities: teenagers who have a particular gene that makes them susceptible to substance abuse are much less likely to use drugs when their parents are involved and supportive.

It *is* possible to teach an old dog new tricks. Even if your children are older, happiness is still a skill that they can learn. Just by fostering gratitude in your home, for example, you can increase children's happiness by as much as 25 percent. You can sow the childhood seeds of adult happiness in your family, and you have plenty of time to do it. Our brains develop rapidly in early childhood, but they don't stop developing once we reach full height. We parents have two solid decades to help our children form happiness habits that can last a lifetime. And as you'll see in Chapter 1, our own brains remain plastic even in adulthood. This means you can even teach *yourself* to be happier. It is never too early or too late to start learning and teaching good happiness habits.

## IS HAPPINESS ACTUALLY IMPORTANT?

Hordes of parents sheepishly—but regularly—ask me about the connection between happiness and success. The crux of their questions: If I focus on my children's happiness, will they still rocket to the top of their classes? Go to Dartmouth? You'd be surprised how often people ask me if my own children are "annoyingly happy." In a culture fixated on high achievement, happiness can seem fluffy. Distracting. Certainly not serious enough to muster the effort and skill it takes to bring about.

Even if you prioritize your children's success over their happiness, here is why you should read this book: happiness is a tremendous advantage in a world that emphasizes performance. On average, happy people are more successful than unhappy people at both work and love. They get better performance reviews, have more prestigious jobs, and earn higher salaries. They are more likely to get married and, once married, they are more satisfied with their marriage.

Happy people also tend to be healthier and live longer. Each chapter in this book details the benefits that positive emotions bring to our well-being, our health, and our performance. In her groundbreaking research on positivity, psychologist Barbara Fredrickson has found that positive emotions

- Broaden our thinking in ways that make us more flexible, more able to see the big picture, and more creative

- Accumulate and compound over time, transforming us for the better by building the resources—strength, wisdom, friendship, and resilience—we need to truly thrive

- Are the most important ingredient in determining a person's resilience in hard times; positive emotions help our bodies and our minds cope with stress, challenge, and negative feelings

But what about negative emotions? Aren't they important, too? Is it possible, or even desirable, to be happy all the time? It turns out that among very happy people, those who are a tad less joyful than the happiest of happy actually have higher incomes, academic achievement, job satisfaction, and political participation than the happiest people. It follows that those with some feelings of discontentment—whether it is dissatisfaction with the status quo or an inclination to improve things—are probably more motivated toward action and therefore success. At work and in civic life, the desire for something better sets us in motion—to elect a new leader, secure a better job, negotiate a raise.

But it also turns out that the happiest group tends to have more friends and be luckier in love. Dissatisfaction with an intimate partner or friend isn't often a big relationship strengthener. In fact, evaluating partners in ultra-positive ways—perhaps even thinking they are more wonderful than they actually are—makes for a happier romantic union. My friend Casey's marriage bears out this research: at her wedding shower she said to us with conviction, "Imagine how many girls around the world are going to fall to their knees in agony the day Mark gets married." We all thought this was hilarious and tease her about it to this day, but she really felt it to be true. I asked her if she still feels the same way nearly fifteen years and two kids later. Her exact response: "Well, look at him! Who doesn't think he is super-hot? And he *has* embodied everything I always knew he had in him."

The takeaway: both positive and negative emotions have many functions, and both are important. To be successful, we should embrace some dissatisfaction in the realms of work and politics. To be truly happy, we should endeavor to appreciate—and maybe even exaggerate—the good in our relationships. Contentment with and acceptance of the people around us are critical for our ultimate happiness, so we need to teach our children to nurture—perhaps even romanticize—their most important relationships. This book will help you teach your kids to cultivate positive emotions and to understand and make negative emotions work for them rather than against them.

All of this is to say that happiness is not a fluffy or frivolous notion; it is the most important thing we can foster in ourselves and our children, for its own value and for its contributions to other things we value, such as professional and social success.

## OUT WITH GUILT, IN WITH JOY

*The most important thing she'd learned over the years was that there was no way to be a perfect mother and a million ways to be a good one.*

—Jill Churchill

As much as we would like to provide it, there is no such thing as a perfect childhood, and I hope you won't use this book to try to create one. In fact, as discussed in Chapter 3, striving for perfection—in our parenting, our children, in anything—rarely leads to lasting happiness. None of us will be a perfect parent, but like any endeavor worthy of genuine effort, we can all work toward being great parents.

Parents have enough to worry about without another expert adding to the list of things they might be doing wrong. I am not worried about the mistakes you are making as a parent: we all make mistakes all the time, especially me. (You will learn about my many errors, do-overs, and "wish I had done that differently" moments throughout *Raising Happiness*.) The trick, of course, is to learn from our mistakes.

Sometimes, guilt about not being a good enough parent is a warning sign that we're making a mistake or doing something wrong. But like many people who strive for excellence in parenting, I sometimes feel angst and guilt about past mistakes or things over which I have no control. In these cases, guilt is not a red flag so much as a choice: consciously or not, I'm choosing to hold myself to an unrealistic standard, or choosing to ruminate about a mistake rather than forgive myself. I feel guilty when instead I could be feeling gratitude for having learned something difficult, or for unintended positive outcomes. And guilt about past mistakes uses up my energy in the present, when I could be parenting effectively if I weren't distracted by the past.

The alternative to unproductive guilt and angst is to focus on what we can do right. We can teach our children happiness habits, such as consciously practicing gratitude. We can model optimism and teach forgiveness. We can make family dinners important. We can help our children forge friendships, and we can help them deal with pain when they are sad and angry. Most important, we can model happiness in ourselves.

But do we need to do all of these things—take on all ten steps outlined in this book—at once? Or ever?

Of course not. Any *one* of the steps outlined in this book is likely to measurably increase our children's happiness. So don't let *Raising Happiness* become another reason to feel guilty for not doing everything right. Let go of the guilt you feel for not being perfect. Learn to embrace your parenting mistakes as genuine paths to growth. Enjoy the effort you are putting into raising happy children and becoming a happier person yourself. All of these things are good enough in and of themselves. Instead of guilt, choose joy.

Parenting is one grand opportunity to find happiness in the messiness of life. When we engage, we will often trip and fall. But more often, hopefully, we will be simply amazed by the beauty and mystery of it all. At dinner last night, my friend Lisa described her most joyful moment this week: watching her kindergartner show off her jump-roping skills on stage at an all-school assembly. With a furrowed brow and fierce concentration, her daughter Helen jumped forward and backward, on one foot and two, to the tune of "I'm Walking on Sunshine." Lisa welled up with pride, not at Helen's stellar jump-roping skills but because her daughter was so *into* *it*. Happiness for Helen was learning to jump rope *and* having the courage to try it in front of 350 other kids.

*Raising Happiness* is about being like Lisa: not simply visiting this world of parenting, but being *in it*. Being continually amazed, moved, delighted. It isn't simply about dipping our toes in the pool; it is about diving in, headfirst. Diane Ackerman once remarked: "I don't want to get to the end of my life and find that I lived just the length of it. I want to have lived the width of it as well." This book is about living the width of our lives and teaching our children to do the same. It is about raising happy kids and, in so doing, becoming happier ourselves.

Ultimately, *Raising Happiness* is about making the world a better place. When we become better parents, our world improves measurably. In our materially rich but spiritually sparse culture, we often forget that this work we do as parents is important, essential. It *matters*—for our children's well-being and for the greater good of the world.

# Raising Happiness

# ONE

■ ■ ■ ■ ■ ■

# Step 1: Put on Your Own Oxygen Mask First

*Nothing has a stronger influence psychologically . . . on children than the unlived life of the parent.*

—CARL JUNG

## CONFESSIONS OF A SELFISH MOTHER

To my friends and neighbors, my life seems pretty crazy. "You're doing too much," people tell me constantly. I write a blog, and I of course wrote this book. I run the Greater Good Science Center at UC Berkeley. I give several talks a month about raising happy kids, and I teach a parenting class, which I love doing. I'm active on committees at schools and our church. I try to pick up my kids from school several times a week. I'm fortunate that my work hours are flexible, which means I do a lot of my work at, um, 4:30 in the morning.

I think the key to staying sane (and healthy) as an involved working parent is actually to do more rather than less: more for yourself, that is. I try to go to the gym several days a week, even though the classes I like best are occasionally during prime family time. I try to spend a good deal of time with my friends, with and without the kids, eating out, sharing belly laughs and soulful confessions. I paint and I read for pleasure. I go on meditation retreats. I might be doing a lot, but I am often wildly happy by any measure.

The only time that I don't do so well is when I let the balance shift too far toward taking care of my children's every need before my own. I get strep throat whenever I am run-down. When I was trying to finish writing this book, I wasn't getting enough sleep (if I wake up at 4:30 a.m. to get my work done, I have to go to sleep when the kids do), and I'd been to the gym only twice in a few weeks. I'd been working a lot, so I was always trying to maximize my time with the kids. To get back on track, I knew I needed to spend more time with my friends than I had been, and I needed to have some downtime—without the kids—doing something that nourished my soul. If I didn't? In addition to the strep throat, I started to feel fried and snippy with the kids. So instead of making the most of my limited time with Molly and Fiona, our interactions were colored by how quickly I became irritated with them because I was so tired and stressed. What I needed to do was trade time with my children for "me time" to exercise or hang out with friends.

Doing this seems pretty selfish, especially for someone who is so wholeheartedly committed to my child-rearing project. *Am* I selfish? Should I be working less and spending more time with the kids, or working *more* in order to provide greater economic stability? Should I be making more and bigger personal sacrifices for my children? Would my kids benefit from more time with me? Would they be happier or better prepared for adulthood if I joined them riding bikes at the local elementary school instead of painting on Sunday afternoons? Is it narcissistic to even think that my children's well-being improves with each additional minute they spend with me?

I know the answers to these questions: my own personal happiness, nourished by the time I take for myself, benefits my children. I've read the scientific studies that prove this.

So out with the guilt, and in with the joy. This chapter will tell you *why* it is so important that you put your own oxygen mask on first—why you should take care of your own happiness before you try to teach your kids the skills they'll need to be happy. Along the way you'll get a tour of the rest of the book and a lot of tips for how to be happy yourself.

This chapter is also about that other thing that is so important to take care of *before* you take care of your kids: your marriage, if you've got one, or your relationship with your children's other parent, if you've got that. The quality of a marriage is a huge component of parents' happiness, and it can have a huge influence on our children. So much so that more than half of this chapter is dedicated to getting along with your co-parent.

*Fix your marriage,* you say? *But aren't you single?* It's true: all the science-based advice given below related to keeping a marriage strong didn't work for me, and believe me, I tried. I thought that I could fix my marriage through the sheer force of my own will. But I couldn't, and now I know that no amount of effort would have fixed it.

So some of you are probably thinking that you shouldn't take my advice about marriage because it didn't work for me. The great thing, though, is that all of the advice in this book is based on scientific research, not my opinion. Which is good, because actually I've failed at a lot more than just marriage. Come to think of it, I have failed at least once in just about everything I espouse in this book. For example, there are long periods of time in my life when I've failed to practice gratitude (Chapter 4), and when I've neglected my friendships (Chapter 2). I spent my childhood as a perfectionist and fixed–mind-set thinker (Chapter 3). I've been too permissive in my parenting at times; other times I've been too bossy (Chapter 7). I *twice* chose terrible child care for my children (Chapter 9). I have made a *lot* of mistakes as a parent.

Which is why I'm a big fan of social science. I have learned and grown as a person and a parent by mining all this research for ways to correct my mistakes. Often what I've found is that the research points me in a direction that is totally different from the path that I was on before, or backs up something I thought I knew but just wasn't sure of. One of the most important things I've learned? Take care of yourself and your marriage first. Before you start worrying about raising happy kids, get yourself—and your marriage if you've got one—to a happier place.

## WHY PUT YOUR OWN HAPPINESS FIRST?

Our own happiness as parents influences our children's happiness in a variety of ways. Extensive research has established a substantial link between mothers who feel depressed and "negative outcomes" in their children, such as acting out and other behavior problems. Parental depression actually seems to cause behavior problems in kids; it also makes our parenting less effective. It bothers kids to see their parents upset and unhappy, and kids' bad behavior expresses this. Depressed parents are also less effective in their parenting, so they are less likely to correct bad behavior in constructive ways. Depressed mothers tend to be less sensitive and proactive in responding to their children's needs, and they are less likely to play with their children in emotionally positive ways. The children of mothers who are chronically depressed—those whose feelings of sadness and despair persist—perform worse on tests of school readiness, they use less expressive language, and they have poorer social skills. And it isn't just depression. Anxiety in mothers (something I'm prone to) is associated with increased anxiety in children.

So if I fail to put my own oxygen mask on first (by not getting the sleep or exercise I need, for example) and I become depressed or chronically anxious, my children may suffer. There is also compelling evidence for the flip side of this equation: when I do what it takes for my own happiness, my children will reap the benefits.

The first reason this is true is simply that kids mimic their parents, especially when the kids are younger. Children imitate their parents' emotions as early as six days old; it is one of the primary ways that they learn and grow. So if we model happiness—and all the skills that go with it—our kids are likely to imitate what we do. If I model key happiness habits such as kindness and generosity, for example, my daughters are more likely to become kind and generous.

And because research shows that people's emotions tend to converge—we become more similar emotionally the more we are together—it follows that the happier I am, the happier my children will be. My friend and colleague Dacher Keltner (we run the Greater Good Science Center together) and his colleagues conducted an interesting series of experiments that show that people in close relationships become more similar to each other over time. The researchers documented that the emotions and emotional reactions of friends and lovers actually become more alike over the course of a year. Moreover, it is the person with the least power in a relationship who becomes more emotionally similar to the other. This is why parents who tend to explain things optimistically tend to have kids who mimic their explanatory styles—as humans, we're wired for mimicry. Another study attempting to determine how much shared genetics account for the similar emotional outlooks of parents and children came up short: although the study did find that happy parents are statistically more likely to have happy children, it couldn't find any genetic component. Like those of roommates and lovers, the emotions of children and parents can be very similar, but not because the people involved are cut from the same cloth, so to speak.

Emotions in general are just plain contagious (more on this in Chapter 5). A political scientist from the University of California, San Diego, and a Harvard sociologist have recently documented that happiness is particularly contagious. Their conclusion, which is based on an analysis of people's social connections over twenty years, is that our happiness depends in part on the happiness of the people we are connected to. Having happy friends, neighbors, and siblings who live in close proximity to you (as adults) increases your odds of being happy. In other words, the positive emotions of one community member spread readily to others.

So I say, take the advice of the airlines: put on your oxygen mask first and *then* help those around you. I'm *not* saying *don't* help those around you; I'm saying that should you become faint from lack of oxygen, you won't be much good to anyone at all. Speaking for myself, I've found that a certain core of peace and centeredness is necessary before I can really be engaged in raising happy, compassionate, and confident children.

## HOW TO BE HAPPY

*Realize that true happiness lies within you. Waste no time and effort searching for peace and contentment and joy in the world outside. Remember that there is no happiness in having or in getting, but only in giving. Reach out. Share. Smile. Hug.*

—OG MANDINO

Scientists have recently had a lot to say—handily explained for you in this book—about what it takes to find true happiness and meaning in life. Although the focus of this book is on children and how to teach them the skills they need for happiness, most of the same principles apply to adults. It is never too late to become a happier person, even if you had an unhappy childhood yourself. Although we scientists once believed that there was a "happiness set point"—that no matter what we do, we mostly stay or return to about the same level of happiness throughout our lives—we now have compelling evidence that this simply isn't so. Consider, for example, that the happiness level of adults in one large study changed significantly over seventeen years for fully 25 percent of the participants. Ten percent of participants' happiness levels changed by three points or more on a ten-point scale. So happiness is better thought of as a collection of habits rather than a genetically endowed trait.

There are lots of ways to increase your happiness, and some aren't necessarily better than others. My blog readers once incited a heated debate about whether or not it is better to, say, save the planet or take care of women in a shelter than it is to spend time on yourself in order to re-center and rejuvenate. I am all for altruism as a route to lasting happiness, and I spend a good deal of time volunteering; Chapter 2 covers the hows and whys of finding happiness through helping others. That said, I tend to see the parents around me giving and doing for everyone else first before taking care of their own needs. Here are some simple things you can do this week to get a little more oxygen.

**Go out with your friends and have a few laughs.** Our well-being is best predicted by how connected we feel to other people. Do we have lots of friends? Know our neighbors? Are we close to our extended family? Care about our co-workers? People with a lot of social connections are less likely to experience sadness, loneliness (duh), low self-esteem, and problems with eating and sleeping.

So to bring on some lasting happiness, we need to nurture our social connections over the long haul. But a date night or a poker night or a girls' night out can—not surprisingly—bring us instant happiness as well, and I'm not talking about the kind you imbibe. The laughter we share with our buddies (or anyone, really) literally changes our body chemistry by retarding that pesky fight-or-flight stress system. A good guffaw—or even a little giggle—causes our heart rate and blood pressure to drop and our muscles to relax.

Because laughter is contagious, hang out with friends or family members who are likely to be laughing themselves. Their laughter will get you laughing, too, although it doesn't even need to in order to lighten your mood. Neuroscientists believe that hearing another person laugh triggers mirror neurons in a region of the brain that makes listeners feel as though they are actually laughing themselves. For more information about how social connections build our happiness foundations, skip straight to Chapters 2 and 5.

**Have your kids or partner give you a massage or a pedicure.** There really is such a thing as a magic touch. Like laughter, being touched in a positive way can also trigger biochemical reactions that make us feel good. Getting a massage or being touched—even just briefly—by a loved one can increase activation in the orbitofrontal cortex, a part of the brain where we feel pleasure. Touch also reduces the cardiovascular stress response and decreases our levels of stress hormones such as cortisol. Touch is essential to our physical and mental well-being; without it we wither and perish.

So a massage is a very appropriate and highly recommended happiness booster, not just a frivolous luxury. Dacher's research shows that touch is the primary language of compassion, trust, love, and gratitude. It promotes the release of oxytocin in our systems, which will make us feel more bonded to the person giving the massage.

**Take some quiet time for yourself.** What does a monk who has clocked thousands of hours meditating have that you don't? Let's see: he has peace and quiet. His clothing is surely free from someone else's spit-up and sandbox dirt. Also, the part of his brain that is responsible for happiness is bigger. This is because the brain is like a muscle, and if you train your mind the way monks do, you will change your brain.

The appeal of a massage or quiet escape for me doesn't come just from the positive effects of touch; it comes from the possibility of some quiet time for reflection or meditation. Want to turn your brain waves that signal stress into those that indicate bliss? Start meditating. Do it enough and research suggests that you will increase activity in the area of your brain that is active when you feel happiness (the left prefrontal cortex).

Neuroscience of yesteryear held that our brains were pretty much done growing when we reached full height. Now we know that our brain is more like a muscle—use a particular area a lot and it will grow. As science writer Sharon Begley describes in her book *Train Your Mind, Change Your Brain,* studies of Tibetan monks show that meditation is a particularly effective way to grow the part of your brain that registers positive emotions. We Westerners freely accept that if we want to excel at something such as music, athletics, or learning a new language, we need to train and practice hard. However, we rarely think that we can also train and practice to be happier—something that Buddhists have long known. Meditation is concentrated happiness training. Chapter 8 will get you started on this.

If after reading the above on meditation, you think, "Huh. I'm sticking to the pedicure," don't give up altogether on taking some quiet time. Instead, create some alone time to begin a gratitude journal. Writing about things you feel grateful for is a simple way to bring more joy into your life. People who "practice gratitude" feel considerably happier than those who do not; they are more joyful, enthusiastic, interested, and determined. In one study, researchers had people list five things they felt grateful for once a week for ten weeks. At the end of the study, participants "felt better about their lives as a whole and were more optimistic about the future." Chapter 4 is all about how you can practice gratitude to become happier.

**Get some exercise.** Lots of new research is showing that exercise, for many people, is probably just as effective as drugs for treating some types of depression. Regular exercise will make you smarter as well as happier, and it will boost your self-esteem. Most of us know we need to cultivate the habit of getting more exercise; read about the method described in Chapter 6 to do this.

**Put yourself in touch with the natural world.** Spending time in nature has been shown to increase our positive emotions and clear our minds. Take a walk in the woods or a hike in the mountains, sit by a river or creek, nap in a meadow or by the ocean: whatever you have available to you will work. One experiment showed that just viewing photographs of nature helped improve people's attention and intellectual functioning, but for the full effect, find the most expansive natural setting you can and spend some time there.

**But don't go shopping.** That is one thing that many of us do for fun that won't result in lasting happiness. Materialistic people are more likely to be depressed or anxious and have low self-esteem. The more we seek happiness in material things, the less likely we are to find it. More about how materialism is a happiness buster is in Chapter 9.

## Fix Your Co-parenting Relationship

To state the obvious: it takes time to work on a relationship. Time you might otherwise be spending with your children. But the research shows that working on your relationship with your co-parent—even if you aren't married—can influence your kids' well-being. So even if it means giving up a little time with the kids to become better friends with whoever is helping you raise them, I say: make it a priority.

There is good news on all fronts. First of all, we don't need to worry that we are spending less time with the kiddos than traditional parents did during that supposedly blissful era of the nuclear family, circa 1965. Research shows that more than half of us feel guilty about how little time we spend with the kids. I'm here to say, let it go. We're not spending less time with our kids than our parents spent with us. Married mothers now spend 21 percent more time caring for their children than they did back then! Dads are stepping up, too: though they still spend less than half the time caring for kids that moms do, they've doubled the amount of time they spend since *Leave It to Beaver* was the gold standard. How can this be? Aren't we all super-busy?

Well, we do a lot of multitasking now. We eat takeout. We don't iron our sheets. We spend less time with our friends and family and—you guessed it—spouse. Which brings me back to my point: prioritize your relationship with that co-parent of yours—even if you aren't married—because your relationship with your children's other parent is very important for their happiness. Psychologists Phil and Carolyn Cowan have been studying marriage and parenting for decades, and this is what they want you to know: if you improve your parenting, you won't necessarily improve your marriage. But if you improve your marriage, you *will* improve your parenting.

Research psychologist and prolific author John Gottman has also been studying strong marriages and healthy relationships for a long time, and he's identified the most important things that partners can do to improve their relationship over the long run. The two main things we need to do, Gottman says, are (1) handle conflict in a positive manner (see "How to Fight," page 18) and (2) become better friends.

### TRY THIS

## Five Hours to a Better Relationship

Gottman has a three-part prescription for strengthening your marital bond. If you aren't married to your children's other parent, I challenge you to follow this prescription anyway. (Save the five minutes of sexually charged grabbing.)

1. **Start building fondness and affection, pronto.** A good friend of mine is a pro at doing this with his ex-wife. Yes, you read that right: his *ex*-wife, the mother of his son. He's always talk-

ing up his first wife's great qualities as a mother. And when he talks to her on the phone, you can hear the appreciation and fondness in his voice, even if they are discussing the logistics of school pick-ups and Saturday games. It isn't that he is still in love with his ex (in fact, there is a lot that she does that bugs him, and he's happily remarried to someone else); he just recognizes that she is doing a good job raising their son, and he appreciates it.

2. **Be aware of—and responsive to—what is going on in your co-parent's life.** The best predictor of a wife's marital satisfaction, according to one study of couples with young children, was her husband's affection and attentiveness.

3. **Approach problems as something you both have control of and can solve together as partners.** In *The Seven Principles for Making Marriage Work,* John Gottman has a whole chapter of exercises for becoming closer to your co-parent. (I also recommend the workshop that Gottman does with his wife, Julie, entitled "The Art & Science of Love.") There is, of course, the all-important date night. But beyond that, John and Julie Gottman have found that small positive actions, done frequently, make the biggest difference. They write about the "magic five hours a week" as being an important intimacy-building tool. Five hours may seem like a lot in a hectic week, but when you look at how they recommend spending those hours, it seems doable.

   - Two minutes every weekday morning: Don't leave for work or school or whatever without knowing something about what lies ahead for your partner.

   - Twenty minutes when you get home: Decompress a little together before you plunge headlong into your evening routine. Listen actively to your partner, and be supportive. Think twice before you start offering advice at this time. The goal is to listen.

   - Five minutes every day: Show a little respect and admiration. Add a little to the economy of gratitude in your household. Every single day, find something you appreciate about your partner. Give genuine praise.

- Five minutes every day: Give a little lovin'. Kiss, grab, hold, hug, and otherwise touch your guy or gal for at least five minutes a day. Here's to hoping it lasts more than five minutes!

- Two hours a week: Schedule time to get to know your partner better. Play games where you ask each other questions, or use the time to resolve a problem. If you don't have time or can't afford to go on a date, be creative. Enjoy a glass of wine in the living room after the kids are in bed, or swap babysitting with another family and just go for a walk together.

The Gottmans' "magic five hours" is a series of happiness habits that will help you *and* your children. Gradually make each of the above "tasks" a routine part of your relationship. Your relationship will flourish and so will your children!

## Your Paltry Sex Life

I remember expecting that after I had kids I might be too busy or too tired or too saggy for a robust sex life, but I didn't think in my wildest dreams that I might be too bitchy. Anyone who has ever had a watermelon-sized miracle come out of her vagina or through her abdominal wall knows that birth itself, and the stress of child rearing that follows, can test even the most vigorous sex lives. But getting or keeping your sex life on track has—you guessed it—important implications for our children's happiness. Read on to learn how to put a little va-voom back in your bedroom.

The quality of a couple's sex life tends to get steadily worse over the course of a marriage, so if it isn't as hot as it used to be, you aren't alone. Sex is less satisfying *and* less frequent when we're married with children: about 50 percent of parents in one study described their sex life as "poor" or "not very good" when their first baby was eight months old.

How often we do it tends to decline the longer we stay married. Most couples have a lot of sex in the first year they are married—the "honeymoon effect"—but all that rabbit-like activity drops off precipitously around the end of the first year. Once we have children, biology starts to grind on us. Rutgers University anthropologist Helen Fisher, who studies the brain circuitry of romantic love, says millions of years of evolutionary adaptation account for a couple's differing sexual interests after kids are born. For instance, when a woman is nursing her child, levels of the hormone oxytocin surge, which makes her feel intense attachment to her baby. Testosterone levels, which are related to sex drive, plummet. "Mom's not just overly tired and making excuses—she's drugged," Dr. Fisher says. "From a Darwinian, evolutionary perspective . . . both parents are fighting a basic evolutionary mechanism that evolved to strengthen the mother/infant and parental bond, not the sexual bond."

One of the most important predictors of how often a couple does the no-pants dance is how happy they are with the marriage, which to a certain extent puts our paltry sex lives back into our control (see "Try This: Five Hours to a Better Relationship," page 11). There are also some other gender differences at work that often leave their mark in the bedroom. Men, on average, want to have sex four times a week, while the average woman would be happy with just once. If you want a more boisterous sex life, here are some insights that might help you stimulate your sweetie's libido.

1. Women often resent men for not helping out more around the house and with the children, and that anger usually does not fire a parallel passion in the loins. If you want more sex from a yummy mummy, rethink your ideas about foreplay. Pre-kid romance: bringing her flowers, commenting on her hot tush, nuzzling her neck. Post-kid romance: folding the laundry without her asking *and* putting it away, then noticing that she seems exhausted and running her a bath while you take on whatever tedious household task she was trying to finish.

2. Another generalization supported by scientific research: sex tends to mean different things for men than it does for women. Women see sex as an expression of pre-existing emotional intimacy, while men see sex as the path to that intimacy. Women tend to be more satisfied with sex and marriage when their partners behave lovingly and affectionately toward them, and they commonly cite things that indicate verbal intimacy—such as having a heartfelt conversation—as something that leads to sexual activity. In contrast, men tend to be less interested in verbal affection and intimacy and more often report that physical desire for their partner leads them to initiate sex. Here's the takeaway:

verbal intimacy—those deep discussions where you really connect in a positive way—can stoke the fire. If you aren't having sex
as often as you'd like, start by connecting with your partner
through conversation.

Despite these dismal gender differences, here's some better news: sexual famine is not necessarily a given after we have kids. The majority of
couples get back to having sex about twice a week, and research supports
what many of my friends and I have experienced: women hit their sexual
peak in their thirties. Studies show that women describe themselves as
"more lustful, seductive, and sexually active" in their thirties than at any
other time in their lives; some experts believe women's sexual peaks occur
even in their forties. I think that a woman's sexual peak also probably co-
incides with her youngest child going off to kindergarten—or at least with
the end of pregnancies and breast-feeding.

But until biology starts working for you again, researchers recommend
finding a way to resist those forces—social, interpersonal, and biological—
that throw water on the flames as best you can. A good number of well-
known therapists recommend scheduling sex with your partner if you can't
seem to make it happen any other way. I don't agree with this suggestion
because it seems cold and unromantic. Sure, we need to block off time to
connect with each other—it's called date night. And I'm certainly not opposed to plotting your moves several days in advance to get yourself juiced
up before a big date with your honey. But scheduling time to do the deed
itself?

Anyway, research shows that time is not necessarily the biggest obsta-
cle to a healthy sex life. On average, busy couples with kids and two full-
time jobs don't have sex less than couples with a stay-at-home parent. The
factors discussed above are what get in the way, so I think you are better off
focusing on those things than blocking out fifteen minutes for a quickie.

On the other hand, any kind of sexual interaction triggers a wash of
feel-good chemicals in our brains. This is evidence enough for me that
once we are happily married, we'll do best to think of sex like exercise: we
might be loath to get off the couch at first, but once we get going we'll be
glad we did. (The first push-up is always the hardest.) Because intimacy
in our relationships is so strongly linked to marital satisfaction, it is important to keep those hearth fires alive if we want our marriages to sur-
vive until our children leave the nest, when many marriages experience a
renaissance.

## SHOULD WE STAY TOGETHER FOR THE KIDS?

This is a question that I myself have pondered a lot. As a society we tend to think that it is better for the kids if we stay together; it is what our grandparents' generation did, or tried to do. Many people believe that a mediocre marriage is better for kids than no marriage. We might think that in part because of a hugely flawed—but influential and well-publicized—study by psychologist Judith Wallerstein that "showed" that kids don't notice that their parents were unhappy in a marriage. Wallerstein argued that unless domestic violence is part of the picture, kids are worse off when parents divorce. The study, while embraced by the press and published as a *New York Times* best-selling book, has been rejected wholeheartedly by social scientists because Wallerstein didn't use a random sample of families that divorce or stay together, but instead used a group of divorced people with mental health problems. Her research doesn't meet accepted scientific standards, and it should not be generalized to families that aren't struggling with the same things that Wallerstein's tiny sample was being treated for (usually histories of mental illness, clinical depression, and suicidal tendencies).

Here is what I've gleaned from the many good studies I've read on the subject: it is the *quality*, not the *status* (married or not) of a parental relationship that matters most for kids' well-being. Parental conflict isn't good for children's happiness, whether or not you are married. "Studies of two-parent families have consistently found that when a couple's relationship is characterized by unresolved conflict and unhappiness, their children tend to have more acting-out aggressive behavior problems, more shy withdrawn behavior, and fewer social and academic skills," say UC Berkeley researchers Phil and Carolyn Cowan. Furthermore, when couples aren't getting along, their irritation or anger with each other often spills over into their relationships with their children. "Some children get a double whammy," say the Cowans. They suffer the consequences of the "heated or frosty emotional tone of their parents' relationship" and the frequent result of co-parent conflict: "harsh or ineffective patterns of caring and discipline."

I know that when my husband and I fought, I would have a hard time managing the powerful negative emotions that surfaced (anger, disappointment, hurt) while trying to keep Fiona and Molly's routines on track effectively. And I could usually win all the awards for poor parenting if I also needed to handle a situation with the kids that required calm, consistent discipline. When I'm already upset, I tend to discipline the kids in a way that is, uh, not calm or collected.

So should you stay together for the kids? It depends on how high-conflict your marriage is, how unhappy you are, and whether or not you can fix these things.

## Fighting Like Dogs and Cats?

Parents fight. But how we fight and how we resolve our conflicts can have a huge influence on our children's health and happiness. A substantial body of research shows that conflict between parents, whether or not they are married, puts kids at increased risk for all sorts of problems: depression, anxiety, disobedience, aggression, delinquency, poor self-esteem, antisocial behaviors, trouble sleeping, academic underachievement, and low social competence—even health problems. Suffice it to say that fighting with your co-parent is not a happiness habit for your kids.

Some conflict may be inevitable, but listen: conflict between parents (whether or not they are married) is a big problem for kids' happiness and functioning. Certain types of arguing with your co-parent can even affect your unborn fetus. Researcher Alyson Shapiro found that how a couple argues when pregnant can predict over half of the variation in the baby's ability to establish calm and focusing attention when it is three months old. (The good news is that the damage can be reversed.)

And if you aren't yet motivated to improve the way you fight, consider this: the way you fight with your co-parent is how your teenager is most likely to fight with you. If you resolve conflicts by becoming angry, so too will your adolescent. On the other hand, if you engage in more constructive problem solving, your teen is likely to mimic that as well.

TRY THIS

### How to Fight

Here is a quick lesson, based on decades of research, on how to fight with your co-parent in a way that won't scar your children. As with most things, we parents are modeling important behaviors for our children when we fight with our beloveds (or ex-beloveds). Conflict is a part of life, and exposure to it can be an important lesson in emotional literacy for kids if it is handled in the correct way.

There are three healthy things, according to researcher John Gottman, that couples in stable marriages do to resolve conflict positively. Remember, what is good for your partnership is also good for your kids.

1.  Sugarcoat your complaints a little bit, as you would with a good friend whose feelings you don't want to hurt. (Gottman calls this the "soft start-up.") I'm a big fan of directness, so I do this wrong all the time. Mike once revealed that he scheduled a business trip in the middle of what was supposed to be our first-ever family vacation. Real-life marriage *don't*: I said, "What were you thinking? Don't you care enough about us to have our vacation on your calendar? What do I have to do, keep your calendar for you? Do you really expect me to be your secretary?" It was ugly, and—not surprisingly—the conversation didn't go well. I should have softened my start-up, saying, "Uh, Mike? Come look at the calendar and check out when you scheduled your trip to Boston. Did you realize your trip conflicts with our vacation?" That probably would have done the trick.

2.  Calm down. Take a break from the discussion if it gets too heated. Research shows that it is particularly important for men to take some time to get their heart rate down if they are starting to get really angry. Agree on a time, maybe a half hour later, to get back together and reopen the discussion. Then go do something to get your mind off the fight for a little while. If you know how to meditate, this is the time to do it. If you struggle with getting too worked up during a fight, you've got to learn how to calm yourself down. Whatever you do, don't go off into some corner to sulk, or plot out your winning arguments, as I am prone to do. (I've been

known to jot down key points to make my argument airtight. This is not a good way to reduce the adrenaline coursing through my veins.) The goal is to chill out so you can come back to the discussion feeling calm.

3. Master the art of negotiation. This means you need to accept the influence of your partner, even if at first you think he or she is being totally irrational. Gottman recommends the "Aikido principle: Yield to win." This is the simple fact that if you want to "win" an argument, you cannot simply counter everything your "opponent" says, as this will only escalate the fight. What we need to do is get our partner to agree with us on at least some points, and to do this we must find something we agree with in what our partner is saying. This is a tough one for me, given my stunning gift for argument and tendency to think I'm 100 percent right.

   Eileen Healy, a family counselor and author of the book *EQ and Your Child,* cautions that this strategy, if done wrong, can lead to a solution that no one is happy with. For example: I give something up, then you give something up, then I give . . . until there is nothing left that either of us wants. That much compromise isn't going to resolve the conflict satisfactorily. Eileen stresses that the art of negotiation involves positive problem solving, and we should work on it until we both feel as though we have a good solution, or at least one we are both willing to try.

Here are some more commonsense things that the research reminds us: high-conflict relationships are more damaging to children when kids actually witness the conflict. (Which isn't to say that lots of conflict between partners that the kids *don't* witness is okay; it is just the lesser of two evils.) Virtually all angry interactions, including nonverbal ones, make your kids feel bad. And, of course, disrespectful fighting—name calling, putting down, swearing—is damaging to children.

Interestingly, simply ending an argument with an apology, by "agreeing to disagree," by withdrawing, or with a simple submission aren't ideal outcomes from the children's perspective. Though these are seemingly low-conflict ways to end a fight, conflict resolution from one (but not both) of the parents' perspectives is not necessarily resolution from the kids' perspective. If you can't resolve the argument in front of the kids, be sure to demonstrate later that the relationship has been repaired, show them that you've reconnected, and tell them how the conflict was resolved.


As Rudolf Dreikurs famously warned, "Children are great perceivers but poor interpreters." Kids feel it deeply when their parents fight or when they are unhappy themselves. Kids are great perceivers of emotion and tension, but most often they think that they are responsible for their parents' fighting, or even for their parents' unhappiness, which can make them distressed, anxious, and even depressed. The good news is that research has shown again and again that conflict that is repaired positively and respectfully has the most beneficial effects on those little people with big ears. When kids see us resolve our differences, and when they see us take charge of our own well-being, they learn skills that will serve them well for a lifetime.

# TWO

■ ■ ■ ■ ■ ■

# Step 2: Build a Village

*Call it a clan, call it a network, call it a tribe, call it a family: Whatever you call it, whoever you are, you need one.*

—JANE HOWARD

What is the key to happiness? Hands down, that is the most frequent question I am asked at parties and when I give talks to professional groups, parents, teachers, and teenagers. Everyone, everywhere wants to know: What really makes us happy? Is it sex? Money? Yoga?

If I had to pick the one thing that matters most to human happiness, I would say that our relationships with other people matter more than anything else. Very happy people have stronger social relationships than less happy people, in part because being happy makes people want to be your friend, and in part because having friends makes us happier.

Truly, our happiness and our relationships are so closely linked that they can practically be equated. People with many friendships are less likely to experience sadness, loneliness, low self-esteem, and problems with eating and sleeping. Our social ties buffer us from stress, making us healthier physically and emotionally. Sharing positive events and feelings with others increases our happiness as well. In his extensive work on the link between relationships and happiness, psychologist David Myers concludes that "there are few stronger predictors of happiness than a close, nurturing, equitable, intimate, lifelong companionship with one's best friend." I would expand that notion to include all of our relationships: there is no stronger predictor of happiness than how robust and positive our "village" is. The same thing goes for our children. We all know that "it takes a village to raise a child," but how many of us feel that our children are truly embedded in a strong network of friends and parents, relatives and neighbors?

Despite the fact that technology and social media (Facebook, Twitter, texting) make it easier than ever to be "connected" to lots of people all the time, Americans are becoming less and less connected to one another. As a parent, it makes me think about how we spend our time: if our happiness is best predicted by the quantity and quality of our relationships with others, how can we foster lots of strong relationships within our family and our communities? I often feel so busy—sometimes too busy to spend time with my friends. But then I think about what I'm modeling. If I'm too busy for my friends, what *do* I have time for? Little is more important for our comprehensive well-being than our relationships, especially for kids: relationships prove to be among those things that have the most significant effect on kids' healthy growth and well-being.

There are two aspects to "building a village" for your children to thrive within. The first way is to teach kids the skills they need to be good at making and keeping friends. How well children establish relationships with other people greatly affects their happiness in childhood and later in life. Children consistently rejected by their peers have more problems; for example, they are more likely to get in trouble with the law, do poorly in school, or have psychiatric problems as adults. But kids who develop strong relationships and are socially intelligent—as emotional intelligence guru Daniel Goleman calls it—tend to flourish.

Socially intelligent kids are able to establish rapport with those around them, reading others' emotions and responding in ways that build friendships and deepen connections. How can parents help their children develop the social intelligence they need to build a thriving village? Many of the happiness habits outlined in this book—such as developing emotional literacy (Chapter 5) or practicing gratitude and forgiveness (Chapter 4)— make us happier because they foster deeper and more positive connections with others. This chapter addresses some other factors that also foster social skills and deepen our relationships: establishing rapport, resolving conflict, and raising kids to be kind and giving people.

The second, and perhaps more obvious, way that parents can build their children's village is to foster kids' relationships with all of their "other-parents." Society as a whole puts a lot of pressure on mothers to be and provide everything that children need for happiness. But fathers are also very important for children's happiness and well-being, as are grandparents, aunts and uncles, and our close adult friends. We need to embed our children in rich communities of relationships with whom they can hone their social skills. These relationships will provide them with a deep sense of security and be sources of joy and growth; they will feed their souls.

## ESTABLISHING RAPPORT

Everyone knows someone who seems to immediately click with anyone they meet. My friend Phillip is like this. Talking to Phillip, you feel his warmth and genuineness. You sense that he really understands you, and that he is riveted by your conversation. When you talk to someone who is as socially intelligent as Phillip, you "experience being experienced," as Daniel Goleman puts it. When you establish rapport with another person, you are so in tune with each other that your nonverbal communication—how you move your hands and eyebrows, your posture—actually start to converge. Talking with Phillip, I notice that when he touches his cheek, I unconsciously touch mine. I lean forward, and so does he. Phillip is so socially intelligent he can tune in to nearly anyone's feelings right away, establishing a warm and engaging rapport.

Researchers have learned that there are tricks (or, for some people, habits) that allow people to tune in to other people, establishing full rapport quickly. Specifically, there are two components that we can practice with our kids:

1. Eye contact. Studies show that eye contact opens our neural pathways for empathy. If we are looking someone in the eye when they hurt themselves, for example, our own facial expression is more likely to mimic the pain on the injured person's face. Similarly, people who are negotiating a conflict are more likely to cooperate—which realizes higher gains for both sides—when they negotiate face-to-face. My friend Jack, who has practiced Zen and Aikido for nearly twenty years and has the patience to show for it, doesn't often rush into verbal conversation with his kid. Instead he'll get down at his son's level and look him in the eye until Logan settles, until they're connected through eye contact. Mutual eye contact also engenders the second element of rapport—positive emotion—because the intense attention we give each other makes us feel good.

2. Positive emotion. We also communicate a significant amount of information nonverbally through our tone of voice and facial expressions. In one study, employees whose managers gave them negative feedback while still exhibiting warm feelings—their voices and expressions were compassionate and positive—came away feeling positive about the conversation. We can use this to establish rapport with our children even when we are correcting them or otherwise delivering bad news: if our faces and tone of voice say "I love you," even when what we are literally saying might be hard to hear, our kids are likely to still feel okay about the interaction. Kids need to practice this somewhat tricky communication skill. For example, Fiona was invited for a playdate at her friend Cecy's house when she already had plans with another girl. She knew that Cecy would be disappointed and maybe even feel a little left out. But Fiona and I practiced delivering the news in a way that showed Cecy just how much Fiona loves her. Watching the girls, you would have thought they were sharing a very special private moment: Fiona approached Cecy, put one hand on her shoulder, and said, "I can't come play because I'm going to Maggie's house." Then the girls shared a long hug. No hard feelings, just a lotta love.

The ability to establish rapport is at the very heart of social intelligence. We can tell when our kids are getting good at it when we start to see "synchrony" in their interactions with others. Synchrony is the only element of rapport that is probably impossible to practice. A high-rapport interaction is like synchronized swimming: it looks like a dance, the conversational back-and-forth flowing freely, as though it was well planned. People who have established rapport draw closer to one another, freely expressing themselves, eyes sparkling and hands animated. They often move their chairs closer together, and they feel comfortable with silences. Research shows that the more people naturally synchronize their movements and mannerisms, the greater their state of rapport. For example, when students unconsciously mimic their teacher's posture, they are more likely to report having felt rapport with their teacher and having been more involved in the subject being taught.

The good news about synchrony is that our brains are hardwired to create it. Scientists have shown that once two people have established rapport, even their breathing falls into synch. Similarly, infants and toddlers have been shown to match their baby talk to the rhythm of their mother's speaking cadence. *Even in the womb,* infants synchronize their movements with speech in the outside world.

The bad news about synchrony is that mimicry can't be faked or created consciously. When confederates (the people in cahoots with the researchers) consciously mimic the postures and gestures of people they are talking with, they aren't particularly well liked. But when confederates spontaneously and unconsciously imitate their partner's motions, they are rated as more likable and appealing. So synchrony isn't something we can coach our children on directly, or teach them to consciously practice. It is something that will naturally come as they learn to express their positive feelings and give others their full attention.

I am confident that Phillip's ability to connect with even the most socially awkward among us is *the key* to his happiness and high satisfaction with life. But make no mistake: this skill isn't just a party trick. It is also essential for righting relationships that have gone wrong and resolving conflict before it damages a relationship. If we want our children to lead happy and meaningful lives, they need skills that will enable them to foster strong friendships, including the ability to deal with conflict by doing more than avoiding it.

## CONFLICT: IT'S A GOOD THING

"He's totally conflict avoidant, so it isn't like we ever fight about this stuff," my friend recently explained, describing how she and her hubby address their differences. She seemed proud that the fighting in her household registers low on the Richter scale. Her meaning: Conflict is bad. Glad we don't have it.

Conflict can be very uncomfortable. Whenever what we want is at odds with someone else's desires, conflict arises. In preschoolers and among siblings, conflict is most often about contested toys or space. My eight-year-old is super-obsessed with rules and fairness, so conflict arises when the rules aren't being followed to her satisfaction. No matter our age, most of us have been known to argue when our heartfelt opinions and beliefs are contested. But conflict is not the same as arguing. You and I can disagree about something—mightily!—and are therefore in conflict about it. But that doesn't mean we're necessarily going to argue or have negative feelings about our disagreement. Once we see that conflict does not always entail anger or suffering, we can understand why conflict is a training ground for positive growth and learning.

Because conflict fuels change, it is what makes life interesting. Think about what snoozers movies would be without conflict. It is entirely necessary for intellectual, emotional, and even moral growth. Good thing, because no matter what we do to avoid it, conflict will always exist. Conflict between children is like the air they breathe: playing kids experience conflict every three minutes.

Although we may avoid conflict between adults, most parents and teachers are constantly addressing it with kids. Kids don't know how to settle disputes constructively until we teach them. One study showed that, left to their own devices, 90 percent of conflicts between elementary school children go unresolved or end destructively. Most kids shun conflict or try to crush their opposition; more than 60 percent rely on adults to resolve their conflicts. After reading a dozen or so studies about conflict resolution, I have found that my own cutie-pies regularly model three unhealthy ways to deal with conflict:

1.  Force. As when Molly simply rips a toy she wants out of Fiona's hand and runs.

2.  Withdrawal and avoidance. As when Fiona says, loudly, "I don't want to talk about this anymore" and then walks out of the room.

3.  Giving in. As when Fiona nags Molly for something she doesn't want to give up. Molly often decides that it isn't worth enduring Fiona's heckling and so—seizing the opportunity to gain approval from me—very sweetly gives Fi exactly what she wants. (Note to self: stop praising the kids when they give in to sibling heckling.)

**Would You Just Knock It Off?**

There are two main ways that we adults intervene when our kids fight. The first is what I'll call the "just stop it" method: we tell them what to do ("give that back and say you're sorry"), physically separate them, or take away the object in question. We are judges and umpires, generating solutions and commandments without much help from the bickering masses. Necessary as all this often seems, these tactics do not teach constructive conflict resolution, nor do they teach kids to resolve conflicts themselves. Effective conflict resolution requires empathy: kids have to be able to take their friends' or siblings' points of view into account, which presents a natural opportunity for children to learn to consider other people's feelings.

The other way that we can intervene is to act as mediators or coaches rather than dictators or judges. Instead of stopping the conflict or imposing solutions, we can help kids see one another's perspectives and encourage them to generate their own solutions. In addition to helping our kids foster strong friendships, research shows that learning positive conflict resolution brings other benefits, including boosting academic performance and increasing self-confidence and self-esteem. It has also been linked to increased achievement, higher-level reasoning, and creative problem solving. Learning how to resolve conflict helps kids cope with other kinds of stress as well, making them better adjusted and more resilient as teenagers—and more successful as adults.

At this point, you might be thinking that this section is for parents of older kids and teens. And it is. But it is also important to start teaching constructive conflict resolution skills pretty darn young. Kids as young as two can be taught to resolve many of their own conflicts without adult intervention.

## TRY THIS

### Ten Steps to Peace in Your Household

Positive conflict resolution is simple, but unless you are a lot smarter than I am (entirely possible) you may need to reference this list a few times to get the hang of it.

1. Breathe. Arguing kids make me tense and prone to, uh, yelling, but obviously we don't make effective mediators when we are angry or upset. I often need to take a few deep breaths to center myself before entering the fray. Unless the action is becoming dangerous, take a second to reread this list, which you can also print out at christinecarter.com and hang on your refrigerator.

2. Address the situation. Paradoxically, peacemaking requires confrontation. We often need to help arguing kids realize that they are experiencing a conflict. It is hard for kids to manage something they can't name or even really see is happening. Kids will probably know that they are arguing, but we can help them by

pointing out that there is a problem to be solved, and engaging them in this problem solving. The other day Fiona and Molly were screaming and grabbing over a doll bathing suit. I said, "Wow, seems like there is a problem here. Let's take a few deep breaths, and then we'll start talking calmly about what the problem is and how we're going to solve it together."

3. Now help them calm down and gain some distance from negative emotions. Conflicts cannot be resolved productively until the "heat" of the moment passes. One way to speed this process is to create a conflict resolution area or time that promotes calm. This can be a peace table, a talking stick, or a family meeting. By making an actual physical space or dedicated time for conflict resolution, you can help kids step back and gain perspective to help them solve the conflict.

4. Have everyone state what they want. In one study, 40 percent of uncoached kids failed to state what they wanted out of the conflict resolution. Rule number one in getting what you want? Ask for it! What does each kid see as the problem? Each might describe something completely different, which is okay.

5. Have everyone express their feelings. How is the conflict making them feel? The best way to do this is in the form of an "I statement," which should be taught early and used for a lifetime. An "I statement" is just what it sounds like: I feel X when you do Y. Molly just used one with Fiona: "Fiona, I feel *so* furious when you mess up my fort!" Miraculously, Fiona replied, somewhat surprised, "Sorry, Molly" in a quiet voice and then left the room.

6. Have them state the reasons that underlie what they want and how they are feeling. Skip this step with younger kids, who probably won't be able to articulate the logic behind their desires.

7. Have everyone communicate their understanding of the other person's wants, feelings, and reasons. This helps kids access their empathy. This is also the time when misconceptions and misunderstandings can be cleared up. At this point the problem is common ground, and they can work together to solve it.

8. Change the focus. Instead of letting your little warriors continue to personalize the conflict, help them refocus on the conflict itself. It is now a problem they will solve together. One approach is to write down the problem and have the kids sit down together to address it.

9. Ask them to come up with three or more solutions together that meet the needs they expressed earlier. Especially with little kids, it is important to realize that these solutions may not seem like good ones to adults. It doesn't matter, though, as long as the kids like their ideas and are able to agree on them. Note that this is not about coming up with compromises; it is about finding the win-win.

10. Agree on the solution that maximizes both people's benefits. Shake hands or hug, and then go have some fun!

If you are overwhelmed by this list and are likely to use it only when you have a world war on your hands, remember that you need not follow each step to the letter to be an effective mediator. Implementing any one thing on the list—breathing before jumping into the fray, or having kids use I statements—is better than the "just quit it" method. Once you make the easiest thing on the list a habit, pick the next thing, and so on. Like you, your kids will best learn conflict resolution incrementally. Eventually they will no longer need your help.

The other important part of teaching kids to resolve their conflicts positively is easier said than done: we have to model positive conflict resolution ourselves. This means that I'll use these ten steps as a guide to solving my own conflicts with the kids, and managing disagreements with their dad. Knowing all the benefits that conflict resolution skills bring, I now encourage my kids to see conflicts as opportunities to listen and learn rather than "just quit it." Each time we help kids resolve a conflict themselves, they learn to solve problems in ways that make them feel competent and effective. They've increased their ability to cooperate, empathize, and build strong relationships.

So conflict really is a good thing. Why? Conflict provides the fuel for growth we all need to become healthy, happy, and resilient adults.

# A VILLAGE IS BUILT ON KINDNESS

*Those who bring sunshine into the lives of others cannot keep it from themselves.*
                                        —JAMES M. BARRIE

Social intelligence is not just the ability to establish rapport or resolve a conflict: it is also an inclination toward kindness. Phillip, with his supreme social skills and ability to establish rapport, is also at heart an exceptionally kind and generous individual. Why? Because he is incredibly empathetic: he literally feels for those around him, and can't help but extend a hand, a simple kindness, or even a loving thought. When we give someone our full attention, connection follows—and kindness and generosity often follow from there.

Altruistic people—those seemingly selfless folks who tend to do things that benefit others before themselves, the *givers* among us—aren't just people who volunteer or give away a lot of money. They have kindness habits in their tool kits that we can teach to our children. Some are as simple as saying a prayer; others are grand gestures of philanthropy. Large and small, acts of kindness, generosity, compassion, and altruism are all happiness habits. They build social intelligence and strong bonds with others, and they can be forms of happiness in and of themselves.

## What We Get When We Give

Sociologists and psychologists spend a lot of time debating whether any altruistic act is ever truly selfless, in part because we benefit so much ourselves when we are kind to others. For starters, helping others improves our physical health and longevity. Kinder people actually live longer, healthier lives. People who volunteer tend to experience fewer aches and pains. Giving help to others protects overall health twice as much as aspirin protects against heart disease. One study found that people fifty-five and older who volunteer for two or more organizations had an impressive 44 percent lower likelihood of dying during the study period—and that's after sifting out every other contributing factor, including physical health, exercise, gender, marital status, and habits such as smoking. This is a stronger effect than exercising four times a week or going to church; it means that volunteering is nearly as beneficial to our health as quitting smoking.

We feel so good when we give because we get what researchers call a "helpers' high"—a distinct physical sensation associated with helping. About half of the participants in one study reported that they felt stronger and more energetic after helping others; many also reported feeling calmer and less depressed, with increased feelings of self-worth. This is probably a literal "high," similar to a drug-induced high: for example, the act of making a financial donation triggers the reward center in our brains that is responsible for dopamine-mediated euphoria.

Finally, nearest and dearest to my heart, kindness makes us happy. Volunteer work substantially reduces symptoms of depression; helping others and receiving help are associated with lowered anxiety and depression.

This may be especially true for kids. Adolescents who identify their primary motive as helping others are three times happier than those who lack such altruistic motivation. Similarly, teens who are giving, hopeful, and socially effective are also happier and more active, involved, excited, and engaged than their less giving counterparts. Generous behavior reduces adolescent depression and suicide risk, and several studies have shown that teenagers who volunteer are less likely to fail a subject in school, get pregnant, or abuse substances. Teens who volunteer also tend to be more socially competent and have higher self-esteem.

## Why Kindness Works

It is important to note that experiments have demonstrated again and again that the effects of kindness on our health and happiness are *causal*. It isn't just that kind people also tend to be healthier and happier (that might be why they are kinder in the first place) but that kindness toward others actually *causes* us to be happier, improves our health, and lengthens our lives. Being kind to others strengthens our social bonds. Giving to others also increases our sense of self-worth—heightening our sense that we have something to offer the world—which makes us feel more satisfied with our lives. But that's not all that is at work here.

Most of us know from experience that when our own worries take center stage—*What did she think of me? Will I get there on time? Will I have enough money this month?*—we stress ourselves out. Though our kids' worries are different, the same thing happens to them. Heart attacks and other stress-related illnesses are highly correlated with how much people reference *themselves* in interviews, using words such as I, me, my, mine, myself: patients in one study at the Baylor College of Medicine with more severe disease were more self-focused and less other-focused.

Indeed, giving to others makes us healthier and happier because it makes us less preoccupied with ourselves, thereby reducing stress and reversing its damaging effects on the body. "One of the healthiest things that a person can do is to step back from self-preoccupation and self-worry, as well as from hostile and bitter emotions," writes altruism expert Stephen Post. "There is no more obvious way of doing this than focusing attention on helping others."

Psychologist Barbara Fredrickson has shown compellingly that positive emotions have an "undoing effect." Emotions—both positive and negative—have biological and physiological effects. Negative emotions such as anxiety and anger put stress on our systems, causing inflammation and heart disease, among a huge host of other illnesses. Positive emotions, on the other hand, "undo" the damaging physiological effects of negative emotions, calming the heart rate and reducing levels of stress-related hormones in our bodies. Kindness, compassion, generosity, love: these are positive feelings. These giving emotions turn off and tone down our stress response in many ways. One study showed, for example, that people who were feeling worried and stressed about their finances felt better by offering social support to others. Kindness works by redirecting our energy toward things that make us feel good, reducing the toll that negative feelings have on our health and happiness.

My guess is that most parents *hope* their children are kind, but few deliberately teach kindness in conscious ways. In young children and adolescents, there is a lot of evidence that parenting practices are significantly associated with kindness in children, meaning that we can, in fact, stack the deck so that our children grow up to be kind and generous adults.

The key to raising kind children is to give them a broad giving vocabulary—to teach them many ways to be kind and generous people. You may not realize that this book is chock-full of ways to teach kindness. In Chapter 4, for example, you will learn how to teach your children to practice being grateful and be more forgiving. ForGIVEness is an act of kindness and generosity—toward ourselves and others. Similarly, an expression of gratitude is a gift, a sometimes tiny but often powerful and generous expression of positive feeling. Chapter 5 covers two foundations for kindness: secure attachments and emotional literacy. Being securely attached to one or more caregivers fosters altruism; secure people are more likely to be actively caring in their relationships across the board. Boosting people's feelings of security makes them more likely to show compassion and help others.

Without the ability to empathize with others (also Chapter 5), our kids can't know how to offer help, sympathy, or compassion, or otherwise show kindness. Altruistic kids tend to be much better at taking others' perspectives—showing empathy—than their less altruistic peers.

## SEVEN WAYS TO RAISE KIND CHILDREN

1. Model kindness yourself. Kindness can be contagious: when we see someone else perform an act of kindness, we are more likely to feel an impulse to help out, too. Research suggests that altruistic children have at least one parent (usually the same sex) who deliberately communicates altruistic values to their kids. Similarly, preschoolers with nurturing caregivers who deliberately model helping others tend to be more helpful and verbally sympathetic to other children who hurt themselves.

2. Be preachy. Not in an annoying way, but in the way that inspirational people such as Martin Luther King Jr. are. Empathetic preaching from competent adults, especially adults who have some direct influence over kids, has been shown to inspire kids to behave more generously. The key word here is empathetic; it works better to help kids imagine the emotions of those they are helping: "I think we should share with poor children, because they would be so happy and excited if they had the money to buy food and toys. After all, poor children have almost nothing. If everyone would help these children, maybe they wouldn't look so sad." Versus "I think that people should share with poor children. It's really good to donate to poor boys and girls. Yes, we should give some money to others poorer than ourselves. Sharing is the right thing to do."

3. Make kids personally responsible in some way. Four- to thirteen-year-olds who were asked to donate their Halloween candy to

hospitalized children donated more (and were more likely to make a donation) when they felt personally responsible. Researchers made kids feel responsible when they said things such as "I will be counting on you and you and you. I will put each of your names on the bag of candy I give tomorrow to the hospitalized children" rather than "please give them as many candies as you want by putting them in the box on the table."

4. Encourage kids to just think about it. Just thinking about giving seems to have an effect on health and happiness that is similar to doing the giving. Students who were asked to watch a film about Mother Teresa helping orphans showed significantly strengthened immune systems after the movie, particularly when they focused their minds on times when they had been loved or had loved someone else. Similarly, praying for others reduces the harmful impact of health difficulties in old age for those doing the praying. Finally, even *remembering* when you helped someone else can induce health benefits for hours or even days.

5. Don't reward helping behavior. Very young children who receive material rewards for helping others become less likely to engage in further helping compared with toddlers who receive only verbal praise or no reward at all. This research suggests that even the youngest children are intrinsically motivated, and extrinsic rewards can undermine this tendency.

6. Be positive. Parents who express positive feelings and use positive, noncoercive discipline raise children who are kinder and more compassionate toward others. Using the ERN method described in Chapter 6 is positive and noncoercive; yelling, spanking, and threatening are not.

7. Expose them to need. Too often we protect our kids from pain and suffering, and in so doing we shelter them from others' needs. Consider the counterintuitive notion that compassion is a positive emotion strongly correlated with happiness, and provide them with opportunities to feel compassion. Teach kids that this compassion is a gift—it is a way to give their time, attention, and energy to another. Added bonus: when we expose kids to others' suffering, they often feel compassion *and* gratitude.

## TRY THIS

## Show Kids the Many Ways
## They Can Give Time and Energy

But wait—there's more! There are an infinite number of ways that we give others our time and energy, and we need to model and teach them all to our children. Here are some ideas to get you started.

1. Help kids find ways to volunteer their time. My kids and I volunteer at the local food bank over the summer and during holidays.

2. Create giving traditions. Many families pick out presents for underprivileged children over the holidays, help clean up parks on Earth Day, or make financial donations to charitable organizations on the anniversary of a loved one's death. Could you start doing volunteer work during family reunions, together as a family? Take a service-oriented vacation during spring break each year?

3. Praise kids for showing empathy and emotional support to others. Teach kids that sometimes the best gift they can give is their quiet support and good listening.

4. Encourage kids to perform small acts of kindness. My kids' preschool taught them to always pick up trash when they see it on the ground. Though this frequently grosses me out, it is a small act of altruism that makes my kids feel great. These small acts of kindness don't need to be much. Multiple sclerosis (MS) patients who were trained to provide compassionate, unconditional positive regard for other MS sufferers through monthly fifteen-minute telephone calls "showed pronounced improvement in self-confidence, self-esteem, depression and role functioning" over two years. These helpers were especially protected against depression and anxiety.

5. Provide kids with teaching, mentoring, or caregiving opportunities. When children are struggling with something, such as learning to read, they benefit the most by helping others who are also struggling. We can take a cue from our primate cousins: monkeys who

have extremely poor social skills due to neglect and isolation re-cover only when given the opportunity to care for a baby monkey.

6. Show kids how celebrating other people and significant events are acts of giving that amplify positive emotions. Encourage the nonmaterial aspects of celebration. Start traditions that celebrate *people* on their birthdays—not toys and cake and balloons—such as telling the story of a child's birth, or having everyone at a party complete the sentence "I'm happy you were born because . . ."

However you decide to foster kindness in your kids, they'll reap the benefits for a lifetime. One particularly impressive study showed that a desire and an ability to help others in adolescence predicted good physi-cal and mental health *fifty* years later. With practice and encouragement, most kids become very good at giving. Finally, remember that your role, even with your distant teens, can be one of great influence. Teenagers whose families were relatively harmonious and oriented toward giving were more likely throughout their lives (starting in adolescence) to have a higher regard for others, broader and more compassionate perspectives on social issues, and a sense of their own competence in caring for them-selves and others.

## TRY THIS

### Practice Loving-Kindness

There is another, very simple way that a new strand of research is show-ing that we can become more connected, socially intelligent, and kind, and it probably isn't what you think.

It's a specific form of meditation. Maybe sitting with your legs crossed repeating phrases such as "May all beings be free from suffering" feels a little too far out for you. I'm a scientist, so you can imagine how I might have felt doing this while surrounded by prominent neuroscientists on a recent seven-day silent retreat. Except that I actually *didn't* feel silly. I felt good.

Why?

Research shows that the Buddhist practice of loving-kindness meditation—the benefits of which science is now bearing out—is actually a good way to build social bonds, making us feel less isolated and more connected to those around us. One study showed that a *single seven-minute* loving-kindness meditation made people feel more connected to and positive about loved ones *and* total strangers, *and* more accepting of themselves. Imagine what a regular practice could do.

Research also showed that, over a nine-week period, this kind of meditation increased people's experiences of positive emotions. The work of positivity psychologist Barbara Fredrickson shows compellingly that the practice actually puts people on "trajectories of growth," leaving them better able to ward off depression and "become ever more satisfied with life." This is because loving-kindness meditation bolsters a wide range of resources that make for a meaningful and successful life, such as having an increased sense of purpose, stronger social support, and less illness. The research shows that loving-kindness mediation even "changes the way people approach life" for the better.

I think that telling kids explicitly about the benefits of this exercise is an excellent motivator. I am partial to the scientific results, of course, but my family and I also like the ones the Buddha taught: Fiona likes that the Buddha said it will make people love you; Molly likes that animals will love you; my mom likes that it will make your face radiant; I like that it makes my mind serene.

### Here's How to Do It

The general idea is to sit comfortably with your eyes closed and imagine what you wish for your life. Formulate your desires into three or four phrases. Traditionally they would be something like this:

> *May I be well. May I be happy. May I be filled with ease.*

Loving-kindness meditation is simply a repetition of these phrases, changing who the meditation is directed toward with each cycle. I often do this with Fiona at night in bed.

1. Start by visualizing the person you are directing the meditation toward. Do yourselves first. I usually say something (*May I be happy*) and then Fiona repeats it after me. After a few repetitions, we usually say these phrases in unison.

2. Next, direct the meditation toward someone you feel thankful for or someone who has helped you. Fiona likes to visualize Mrs.

Adams, her superstar teacher. So we say, *May you be healthy. May you be happy. May you be peaceful. May you be free from suffering.* All the while we're thinking of Mrs. Adams.

3. Then direct your meditation to various loved ones. Fiona's dad often features prominently here. Usually we visualize each other since we are each other's loved one.

4. The hardest one for us is visualizing people we feel neutral about—people we neither like nor dislike. Fiona suggested our postman, and then she decided that she *loves* him. We usually settle on the people in our neighborhood whom we've never met, though they too are hard not to like just because they are our neighbors. This visualizing makes us realize how quick we are to judge people.

5. Ironically, the next one is easier: visualizing the people you don't like or are having a hard time with. This is usually the fourth grader who bullies Fiona a little bit, and she feels empowered when sending her love.

6. Finally, direct the meditation toward everyone universally: *May all beings everywhere be happy.*

Doing this with kids of all ages doesn't need to be complicated; most kids are good at using their imaginations to send love and good wishes.

## WHO LIVES IN YOUR VILLAGE?

Mothers tend to get all the credit—and shoulder all the blame—for the happiness and health of their kids. The old-school feminist in me instinctively thinks this is unfair baloney, but the single mommy in me had always wondered: can I do it alone, and are dads really as essential as moms? The short, emphatic answers to these questions are *no,* I can't do it alone, and *yes,* dads are essential.

Although much attention has been paid by researchers to the mother-child bond—we mothers do matter a lot—children are equally likely to form secure attachments to fathers as they are to mothers. Indeed, most of the world's children are *not* cared for exclusively or even primarily by the mother. Our sense that children will be best served when cared for exclusively by their moms is a product of Western industrialization. Mothers serve as the exclusive caregiver in only 3 percent of nonindustrial societies.

Multitudes of studies show that fathers and other caregivers matter a lot for children, and that children don't just benefit from multiple attachments but are also naturally predisposed to forming them.

Children are *much* better off when their relationship with their father is sensitive, secure, and supportive as well as close, nurturing, and warm. One of the biggest problems with divorce is that when a father moves out, the father-child relationship frequently falters. If he stays in the game, his kids will cope far better with the divorce. In general, kids with dads who actively participate in their care and interact with them a lot are more likely to reap a host of benefits, detailed below. But before I cite that research, there is one important question that I know is in the minds of many single mothers out there: Do fathers really deserve all that credit? Research results like those cited don't necessarily show that father involvement *causes* all those great benefits for kids—we just know that kids who have involved fathers are more likely to have those qualities. Although many studies show the unique benefits of having an involved dad by controlling for other factors, the relationship between father involvement and positive child-outcomes is complex.

For example, it could be in part about money: maybe having an involved dad also means that family income is higher, and the positive effects come from being able to live in a safer neighborhood and go to better schools. Or maybe having an involved dad means that your mom has to work less, and so some of the positives for kids come from the increased time that their mothers are able to spend with them. But in general, research shows that kids with positively engaged dads tend to exhibit the following:

1. Are smarter and more successful in school and work. Kids with involved dads are better problem solvers as toddlers and have higher IQs by age three. One theory about why this is: fathers tend to speak with their children differently than mothers do, and as a result children talk in longer sentences and use more diverse vocabulary when talking with their fathers. School-aged children with positively involved fathers are more likely to have higher

grade point averages and better math, reading, problem-solving, and language skills. These kids tend to enjoy school more and have a greater ability to take initiative and use self-direction and control. Later in life, children of positively involved fathers are more likely to have greater success in their careers, and to earn more money.

2. Are happier. Children with positively involved fathers are more likely to be satisfied with their lives overall. They experience less depression, distress, and anxiety, and fewer negative emotions such as fear and guilt.

3. Have more friends and better relationships. Children whose fathers are positively involved have better social skills, and tend to be more popular and better liked. They have fewer conflicts with their peers. They are also more likely to grow up to be tolerant and understanding. They have more positive interactions with their siblings, have supportive social networks made up of long-term close friendships, and have more successful marriages and intimate relationships.

As if all that isn't enough, kids with positively engaged fathers are also less likely to get into trouble or otherwise engage in risky behavior: father involvement protects kids from substance abuse in adolescence. While it is true that happy and successful kids could also be inspiring their fathers to be more positively involved, there are lots of studies that take these factors into account in one way or another and, not surprisingly, the results still show that when fathers are positively engaged, their children benefit in a multitude of ways. So when we talk about building our children's village, it is important to remember that dads need to dig in as well.

Here is what all of this research means to me as a mom. First, positive father involvement is really important and we moms should do whatever we can to encourage it—even if we aren't married to the dad, or we find having him around difficult for ourselves personally. Second, the key takeaway here is that more positive relationships with adults are better; this research looks at relationships with moms and dads, but I believe that positive and lasting relationships with grandparents, aunts, uncles, and close friends function in the same way.

## TRY THIS

# Get Your Kids' Dad More Involved

At this point, there are probably some moms reading this who are a little annoyed with all this emphasis on the importance of dads when they are the ones who are shouldering most of the child rearing in their household. Even today—generations after women have reentered the workforce—we still take for granted the supreme importance of mothering. And of course I'm hopeful that many of the readers of this book are dads, who are likely to be annoyed that the bulk of this discussion assumes that they are not the primary readers of this book. What can I say other than this: congratulations if you are a positive and involved parent. You get to skip this section.

The reality is that not all, or even most, kids are lucky enough to have positively involved dads. In general, times have changed and fathers are more engaged in parenting than Mr. Cleaver was. My dad was considered involved back in the day because he coached softball twice and took me to father-daughter dinner dances. But dads today need to do more than just the fun stuff. My own dad has done more work—changing diapers, picking up prescriptions, cleaning up dog barf—in my household with his grandchildren than he ever did when my brother and I were kids.

But my father is an exception in terms of the amount of child care he does with my kids. Family sociologists often conclude that despite all the gains that women have made in the workforce, they are still facing a stalled gender revolution at home: men aren't typically doing their fair share of housework or child care. The good news is that the amount of time men spend doing housework has doubled over the past three decades. The bad news is that women are still doing 70 percent of that work. Change takes time.

"Seriously," one mom recently said to me, "how do we get dads to be more involved?"

There are three things that make men more likely to be involved dads.

1. A mother's support. Men are more likely to be involved dads when mothers expect and believe that parenting is a joint venture. When a mom believes that the role of fathers is very important, the dad tends to place greater importance on his own role, which in turn leads to greater involvement on his part.

Mothers sometimes serve as "gatekeepers" to father involvement. Women who are ambivalent about the competency of a dad and those who don't want to lose control over parenting tend to block greater father involvement (whether or not they are conscious that they are doing it). On the other hand, support from mothers can improve the quality of a father's parenting. Differing standards for housework and child care can be a common barrier to greater father involvement. The more moms support and provide encouragement—rather than complain about how a job was done—the more involved a father is likely to be.

2. A good co-parenting relationship. The best predictor of a dad's involvement is the quality of his relationship with his children's mother (whether or not they are married). If a marriage or a co-parenting relationship is fraught with conflict, fathers tend to have a difficult time being involved with their children, which of course weakens the father-child relationship. Good fathering can also strengthen a marriage. Fathers who are positively involved in their children's lives are significantly more likely to have successful marriages.

3. Reasonable work hours. Fathers report that long work hours are the most important reason for low levels of paternal involvement. Organizations that want to improve the health and well-being of employees' children need to find ways to reduce the workloads of fathers working long hours.

## DO FATHERS HAVE TO LIVE WITH THEIR KIDS FOR THE KIDS TO REAP THE BENEFITS?

Fathers who don't live with their children can have just as big an impact on their well-being and success as residential fathers—*if* they maintain strong ties with their kids. Unless the relationship between parents is marked by extremely high conflict, kids consistently do better following a divorce when they are able to maintain meaningful relationships with both parents.

The best predictor of the quality of fathers' relationships with their kids is the quality of their relationship with the kids' mother. When parents who live apart can cooperate effectively, father-child contact tends to increase, which in turn promotes better parenting and stronger ties between nonresidential fathers and their children.

It also matters a lot *how* dads parent. Children do better across the board when their fathers are involved in a way that is not too permissive and not too strict. These "authoritative" fathers are engaged in

- Setting and enforcing rules and providing consistent discipline
- Monitoring and supervising their kids
- Helping with homework
- Providing advice and emotional support
- Praising children's accomplishments

Participating in "leisure activities"—such as going out to dinner, buying kids things, or seeing movies together—does *not* tend to influence children's well-being. Nonresidential parents do well when they stay involved with the nitty-gritty of parenting instead of becoming someone who just takes the kids on weekend outings.

And let's not forget that one of the most important ways that non-residential fathers contribute to their children's development and well-being is to pay child support. The amount of child support received influences a child's

- School success and cognitive test scores
- Social skills
- Emotional well-being
- Behavior problems
- Health and nutrition

The amount of child support paid by a nonresidential father impacts children hugely, even after taking into consideration the influences of maternal income, frequency of contact between the father and child, and conflict between parents.

## Be a Part of the Village

You need not be a biological parent to help raise happy kids. As Western households get smaller, parents need "other-mothers"—grandparents, stepparents, aunts, uncles, close friends—to step up and be a part of their children's village, now more than ever. If you are a nonresidential parent, "other-mother," or "other-father," you can have a profound and lasting impact on the health and well-being of the kids in your life. Although I am not married to my children's father, I don't think of myself as a single mother. Why? First and foremost, Mike is an involved dad who makes lunches, helps with homework, and is engaged in the dirty details of child rearing. In addition, my parents live close by and see the kids once or twice a week, picking them up from school or bringing dinner over, babysitting or simply stopping by to help out with homework and bath time. And the kids have longer-distance grandparents whom they have special traditions and rituals with; these traditions create strong and real social bonds. When these grandparents support me and Mike, they strengthen our village and our parenting.

My brother also lives nearby and comes for dinner every other week. His routine with the kids involves tricking them in some way or teaching them a prank, which often leads to lots of revenge plotting in the interim before we see him next. So although we don't see him on a daily basis, his connection with the kids is strong.

I am especially lucky because I have a childless friend who loves Fiona and Molly as though they were her own. She eats dinner with us each Monday, and babysits (for free) a few times a month. Jane has a special relationship with the kids based in large part on their common interests: she is an artist and a zoologist. She teaches the kids about every vertebrate under the sun and is always cooking up a new art project. Because Jane has taken a reliable interest in the kids for as long as they can remember, their bond is also strong.

Also key: I have a large network of good local friends who pick up my kids at school when I get stuck at work. We cook for one another regularly, and treat one another's children like our own. These other-mothers are as critical for my kids' security and happiness as they are for my sanity. I feel great joy when Molly runs out of her classroom and gives my friend Adrienne a big hug before she sees me; I feel similarly happy when Fiona decides to talk over a problem with my friend Kathleen. I may be a single mother, but I'm not raising my children alone by any stretch of the imagination.

Any of the steps in this book can be practiced by other-mothers and other-parents. Doting grandparents, aunties, and uncles—and anyone else who wants to have a place in a child's village—can master growth–mind-set praise (Chapter 3) if they want their adoration to have a huge impact on the success and engagement of the children in their lives. Consciously practicing gratitude (Chapter 4) by creating gratitude routines and rituals in your neighborhood, friendship groups, or families will make you a positive and central part of a kid's village.

It doesn't take much to be a positive part of kids' villages. Is your relationship sensitive and warm? Encouraging and affectionate? Supportive, nurturing, and accepting? Here are some of the simple things that you can do to be positively involved in kids' lives:

1. Take the time to talk with them. Often what kids need most is a good listener.

2. Teach them how to do something you love.

3. Encourage and support their activities and interests. Go to their athletic games and plays, take them to the skate park when you know they need a ride, give gifts that support their hobbies.

4. Supervise them when they are with friends, or help them with their homework.

5. Run errands with them. You never know when a quick conversation in the car or grocery store will have a huge impact.

6. Participate in giving them basic care, such as feeding and bathing them.

7. Find your common interests, and engage the kids in those activities. Can you read together? Toss a baseball? Play checkers?

8. Simply make yourself reliably available to talk, drive, or otherwise help them or their parents.

9. Spend time planning with them. What do they want to do this weekend? What are they planning for their birthday? How can you help make their plans happen?

10. Show them affection and love. Just being present and loving is valuable.

11. Be there for them emotionally with your support and encouragement when times get rough.

None of these many ways that other-parents can be positively involved is contingent on coresidence, but all will help you build your children's village. When we deepen our relationships with one another, we all benefit. It feels just as good to an auntie to establish rapport with a child as it does to the child; uncles and grandparents benefit from being needed by kids just as much as the kids benefit from their help. What is the key to happiness, if I had to pick only one? A big pool of loving friends, family, and neighbors.

# THREE

■ ■ ■ ■ ■ ■

# Step 3: Expect Effort and Enjoyment, Not Perfection

*Only those who will risk going too far can possibly find out how far one can go.*

—T. S. ELIOT

"Y ou're so brilliant!"

"She loves music, but she didn't seem to inherit her dad's talent."

"You're so creative!"

"Look at what a math whiz you are!"

"Try not to get so frustrated, honey. Maybe soccer just isn't your thing."

I used to say things such as this to (or about) my kids constantly. That is, until I found out that certain types of praise can make kids underperform in the long run, not to mention make them anxious and unhappy. Praise in and of itself isn't bad, but the right kind—growth–mind-set praise, which I explain below—is highly counterintuitive for most people. Once mastered, the growth mind-set helps kids

- Learn more and perform better
- Enjoy their activities more
- Embrace challenge

This chapter will teach you how to praise your kids effectively. You'll also see why embracing children's failures invites success, and why it is important *not* to praise, celebrate, or otherwise focus on kids' grades and other achievements.

## UNDERSTANDING THE GROWTH MIND-SET

Stanford psychologist Carol Dweck's research on the psychology of success shows that a parent's "mind-set"—in this case, our beliefs about what makes someone successful—can profoundly influence how kids feel about school and how successful they are academically, athletically—even socially and artistically.

There are two basic mind-sets. People with a **fixed mind-set** believe that talents and personalities are more or less inborn, carved in stone. People with a **growth mind-set** believe that success is a result of effort as much as or more than aptitude.

In my experience, most parents describe their children's personalities in fixed–mind-set ways: they see how easily math comes to their firstborn, that their youngest is good at language, how one child inherited her father's talent for music and the other his mother's hand-eye coordination. This emphasis on what appears genetic seems harmless, but it actually sends our kids a powerful message about learning and effort. Nearly three decades of research have shown profound consequences when kids believe that their intelligence (or athletic ability or anything else, for that matter) is innate rather than believing that talents are something they can develop.

When we send the message to our kids that their talents are inborn—as when we tell them that they are a "natural baseball player" or "good at math"—we create an urgency in them to prove their "gifts" over and over. It isn't that kids don't like this praise: they do. It puffs them up and even encourages them to keep doing whatever it is they are doing. Unfortunately, when kids want to keep their special label as talented, they also start to avoid learning new things, and they start choosing activities based on whether or not they think they will succeed or fail, look smart or dumb, be accepted or rejected. As naturally as it comes to parents, the problem with fixed–mind-set thinking is that it undervalues the role of effort in the learning process.

For example, my friend Elizabeth's fifth-grade daughter Madeline has always seemed "naturally" good at gymnastics, seeming effortlessly able to turn cartwheels and slide into splits without inducing empathetic pain in her audience. Madeline was thrilled when Elizabeth offered her gymnastics lessons—until Madeline heard that there would be other fifth graders there, all of whom had been taking lessons for years. Madeline knew that she would not elicit the same sort of praise (*Wow, Madeline, you are a great gymnast!*) that she was used to, and so began the excuses: *I don't think I have enough time. It's not my thing. It's a babyish gym.* She didn't want to be the beginner in the class and risk losing her status as a natural gymnast. Although Elizabeth's instinct was to reassure her with fixed–mind-set praise—*Don't worry, you're built for gymnastics*—she bit her tongue and cooked up some growth–mind-set encouragement: *The other girls probably will be better than you, but how great! You'll learn a lot from them. All that matters, really, is that you have fun, and it seems like you have fun learning new gymnastics moves.*

For kids and parents who attribute success to natural talent rather than something such as practice, having to make an effort is an indication that they aren't naturally gifted. For example, think about what happens when a kid who has been told he's brilliant can't figure out something easily. Does that mean everyone was wrong—he's not brilliant? This becomes a problem anytime we need to learn something new. It takes effort and often hard work to master a new skill or learn a new subject.

My friend Jackie saw the problem with the fixed mind-set when her daughter Brook was about six. Brook could draw an incredibly detailed, elaborate flower—unbelievable for a kid her age. When a new babysitter came over, Brook would draw her flower for the millionth time. Predictably, the sitter would gush about what a great artist Brook is, and Brook would just beam. But we all knew that if the sitter asked her to draw a tree or an apple, Brook wouldn't even try because she didn't want to look bad. Brook was limiting her artistic repertoire in order to look like a great artist.

Like Brook, I was very much a fixed–mind-set student in grade school, and I'm here to tell you that it is very uncomfortable to go through life worrying about whether or not people think you're good at whatever it is you're trying to be good at. Fortunately, we *can* teach our kids to evaluate situations differently than I did—in terms of whether they are going to have fun, learn something, contribute to a group. Not whether they are going to win, succeed, or be the best.

It is easy to create growth mind-sets in just about anyone: researchers are able to do it with just one sentence. All we have to do is clearly send the message that effort is more important than achievement. When we define success as how hard kids try rather than what kind of grades they get or whether they win the game, we foster the growth mind-set. I know that for many parents this is far easier said than done. We might intellectually understand the difference between the fixed and growth mind-sets, but the fact is that our fixed mind-sets often reflect deep-seated beliefs about and desires for our children, and ourselves.

What about colleges? you ask. After all, they aren't looking at effort expended; they are looking for feats of achievement. I do realize that our culture usually values achievement over effort, but I'm not saying that your kids won't be successful if you emphasize effort. And I mean successful defined traditionally, as high achievement and elite performance. Growth–mind-set thinking does lead us to define success a little differently for our children; it also leads to greater success in the traditional sense of the word.

## THE SCIENCE OF SUCCESS

Is it true, you ask: if I stop emphasizing my kids' "natural" talents and praising their achievements, will they be happy *and* successful? Or will they be happy but possibly successful only in less conventional ways? Can success really come from hard work alone?

There is a solid link between happiness and success. Happier people earn more money, perform better, and are more helpful to their coworkers. Most people assume that this link exists because people feel happy when they are successful. But happiness often precedes success; moreover, fostering happiness and other positive emotions can lead to better performance.

Happiness obviously isn't the only—or even the most—important factor when it comes to achieving greatness. Though Tiger Woods might golf better because he's a happy person, few would say he rose to greatness on the back of happiness. Instead, most people would point emphatically to Woods's incredible talent. But researchers across a wide array of disciplines have produced remarkably consistent findings: innate ability has relatively little to do with why people go from being good at something to being great.

People who rise to greatness tend to have five things in common. First, they practice hard, in a specific way. Accomplished people devote hours to "deliberate practice." This isn't just poking around on the piano because it is fun; it is consistently practicing to reach specific objectives—say, to be able to play a new piece that is just beyond their reach.

Second, very successful people practice consistently. K. Anders Ericsson, a psychologist and the author of a landmark study on this topic, says that "elite performers in many diverse domains have been found to practice, on the average, roughly the same amount every day, including weekends." Knocking out a bucket of balls on the weekend won't make you a great golfer, but doing it every day might.

Third, elite performers gain experience over the long haul. Researchers call this the "ten-year rule." Most successful people average ten years of practice and experience before becoming truly accomplished. Even child prodigies generally work at it for a decade or more. Bobby Fischer became a chess grandmaster at sixteen years old, but he'd been studying since he was seven. Tiger Woods had been working on his golf game for fifteen years when he became the youngest-ever winner of the U.S. Amateur Championship.

Fourth, what kids need is *passion* to stick with their deliberate and consistent practice for upward of ten years. My friend Sara's twelve-year-old daughter, Parker, loves to sing. Sara is the first to point out that Parker lacked "natural" talent when she first started. But her heart is in it. She sings all the time for fun, and consequently she's getting better—good enough to perform in musicals. Bottom line: Parker's practice and effort are fueled by her intrinsic desire, not by her hard-driving parents. In fact, Parker's hobby is probably developing better—and her chances at success increased—because Sara doesn't push and isn't emotionally invested in the outcome. Musical theater is a hobby that Parker has taken ownership of and made her thing.

And most greats aren't just piling up one success after the next. Successful people tend to have experienced some significant failures. Failure seems to be a key part of growth and eventually elite performance. J. K. Rowling's first Harry Potter book was rejected by twelve publishers, and before she even wrote the book she suffered a stream of potentially devastating personal failures. Michael Jordan was cut from his high school varsity basketball team. The great football receiver Jerry Rice was passed up by fifteen professional teams for being too slow.

Fifth and finally, great performers have been shown to believe that their persistent effort will lead to success; researchers call this self-efficacy. Parents and teachers can build self-efficacy in kids by giving them effective encouragement, helping them find effective strategies for mastering an activity, and helping them model their practices on the behavior of others who have succeeded.

Will stunning success bring your kids true happiness? Not necessarily, and especially not if they don't genuinely enjoy what they're doing. But knowing that it is practice rather than innate talent that makes a person successful can help kids take risks to rise to the top of their field—or to try something new in order to find their true passion. More than that, though, seeing effort and engagement as the key to success helps kids enjoy their activities more than they do when they are worried about proving their special talent to the world.

## Repeat After Me: "I Don't Care Whether You Win or Lose."

Valuing effort over achievement is probably easier for the parent of an elementary school kid than a high school sophomore, whose grades or athletic performance might seem to matter more. But even when kids are young, often it is hard to embrace their mediocrity. In fact, it can be anguishing for parents, especially perfectionists, because we love our kids and want to see them fulfill their potential and also because their setbacks or low achievement feel like a reflection on us, the parents. "What did I do wrong?" is something parents ask themselves when children make mistakes or perform poorly.

I have been trying to figure out where to spend our time and money on the kids' activities. Fiona wants to take languages—in first grade she took Spanish *and* Mandarin—but so far she doesn't seem very good at them. In fact, at the end of the year I was hard-pressed to find anything she'd learned in either of these classes. I tell Fi that it doesn't matter if she is good at languages, only that she makes an effort and enjoys the class. But honestly, do parents want to invest money in classes if our children are never going to be able to speak the languages?

Then I catch myself. The message I'd be sending Fiona by pulling her out is that something is worth doing only if you are good at it. The thing to remember is that most people who are really good at something often started off not so good; it was their interest that led them to practice enough to succeed. Kids who choose challenge and improvement over an easy win learn more *and* are happier.

Parents who overemphasize achievement are more likely to have kids with high levels of depression, anxiety, and substance abuse compared to other kids. It's easy to do, because we live in such a fixed–mind-set world. Look at what we hang up in our homes. Listen to what we tell our parents about their grandchildren. I catch myself all the time jumping up and down about home runs and hat tricks. But thirty years of research on mind-sets clearly shows that we need to emphasize effort and enjoyment, not achievement and perfection.

## Praise Your Children in a Growth–Mind-set Way

The easiest way for most parents to foster the growth mind-set is through praise. Most parents encourage and praise their children naturally. When we want to build up their confidence, we say, "You can do it, honey. You're a smart kid." But that's a mixed message. The fixed–mind-set part—telling them they're smart—is tempting, but that's exactly the kind of praise that causes problems. We need to make the message constructive by saying something such as "I know you can do it if you put your mind to it."

Carol Dweck's research team conducted an experiment where they gave kids a short test and then one line of praise. They said, "You did really well; you must be very smart" (fixed mind-set) or they said, "You did really well; you must have worked really hard" (growth mind-set). After the first puzzle, the researchers offered the kids a harder puzzle that they could learn from or one that was easier than the one they completed successfully. The majority of the kids praised for their intelligence wanted the easier puzzle; they weren't going to risk making a mistake and losing their status as "smart." On the other hand, more than 90 percent of growth–mind-set–encouraged kids chose a harder puzzle.

Why? Dweck explains: "When we praise children for the effort and hard work that leads to achievement, they want to keep engaging in that process. They are not diverted from the task of learning by a concern with how smart they might—or might not—look."

When we praise our kids by unintentionally attributing their success to their innate gifts, we hand them a recipe for anxiety and joyless achievement. In Dweck's study, during the first puzzle, almost everyone had fun. But when the "very smart" kids were given a harder puzzle, they said it wasn't fun anymore—it's no fun when your special talent is in jeopardy. Besides making them insecure and crushing the fun of learning something new, telling kids how smart they are actually hinders performance. On the other hand, the effort-praised kids continued to have fun even when they weren't doing as well.

Remember: praise itself isn't bad. We can praise our kids all day long—as long as we are attributing success to things such as effort, commitment, resourcefulness, hard work, and practice. Those are the things that truly help them grow, succeed, and be happy—the things most worth praising.

## HOW TO CRITICIZE YOUR KIDS

What if you just don't feel like praising your kids today? What if they are driving you nuts, or if they stumbled in a way that bears pointing out?

If you are anything like me, you might often be overcome by a burning desire to point out your children's clear shortcomings so that they might do better next time, or in the hopes that they might *just cut it out*.

When we feel disappointed in a child, it is important to approach the topic constructively. Outright criticism rarely achieves the results we are after. The best first step is often to do nothing. Cool off and wait until you have your emotions in check; bring it up later when you're able to use a tone of voice that sounds loving and inquisitive rather than disappointed and critical. Once our own emotions aren't in the picture, we can ask them to evaluate their performance or behavior themselves with questions such as "Are you happy with how you did?" and "Is there anything you'll do differently next time?" Remember that tone matters: your tone should communicate love and support, not accusation and judgment. Ask them why they feel the way they do, and what they learned. With younger kids, a better starting place might be asking why they were behaving a certain way ("What was going on? What were you trying to do?"). Really *hearing* them might help you see that they need a tutor, or that they'd benefit from more regular family meals, or that they need a plan for how to watch less TV.

Second, make it clear that you see failure as an event, not an identity. If a child is disappointed in her performance or an outcome, empathize ("I can tell you are pretty upset about this") and then help her strategize about how she can make things go differently next time. The hardest thing for me is to leave the "I told you so" out of the discussion; I find it easy to say things such as "I asked you a thousand times to put your homework folder in your backpack as soon as you were done instead of waiting until the morning." Better to ask about times when things worked out well: "Last week you remembered your homework. What did you do then that you didn't do today?" Teach kids that the way to do better the next time is to understand which efforts pay off and which strategies work.

We may be disappointed when children make mistakes, but it is important not to express anger or imply that we love them less. Mistakes are just mistakes; although they might need to be dealt with, they are never grounds to withdraw love.

If we are perfectionists ourselves, we need to accept that sometimes second best is good enough, and communicate this. And if our children are as upset about their flub-up as we are, our energy is better expended in empathy than criticism: ask them how they feel and then repeat that back to them. For example: "I can tell you are really disappointed" or "It sounds like you felt really embarrassed." Don't just replay how bad it feels—get to the part where having a failure doesn't matter anymore: "It sounds like that was really hard at first, but I'm glad to see that you can laugh at yourself now."

## THE PERILS OF PERFECTIONISM

All this emphasis on effort and hard work might be misleading. I'm not talking about fostering a put-your-nose-to-the-grindstone and stick-with-it-forever mentality. (Remember, this is a book about happiness. Sweating it out through the sheer force of will doesn't sound like fun.)

There is a fine line between persistent practice and perfectionism. Perfectionism is the dark side of consistent hard work; it produces a chronic feeling that nothing is good enough and the worst thing in the world is failure. Instead of enjoying the process and deriving satisfaction from a job well done—not to mention growing and learning from mistakes—elevated stress hormones coursing through perfectionists' blood make them prone to a host of health problems, including depression, severe anxiety, and a higher incidence of suicide.

A lot of people incorrectly assume that perfectionism propels kids to the top of their class, their teams, and eventually their fields. Though perfectionism can *seem* like a straight road to success, it isn't, and it certainly isn't a route to happiness. To the contrary, perfectionism tends to detract from success and happiness by creating a steady state of discontent fueled by a stream of negative emotions such as fear, frustration, and disappointment. Perfectionists can't even enjoy their successes because there is always something they could have done better. All that fear diverts energy from more constructive things, making perfectionists less able to learn and be creative. Ironically, perfectionists expend a lot of energy on the things they are desperately trying to avoid: failure and the criticism they imagine it will create. This preoccupation has been shown to undermine performance in sports, in academics, and in social situations.

Like all fixed–mind-set thinking, perfectionism keeps kids from taking risks and embracing challenge (think of Brook and her flower). For this reason, sometimes perfectionism leads kids to underachieve: they give up or don't even try because they assume they can't be good enough. Rising to a challenge, especially if we won't necessarily succeed at first, is one of the best ways to go from being good at something to being great.

Furthermore, perfectionism leads kids to conceal their mistakes and avoid getting constructive feedback. In nearly every field—writing groups are the most obvious example here—group critique is a rapid way to get better at something. As a perfectionistic undergraduate at Dartmouth College, what I feared most was having my work read aloud by a professor or my paintings critiqued by a class. Though I couldn't prevent these things from happening except by skipping class, when I did have to endure group critique I was so paralyzed by fear of judgment and having my mistakes exposed that I couldn't learn from (or even really hear) the constructive feedback being given to me.

To be clear: perfectionism is not about setting high expectations or being successful in our endeavors. It is about being concerned about making mistakes and worrying about what others think.

We know that, for the most part, kids aren't born perfectionists; their environment creates them. Are you overly concerned about making mistakes yourself? Chances are your children will be, too. Since no child *is* perfect, when parents push for perfection, kids feel criticized.

As parents put more and more pressure on their children to achieve, more and more children become perfectionists. Sometimes parents' well-intentioned perfectionism emerges more subtly, as when we try to help kids by pointing out their mistakes in ways that make our kids feel judged and criticized. Kids conclude that they're never good enough or can't do anything on their own without us helping them. Many kids give up and become underachievers who feel helpless and hopeless. This is what started to happen to my friend Jeff's son Henry in second grade. Jeff had too-high standards for Henry and ended up "fixing" a lot of his homework.

Henry basically gave up on math and writing, concluding that he couldn't do it without his dad's constant and vigilant help.

So we have a choice. We can focus on whether or not our kids win or lose, look smart or dumb, seem talented or average. Or we can help them see that there is more to life—and to them—than their achievements. Ironically, focusing on kids' short-term achievements can prevent them from achieving more in the long term.

Even when children are doing very well, perfectionism-creating parents find faults: we raise an eyebrow at the one B on a report card full of A's, we point out the bad pitch in a game well played. Instead, praise kids for a job well done without pointing out what they could have done better. A good job is just that: a good job.

Even better, use only growth–mind-set praise. There is a fine line between failing to recognize a job well done (by pointing out what could have been done better) and praising kids for anything and everything they do. If a kid didn't try very hard or put any effort into a project, save the praise for something else.

Do we really not praise them for a job well done? We don't, or they won't want to move on from their list of easy achievements (think of Brook and her flower). When kids do something quickly and perfectly, Dweck recommends saying to them: "Whoops! I guess that was too easy. I apologize for wasting your time. Let's do something you can really learn from!"

Finally, we parents create perfectionists in children when we are unable to see the positive aspects of mistakes, failures, and jobs left undone, fearing that our children's poor performance will reflect badly on us. If you find yourself doing everything within your power to prevent your children's failures—bringing forgotten homework to school, staying up late to "help" rewrite a paper, manipulating the system to your child's advantage—take a step back and ponder whether you really want to prevent your children from learning to deal with challenges and mistakes.

## Embracing Our Children's Failures

Chronic failure is never good, of course, but the ability to learn and recover from failure is an essential life skill. Rather than seeing failure as fertile ground for learning and growth, though, too often we treat it as something to be avoided at all costs. Wikipedia defines failure as "the state or condition of not meeting a desirable or intended objective." That's all, just a mark missed. Nothing so awful. Nothing to be ashamed of or chronically avoided.

Yet we protect our kids from failure as though life depends on their never feeling the pain of a missed mark. We bring them their homework when they forget it, jockey to get them into the classroom where we think they'll shine, hold them back a year so they will be the oldest at a sport, and likely the biggest and perhaps the best.

When parents communicate to their children that they care less about the outcome than the process itself—when parents show kids that they aren't personally invested in whether they make the team or ace the test or get into an elite college—they free their children from the fixed mindset. Kids who are free from the fear of failure don't need the good opinions of others to get through life. They can lead their lives according to higher principles, driven by virtues such as gratitude or respect, or simply by being authentic. They can laugh at their mistakes, and most importantly they can learn from them.

If we intervene when our kids are on the brink of making a mistake—preventing the mishap or just making things easier for them—we send the message that we think they are incapable in some way or that failing would be too traumatic. We need to protect our kids not from failure but from a life void of failure.

A good way to help kids, then, is simply by helping them figure out what went wrong. If they seem to be stuck in a particular area, we can help them make a plan, help them see a new way to reach their goals. Discuss strategies. Give them the coaching they need to improve but let them make the improvements. Maybe Fiona doesn't seem good at softball because she isn't practicing enough, or she's got the wrong idea about how to make the bat connect with the ball. All we can do is help our kids with their approach and send the message that, while we expect their full commitment and solid effort, we're also okay with their mistakes and their fumbles.

## TRY THIS

### One Mistake I Made Today . . .

At dinnertime, or anytime you are hanging out with your family looking for something to talk about, ask each person to describe a mistake they recently made or a setback they experienced and what they learned from it. Parents can share their own mistakes first, and then ask kids if they can come up with an example when they made a mistake or overcame a challenge. An example: One night at dinner I was feeling discouraged because my magazine editor had asked for a rewrite of something I thought I was done with. I talked about it over dinner to let my kids know why I was frustrated and how I doubted my ability. Then I forced myself to take a more upbeat tone and say, "Well, a lot of times I don't get things right on the first try. See, you guys? Everyone has to do things over sometimes." When the article was published, I showed it to them and said, "This took a lot of work, but in the end I'm glad my editor made me rewrite it. He helped me make it a better essay."

An oddly carved pumpkin, illegible homework, a poorly played game: when our children learn to cope with these things and rise again in the face of failure, they will become resilient to life's inevitable challenges.

## WHEN QUITTING IS A GOOD THING

If we want our kids to be successful *and* happy, we need to teach them the value of hard work and practice. But we also need to teach them when and how to quit.

It is a myth that "winners never quit and quitters never win." From a stress-management standpoint, we need to be able to disengage when the cost of reaching a goal is outstripping the benefit. One study showed that teenage girls who couldn't disengage from pursuing a difficult goal showed increased levels of the damaging stress-related chemicals in their bloodstream that are linked to diabetes, heart disease, and early aging. It didn't matter whether or not they eventually reached the goal; too much perseverance can elevate stress hormones and exact a high cost physically.

People tend to feel better physically and mentally when they disengage from a too difficult goal and reengage with one that is more attainable. For example, in college my good friend Vanessa was failing calculus but doing well in her other classes. Her advisor coached her to admit she was failing the class, and instead of continuing to throw good effort at a lost cause, rededicate herself to the classes that she enjoyed and could learn from—which she did. Her advisor was concerned that she would spend so much time and mental energy on calculus (passing was a mathematical impossibility at that point) that she would also tank in the other two classes. That advice—to choose to fail—was revolutionary for Vanessa, and she'll never forget it. She left calculus behind and did well in all of her classes from there on out. Moreover, she enjoyed college, went on to grad school, loves learning, and now laughs about calculus. Failing that one class had no negative impact on her life.

Hard work may be a key to success, but we also need to teach kids that *rest* is an important part of growth and learning. Kids who sacrifice sleep put their physical and intellectual growth—and, ironically, their performance—in jeopardy. *The Power of Full Engagement* authors Jim Loehr and Tony Schwartz emphasize that growth occurs in cycles of challenge and rest. Challenge your muscles, then let them rest and recover. The same thing is true mentally: rest is necessary following effort for our brain to process what we've learned. Life is too short to keep our noses to the grindstone 24/7. Not all mountains are worth climbing all the way to the top, especially if the costs of doing so are great. So if you have extremely busy kids in your life, or goal-oriented teens, make sure they can rest when they are tired.

The social pressure *not* to quit can be tremendous, and for some people quitting will take a great deal of courage. Is your child embarrassed to admit that she just can't do it? Are we, as parents, having a hard time letting our child abandon a project or give up on lessons that we've already paid for? Remember that there are good reasons to quit—when the stresses and costs of continuing outweigh potential gains—and there are bad reasons, such as fearing failure.

Downtime, rest, play—and sometimes quitting—are not indulgences or a waste of time. They are necessary for strength and growth.

## TRY THIS

### Combating Perfectionism

If you read the part of this chapter about perfectionism being a drag on happiness, and you kept thinking to yourself, *dang it, I've created a perfectionist,* and now you're worried that your daughter is going to end up depressed and stifled or your son is going to turn out to be an anxious meth user, stop it. Everyone is going to be fine. You don't need to be a perfect parent to raise happy kids.

To recap: Perfectionism is all about fear of failure. The worst-case scenario for perfectionists, then, is that we make a mistake or fail and someone finds out about it. Perfectionist logic:

I stop obsessing about being perfect → I won't be perfect → I'll feel terrible.

This is faulty logic, of course. The way to wean someone from perfectionism is to show them that when they make mistakes and fail, they don't feel terrible. In fact, they might feel free. Once we learn that we can emerge from a failure—or just a minor mistake—still breathing, often we feel free to take on greater risks and opportunities for growth.

According to researcher Randy Frost, perfectionists believe that their self-worth is contingent on their performance—if they don't do well, they are worthless. That's why they think they are going to feel bad when they stop trying to be perfect. Perfectionists tend to think that failure to achieve will seriously diminish the affection and high regard of their parents.

Here's how to help the perfectionist in your life quit it.

1. Have your perfectionists engage in whatever they tend to be perfectionistic about. (This goes for you, too, if you are a perfectionist.) Pick a quick task that they don't want to be bad at but are unlikely to be able to do perfectly on the first try. This would mean having Brook, in a previous example, draw an oak tree instead of her multimillion-petal flower.

2. Ask the perfectionists to give it a go, even though it is unlikely they will do well. When I was in high school, my dad used to beg me to get a C just so I could see that my heart wouldn't stop beating if I wasn't a star student all the time. I finally learned this lesson while rock climbing; the first thing my instructor made me do

was fall off a rock at fifty feet up. Once I felt the ropes catch me, I knew viscerally that I would live even if I did fall, and my legs stopped quaking with fear. Perfectionists need to learn this lesson: usually failing doesn't hurt very much or for very long.

3. Talk about the experience. How did it feel to do something badly? If Brook's oak tree was really bad, her mother could ask her if she thought that meant she wouldn't ever be able to draw a realistic oak tree. Does not being good at something in this instance diminish a kid's self-worth? Point out that Thomas Edison had to try more than a thousand times before he invented a functioning lightbulb. If kids actually did pretty well in their own eyes, ask them what they think that means. Often whether something "is" an oak tree or not is in the eye of the beholder. Let them see that you don't care whether or not their performance actually *was* any good. You love them just the way they are.

   As you ask them how they feel, you might notice that they don't actually feel terrible. Chances are they'll feel loved and cared for by you. Point this out empathetically: "Sounds like you feel okay even though you did something you were afraid might make you look bad." Offer enthusiastic congratulations: "How great! You're learning to try new things and take risks! Whoo-hoo!"

At this point, you can help develop a strategy that might work better on their next attempt. Try to keep this lighthearted. And if you find your kids laughing at themselves as they reflect on their jobs imperfectly done, you know you've succeeded.

## CHOICE CAN BE A CURSE

Barry Schwartz, the psychologist who wrote *The Paradox of Choice,* has done interesting research on the consequences of living in a culture that assumes that more choices are better than fewer choices. Schwartz divides the world into people who maximize and those who "satisfice" in the face of their many choices. Maximizing is a form of perfectionism; we maximize by searching out all the best possible options when making a decision, hoping to make the "perfect" choice. We satisfice when we choose something based on preset criteria and move on. Satisficing doesn't mean settling for something less than you really want; it is just a different way to go about making a decision.

Happy people have different decision-making processes than unhappy people; they tend to satisfice. Maximizing is tempting for perfectionists, and it is associated with unhappiness and discontent.

This may be hard to believe, especially if you are a perfectionist, because it seems as though maximizers would have higher standards and could be expected to make better decisions that they are happier with. Not necessarily. Maximizers tend to be less happy with the decisions they make (when they finally make them). Why?

Consider this example from my own family. Last year when the rec center activity catalog came out, I let Fiona peruse it and circle things she was interested in. She circled more than a dozen things she "really really really" wanted to do. How to decide? If she took Spanish, she could walk to the center with Kate and Hannah, who she knew would also be taking it. She said carpentry would be cool because she'd get to make a birdhouse, and pottery would be awesome because she wanted to make a teapot. Sewing was a definite must—she *needed* to make a shirt for Zoe, her favorite doll. She ended up taking Spanish *and* Mandarin *and* knitting *and* drama—and lamenting the fact that she didn't get to take sewing and softball, too. In letting Fiona ponder her multitude of options, I encouraged her to think through how cool each was, and then I forced her to give up a lot of them. The more choices you have, the more you have to give up.

This year I gave Fiona two choices: carpentry or soccer. She said, "What about drama?" I said, "Not an option until spring. Wrong time, wrong day of the week." Fiona chose soccer and hasn't looked back since.

Here is how to satisfice instead of maximize.

- Have your kids outline their criteria for success. What are the objective signs that a project is finished or an option is good enough? If your teen is trying to decide where to apply to college, for example, what are the things that she can't live without? No need to set your sights low; just set your sights on something specific.

- Encourage your kids to choose the first option that meets their criteria, or stop working the moment that the predecided "finished" signs appear. People with decision paralysis or perfectionists who have a hard time calling it quits might also want to set time limits—say, two minutes to decide or no more than a half hour a day browsing college websites.

■ Once the decision is made or the job done, focus on the positive aspects of the choice or accomplishment. Maximizers who don't have regrets are no less happy than the average satisficer. Focusing on what might have been is not a happiness habit. Enjoy the fruit of your work.

The gist of Schwartz's research is that having a lot of choice is a curse on our happiness. Knowing this makes me feel better about restricting the choices my kids have. And I no longer think of myself as settling when I make a decision without exploring all the options. I'm modeling satisficing for my kids; and if they pick up on it, they'll be happier in the long run.

# FOUR

■ ■ ■ ■ ■ ■

# Step 4: Choose Gratitude, Forgiveness, and Optimism

*The greatest revolution of our generation is the discovery that human beings, by changing the inner attitudes of their minds, can change the outer aspects of their lives.*
—WILLIAM JAMES (1842–1910)

P arenting would be considerably easier if childhood happiness were just a function of ice cream cones eaten and time spent swimming. But a joyful life at any age is a function of the positive emotions we experience, and, as I've said before, positive emotions are in large part skills and habits that we can teach our children. In this chapter we look at important choices we make when it comes to teaching happiness—choices we often don't even realize we are making.

Thinking about making choices in the emotions we feel is a bit of a paradox; aren't emotions by definition not rational? In general, emotions activate different parts of the brain than logical thinking does, so this might account for why we think of emotions as irrational. But things we think and do every day evoke different emotions in us, and emotions such as gratitude, forgiveness, and optimism require us to make rational choices we often don't even realize are in front of us.

If you are anything like I was before I started studying happiness, you might have a hard time believing that qualities such as optimism are choices and habits rather than personality traits. A lot of who we are *does* come from our genetic makeup and life circumstances, such as whether or not we are rich or urban or married. But fully 40 percent of our happiness comes from intentional choices about what activities we pursue. Using sophisticated statistical techniques and lots of studies involving twins, several researchers have concluded that about half of the differences in people's happiness levels are due to genetic factors, over which we have little control. Another 10 percent can be accounted for by our life circumstances: whether we are "rich or poor, healthy or unhealthy, beautiful or plain, married or divorced, etc." This means that if we put a hundred people in the same life circumstances—gave them the same level of physical attractiveness, with the same demographics, in the same house in the same neighborhood—the differences in their happiness levels would be affected by only 10 percent. That leaves 40 percent to behavior: the things we do on a day-to-day basis. Do we feel grateful or entitled? Do we forgive or hold a grudge? Are we pessimistic or optimistic?

Forty percent is a heck of a lot of influence. Will we let our culture influence how happy our children are when it insidiously models cynicism, revenge seeking, and entitlement? Or will we consciously teach our children to practice gratitude, forgiveness, and optimism?

Even knowing what I do, I still find myself barreling along the road of life fairly reflexively (now with kids in the car). I have learned that throughout my day I'll have dozens of opportunities to change direction— choose between optimism and pessimism, for example, or forgiveness and anger. Sometimes I cruise through the intersection, missing my turn. There are lots of possible roads, but only some of them lead to happiness. This chapter is about learning to recognize the choices we have in how we influence our children's happiness. The best thing about this? When we teach children the road signs that point to happiness, we tend to find ourselves taking those same roads as well.

## ENTITLEMENT V. GRATITUDE

Why does it feel as though we are raising a generation of kids who are cynical and feel more entitled than thankful for all they have? Children are born feeling entitled to our care; they aren't, however, born knowing how to feel grateful for all that life gives them. Gratitude is a learned skill to be practiced, like kicking a soccer ball or speaking French.

Practice gratitude? Like multiplication tables? Yes. Americans live amid such incredible abundance that we tend to be out of practice when it comes to feeling appreciation for what others do for us. Our culture glorifies independence and undervalues how much others help; we see our blessings as hard earned. One gratitude researcher, in an article for

*Greater Good* magazine, describes a scene from *The Simpsons:* "When asked to say grace at the family dinner table, Bart Simpson offers the following words: 'Dear God, we paid for all this stuff ourselves, so thanks for nothing.'" While we might think this is funny, it won't teach viewers the skills they need for lasting happiness.

My own kids have picked up rich notions of what romantic love is from watching Disney princess movies, but until I gave them an earful about it, they couldn't say a word about what Cinderella might feel thankful for. I asked Molly, then four, what she thought Cinderella would say to her fairy godmother the day after she made all of Cinderella's dreams come true, what with the schmancy gown and last-minute carriage ride to the ball. Molly thought for a second and then said, "Faiwy godmuddewr, next time can I have a pink dress?"

## Practicing Gratitude: Here's How

Practicing gratitude is blissfully easy: simply count and recount the things in your life that you feel thankful for and ask your kids to do the same. Admittedly this is not so simple if it feels hokey or if your spouse or kids are cynical about it. Persistence is key: choose a gratitude practice and stick with it until it feels natural for everybody.

At night before bed, I ask my kids to tell me about three good things that happened during the day. What went well and why? Their answers vary from the trivial to the profound. Some days they have dozens of good things; other days they only whine and complain. Most of the time, though, Molly and Fiona end up simply recounting little things that made them happy that day.

Here are some other ways we can get our children in the habit of counting their blessings.

- A family in our neighborhood has a "gratitude box" on their dinner table; every day each family member writes down something that they are thankful for on a scrap of paper and adds it to the box. On Sunday nights they take turns reading "gratitude fortunes," as they call them, from the box.

- Another family I know does "appreciations" at the end of family dinners: family members take a turn saying what they appreciate about each of the other people present.

Appreciation is one of the most important ways that we teach our kids to form strong relationships with others. So much of our human relationships are about giving, receiving, repaying—the stuff of connection. Expressing gratitude acknowledges just how deep those connections run. For this reason, we need to remember to practice expressing gratitude to the people who help us outside of our families as well. The best way to do this, I think, is to write thank-you notes.

Psychologists have tested a particularly effective take on thank-you notes called the "gratitude visit." Help your child write a thank-you note to a teacher, friend, or relative who has meant a lot to them, and then encourage them to deliver it in person and read it out loud. My friend Kendra's kids, Keith, age seven, and Avery, eleven, don't like writing thank-you notes, but these gratitude letters are different. Keith and Avery paid end-of-the-school-year gratitude visits to their teachers this year, and Kendra reports that Keith's and Avery's letters came from the heart. Both kids look forward to writing and delivering their next gratitude letters. Paying gratitude visits teaches children to express appreciation for more than things such as birthday presents, and to recognize that meaningful gifts are often nonmaterial. And adults who do this feel measurably more satisfied with their lives a full month after the initial gratitude visit.

## The Abundance Paradox

Difficulty and scarcity inspire gratitude. My cousin and her husband took their four children to live in Kenya, and never once in two years did she see a Kenyan child express anything but gratitude for the food before them. My cousin's whole family came back from Kenya deeply thankful for all that their upper-middle-class American life provides. Helping others who are less fortunate makes kids aware of the ways that they are blessed, calling attention to what they previously took for granted.

My friend Brian has his ten-year-old-son, Max, choose one toy each week to give away to poor families. If you think this sounds a bit drastic, consider that on average American kids get seventy new toys per year. Max has come to value the toys he keeps far more than before he started giving some away. Similarly, my friends Gabe and George have their kids donate toys each year around Thanksgiving—the same number as their respective ages—so that other kids will have Christmas presents as well.

When kids come to expect that we will anticipate their every need, they feel disappointment—not gratitude—when they don't get exactly what they want. For this reason, we need to make sure that all of our kids' fantasies *don't* come true. Although we often instinctively protect our children from distress, we don't want to lead them to believe that they live in a magic land where they will live happily ever after without having to contend with deep sadness or disappointment. Max wasn't happy about giving away his toys until the fourth or fifth week, but once he learned to cope with the loss, he could experience great gratitude and joy.

And though our American life tends to be abundant, it isn't necessarily easy. When things aren't going well, we can use gratitude to cultivate the growth mind-set, or the understanding that success comes from effort and practice, not from doing things quickly and perfectly the first time (see Chapter 3). When we think of failure as something to be thankful for because it is a necessary step in learning, we get better at overcoming challenges.

---

## THE BENEFITS OF GRATITUDE

Getting kids in the habit of practicing gratitude comes with all sorts of other bonuses besides less brattiness. For example, scientists have found that, compared to those who aren't practicing gratitude, people practicing gratitude

- Are considerably more enthusiastic, interested, and determined
- Feel 25 percent happier
- Are more likely to be kind and helpful to others
- Sleep better

I don't know anyone who doesn't want happy, kind, and helpful children who sleep well at night!

---

Encouraging kids to look hard for a reason to feel grateful for unpleasant events or difficult relationships teaches growth and promotes change. Looking for the silver lining is not superficial Pollyannaishness but a decision to replace bad feelings with good ones. For almost a year I ruminated endlessly on what was a difficult time for our family. Because of what seemed like extremely bad luck, we had to move out of a house that we loved and otherwise would never have chosen to leave. The move was extremely stressful for everyone in our family. But we now live in an ideal

place surrounded by neighbors we love and wouldn't have known otherwise. Our neighbors have brought a host of good fortune to us; I wouldn't
even be writing this book if it weren't for two in particular. It wasn't until
I was willing to see how much good had come out of the move that I
stopped feeling resentful that we'd had to do it. This shift was not hard to
teach my kids, who still sometimes long for the "old house." When they
do, we practice thinking of the good things in our life that came out of
having to move. We can usually talk for a long time about the benefits of
living near a park, their school, and our neighborhood friends.

A word about persistence: many parents I know have reported back to
me that their spouse or teenager initially mounted stiff resistance to practicing gratitude, which might feel hokey to those out of practice. Stick
with it. Particularly tough cases probably need a hefty serving of altruism
to inspire them to convert; see Chapter 2. Remember, practicing gratitude
is inherently rewarding, so even the coolest and most entitled among us
usually come around.

## TRY THIS

## PRACTICE GRATITUDE

1. Keep a family "gratitude list" or collection of things that family
   members feel thankful for. Post a big sheet of paper on your fridge
   and ask everyone to contribute to it on Sundays, or at some set
   time every day when it can easily become a habit. Anything can
   go on the list, no matter how large or small—people, places, toys,
   events, nature. Let older kids be list keepers; younger kids can
   dictate. Variations on this theme are endless; for example, at
   mealtime you can go around the table and ask each family member to talk about three good things that happened that day.

2. Slow down and smell the roses. Savoring good experiences can
   heighten positive emotions. Adults can teach kids to savor positive events by habitually expressing gratitude when nice things
   happen, even if they are very small things. Simply stop what you
   are doing and express thanks for the moment—a beautiful sunset, the chance to smile at a baby, the opportunity to be with
   your child. Celebrating good news is a form of savoring. Repet-

itively replaying and reveling in happy moments—such as a graduation, a fantastic soccer game, or a vacation—can make us happier.

3. Write gratitude letters large and small. Large: Help kids write a thank-you letter to a person who is important to them, and then encourage them to deliver it in person and read it out loud. Small: Encourage kids to write unexpected thank-you notes for things other than gifts. Write notes for kind words spoken, to someone who lent a helping hand, or to say thanks for a fun day.

## ANGER V. FORGIVENESS

*Holding on to anger is like grasping a hot coal with the intent of throwing it at someone else; you are the one getting burned.*

—Buddha

Forgiveness is another important ingredient for a happy life. Few people fully realize the impact that the ability to forgive can have on their happiness. Nor do most people think of this as a skill that they need to teach and practice with their children. But important it is: forgiving people tend to be happier, healthier, and more empathetic, and, like the Buddha, more serene, agreeable, and spiritual.

The inability to forgive, on the other hand, tends to make us into those people who can't seem to stop plotting revenge or ruminating about how they've been wronged. Researchers find that unforgiving people tend to be hateful, angry, and hostile—making them anxious, depressed, and neurotic as well. Which is why we need to teach our children how and why to forgive others.

Childhood can be particularly fraught with meanness and bullying. As we learn to become kinder and better people, we inevitably make mistakes. For that reason, we need to learn to apologize and forgive others. We also need to teach kids that, contrary to popular belief, forgiving does not necessarily mean forgetting, excusing a hurtful action, or becoming friends with the person who hurt you. My friend Amy periodically reminds her nine-year-old son, Zach, to keep his guard up around a schoolmate who has bullied him in the past. Zach has successfully forgiven his schoolmate, but he thinks of the forgiveness as something he did for himself in order to let go of all the painful feelings that the bullying incident brought into his life. Zach is a particularly articulate advocate for the many ways that forgiveness makes us feel better.

In watching my daughter Fiona with her school friends, see that most transgressions are naïve, but they still require apology and forgiveness. I particularly remember one incident when Fiona was in the first grade. She was walking to school with her two best friends, Catherine and Quinn. Fiona had definite ideas about what game the three of them should play at recess. Catherine had other ideas, but Fiona was so excited that she didn't even acknowledge Catherine's resistance.

Catherine pulled Quinn ahead and whispered, "Don't you think Fiona is bossy?"

Fiona was crushed. "That's *so mean*," she shouted at her buddy.

"You're so *mean!*" Catherine shouted back. More accusations and tears ensued.

Until kids apologize and forgive one another, an exchange such as this one tends to consume them emotionally and, of course, hinder their friendship. One of the most difficult but important lessons we can teach our children is that when we hold a grudge—for something large and seemingly justified, or for something small but irksome—we continue to injure ourselves.

Fiona's instinct when she's hurt is to avoid the person who hurt her. Avoidance is a common response to a transgression, and it is a sign that forgiveness has not occurred. Catherine tends to replay the transgression in her mind over and over again—another common response to a hurt called rumination. Each time she thinks about Fiona accusing her of being mean, she feels hurt all over again. Ruminating is stressful and unpleasant, and it makes us feel out of control, angry, sad, anxious—and less forgiving. So a big part of forgiveness is the decision to stop thinking about the offense and start directing our energy toward finding a way to forgive.

Other times—often understandably—we feel angry and hostile toward our offenders when we are hurt, and our thoughts turn to revenge. Hostility harms our health (putting us at increased risk of heart disease, for example). Wanting revenge rather than forgiveness creates more conflict with the person who hurt us, increasing our anger and anxiety. When we hold on to negative emotions such as anger, bitterness, and hatred, we can't experience joy or gratitude.

So it is key for me to help Fiona and Catherine find ways to forgive each other so that they can get on with their friendship and feel better.

The surest road to forgiveness is a sincere apology, of course. (For tips about making apologies effective, see "You Don't *Seem* Sorry" on page 77.) People are also more willing to forgive if they see that the offender is willing to sacrifice something. In Fiona and Catherine's case, each needs to consent to play the other's game as part of the apology.

It won't help to have Fiona and Catherine talk about what is and isn't fair. The brain registers forgiveness deep in its emotional center (the limbic system), not the areas of the cortex that are associated with reasoning and judgment. The best way to activate the forgiveness area of the limbic system is empathy, not reason. To help Fiona and Catherine forgive, we need to steer them away from discussions of fairness and encourage them to stand in each other's shoes, imagining how the other feels. If Catherine starts pointing out that it isn't fair that they always play Fiona's games, we can simply redirect: "Catherine, imagine that Quinn pulled Fiona ahead of you and whispered to her, 'Catherine is *so bossy!*' How would that make you feel?"

---

### THE BENEFITS OF FORGIVENESS

Compared to their unforgiving counterparts, more-forgiving people report having

- Better and happier relationships
- Better moods
- Higher self-esteem

Forgiveness can

- Reduce stress, blood pressure, anger, depression, and hurt
- Increase optimism, hope, compassion, and physical vitality

In a study of Protestants and Catholics from Northern Ireland who had lost a family member to violence, participants reported a 40 percent decline in depression after practicing forgiveness.

---

In addition to empathizing with the person you'd like to forgive, we can prepare the ground for apologies and forgiveness by consciously evoking positive emotions about the person we are in conflict with. When I'm mad at my kids' dad, Mike, but I know that I need to forgive him, I make myself think of all the sweet things he's done for me recently. This to-gether with imagining things from Mike's perspective—visualizing myself in his shoes, thinking the thoughts that he'd probably think—often makes me feel ready to forgive much sooner.

For Fiona and Catherine, it works to have them share what they like about the other person or recall fun times they've had together. Having a smile, a laugh, or just a series of positive thoughts can actually change our physiology to make us feel better—lowering our blood pressure and heart rate as well as loosening our frown muscles and making us more likely to feel forgiving.

## PRACTICING THE SKILLS WE NEED FOR FORGIVENESS

As parents, we teach forgiveness when we forgive others because our chil-dren learn what we model. We also need to teach our children directly how to forgive. But forgiving other people is challenging. If practicing gratitude is like a stroll through the park, practicing forgiveness is running a marathon while carrying a bowling ball. Though it is a skill that almost anyone can learn, forgiveness can be a long haul. As with most difficult tasks, the more time we spend trying to forgive, the more successful we are. It is not about forgetting, as the adage would have us believe, but about letting go; that bowling ball is heavy. Forgiveness is about choosing positive emotions over negative ones; it is a decision that results in an en-tirely different emotional experience.

### How to Forgive

Fred Luskin, the director of the Stanford Forgiveness Project, has spent decades researching and teaching about forgiveness. He has developed a program to help people learn to forgive even the most heinous acts. Here is Luskin's forgiveness program translated into skills and concepts that we can teach and practice with our kids.

1. Help kids develop the ability to understand their emotions and articulate them when something is bothering them. Practice this by asking kids to identify and talk about their feelings, particu-larly when they are hurting. Kids can learn to talk about their feel-

ings at a very young age; see Chapter 5 for more about how to "emotion-coach" your child.

2.  When kids feel hurt, help them recognize that what they are feeling is distress coming from what they are thinking and feeling *right now,* not from the original offense, whether it was months or just minutes ago. Yesterday, Fiona and Molly collided on their scooters, resulting in minor skinned knees. Both started shouting blame at the other, wailing in melodramatic pain. I could see that neither was hurt from the accident, so I pointed out that the pain from the situation was coming not from the accident but from all the blaming. (A little of the pain was coming from the fact that each was trying to make herself look as though she was bleeding more than the other, when in fact neither was bleeding much at all.) Once they had decided to forgive each other and move on, poof! No more pain or suffering.

3.  When kids are upset, help them practice the mindfulness techniques outlined in Chapter 8. This will help turn off their fight-or-flight response so that they can respond to the upsetting situation more effectively.

4.  Teach kids that they suffer when they demand things that life is not going to give them. They can hope for things, of course, and they can work hard to get what they want. But they cannot force things to happen that are outside of their control. When we expect something outside of our control and it doesn't happen, we feel hurt and wronged. Help kids practice letting go of the desire for things that they have no influence over, and redirect their energy toward things they do have control over.

5.  Help kids understand that forgiving does not mean forgetting, excusing an action, or even reconciling with someone who hurt you. Forgiveness is a choice we make to *feel better ourselves.* Talk with kids about how awful we feel when we ruminate about how we've been hurt. Remind them of all the positive benefits *for themselves* of forgiveness.

6.  Talk with your kids about the desire for revenge, and show them that the best revenge is a life well lived. Explain that when we focus on how we've been hurt, we give power to the person who hurt us because it causes us to continue hurting.

Forgiving is tough business. It takes courage and resolve to let go of negative feelings when we've been wronged. This gets easier with practice—especially if we start with the small stuff and get into the habit early on—and it makes us stronger and better people.

## TRY THIS

### Three Ways to Practice Forgiveness

Forgiveness training raises the self-esteem and hope of people who have been hurt, and it lowers their anxiety. Here are some exercises to teach kids (and ourselves) how to forgive.

1. Tell family stories about times when you have hurt others. During dinner, for example, take turns reflecting on a time when you each were forgiven. Recall a time when you hurt someone else, either intentionally or accidentally. Then discuss whether or not you feel forgiven for the offense. If you feel as though you've been forgiven, here are some questions to discuss.

   - How do you know you've been forgiven?

   - Why do you think the person forgave you?

   - Do you think the person you hurt felt better or worse after they forgave you?

   - How did you feel after you were forgiven?

   - What is your relationship like with the person now?

   - Did being forgiven make you more or less likely to repeat the hurtful behavior?

   - If you do *not* feel that you've been forgiven, talk about how you might ask for forgiveness.

2. Role-play empathy and forgiveness. Pick a family member to describe a particular person whom they blame for something hurtful. Then take turns standing in the offender's shoes. Why might he have done what he did? What emotions might he have been feeling? Try to give the offender the benefit of the doubt; imagine lots of different things that the offender might have been going

through. Remind everyone that practicing empathy is not the same as excusing bad behavior, but it is simply a technique for letting go of anger. Finally, role-play forgiving. What can you say to the offender? What emotions are you feeling as you do the role play? Try on the facial expressions that you think you might have when expressing forgiveness. What does your body feel like when you're feeling or expressing forgiveness?

3. Write a forgiveness letter. Help kids write about a time when they were hurt in a letter that they may or may not ever send to the person who hurt them. Have them illustrate how they were affected by the hurt at the time and the bad feelings they are still experiencing. They can state what they wish the offender had done instead. Have them end this forgiveness letter with an explicit statement of forgiveness, understanding, and even empathy if they can muster it. For example, "I imagine that you didn't realize that what you said would make me cry, so I forgive you for hurting my feelings."

## YOU DON'T *SEEM* SORRY: FOUR PARTS OF AN EFFECTIVE APOLOGY

All parents eventually have to contend with the ridiculously disingenuous apology. In our household, I've been known to follow this up with an equally ridiculous insistence that the offender make her apology sincere (and right *now*, dang it). However, if we can't apologize sincerely, we shouldn't do it at all; insincere apologies make people angrier than if there had been no apology. This means not insisting that our children apologize right away if they can't do it sincerely.

According to Aaron Lazare, who has studied the psychology of apologies, effective apologies include some or all of the following: (1) clear and complete acknowledgment of the offense, (2) explanation, (3) expression of remorse, and (4) reparation.

Take the case of Fiona and Catherine, described previously. This is what it would take for their apologies to be effective.

1. Each girl needs to acknowledge her offense without mentioning what the other did wrong. Fiona needs to say, "I'm sorry I called

you mean," *not* "I'm sorry I called you mean, but you called me bossy." For an apology to work, the offender needs to fully confess to the crime without hemming, hawing, or making excuses.

2.  Each can offer an explanation, especially if they explain that they did not intentionally hurt the other's feelings or that it isn't likely to recur. Fiona can say, "*I* was hurt that you were whispering about me. In the future, I'm going to practice telling you I feel hurt without using mean words."

3.  Expressions of remorse, shame, or humility that recognize why their comments hurt the other. "I know how much it hurts my feelings to be called mean, and I feel bad that I said that to you. I am so sorry."

4.  Good apologies often include a reparation of some kind, either real or symbolic. Fiona and Catherine each need to agree to play the other's game for a little while.

# PESSIMISM V. OPTIMISM

Many kids naturally savor the future—eager anticipation of a birthday party or a big game, for example. This future savoring is a natural part of optimistic thinking, and optimism is also a skill that parents can teach their children. Optimism is so closely related to happiness that the two can practically be equated. The benefits reaped by optimists are numerous. Compared to pessimistic people, optimists are

-   More successful in school, at work, and in athletics
-   Healthier and longer lived
-   More satisfied with their marriages
-   Less likely to suffer from depression
-   Less anxious

Who wouldn't want that list of benefits for their kids? Here are three ways that kids learn to be optimistic from their parents.

## Parental Affection

I love that parental affection can influence kids' outlook on life. My brother thinks my propensity to stand close and touch the people I'm talking with is annoying, but I like to think I'm fostering hope in my kids. The researchers who direct the Penn Resiliency Project at the University of Pennsylvania say that kids whose parents are caring and affectionate are more hopeful. Parental affection and care is—no surprises here— essential for kids to develop trust in the world. When kids have a secure base in their parents, they tend to believe that the world is a good place. In addition to fostering optimism, this allows them to take risks and explore—another way they learn to be optimistic.

## Taking Risks and Failing

The ability to cope with challenge and frustration is critical for the development of optimism. Research shows that kids who are protected from failure and adversity are less likely to develop optimism. Why? When we make mistakes and learn from them, we also learn that we can overcome the challenges that likely lie ahead. This makes us feel hopeful about the future.

Optimism is contagious, especially with younger children. When Todd's daughter Suzie is apprehensive about doing something, he simply says in an excited voice, "Let's see! Let's see what happens." Suzie's anxiety, which is a form of pessimism about what the outcome might be, is usually transformed into curiosity. I love this practice because of the inherent optimism in it: no matter what the outcome, the fact that Suzie will give it a go is a good outcome in and of itself.

On the other hand, repeated failures lead to learned helplessness, not optimism, so it is important that the challenges that children face are developmentally appropriate. Too much hardship—challenges that children have little chance of rising above and can't opt out of, such as poverty or a high-pressure academic environment—can overwhelm children, making them anxious and insecure.

## Modeling

Pessimistic parents are more likely to have pessimistic children. More than modeling how optimistically or pessimistically we interpret events in our own lives, parents model how we interpret events in *their* lives. In other words, kids are more sensitive to the feedback they get from their parents than they are to their parents' explanations about their own life events. This means that when we criticize our children we make them more vulnerable to pessimism.

Here's a real-life parenting don't. The other day Fiona took out a crazy build-a-robot toy that a relative sent her for a birthday. It was intended for kids twice her age, so I was pessimistic about her ability to put it together. "You won't be able to do that," I warned her, "and I don't have time to do it for you." Deflated, she flipped through the fifty-plus-page instruction booklet and then found something else to do. I had unwittingly taught her to question her ability without testing it first. That afternoon, her god-mother, Jane, came over and saw the box of robot parts on the table. Fiona explained to her that she wanted to make the robot with pigtails but it was too hard for her. "Really?" Jane asked optimistically. "Should we try it out and *see* if it's too hard?" An hour later, the two of them had the robot functioning. Fiona was bursting with joy over her creation, which she actually ended up doing mostly on her own. "You were right, Mom," she said to me with pride. "It *was* hard. But turns out I'm good at making robots."

## THINKING OPTIMISTICALLY

Ten-year-olds who are taught how to think and interpret the world optimistically are half as prone to depression when they later go through puberty. There are lots of ways to think optimistically.

- Identify the good that comes out of difficulty.

- See the glass as half full: point out what is good rather than what is bad, even if both are present.

- Reflect on what learning comes from failure.

- Choose to trust: give yourself and others the benefit of the doubt rather than succumbing to self-doubt, blaming, or feeling offended.

Famed psychologist Martin Seligman, who has studied optimism for decades, shows that how optimistic or pessimistic we are can also determine how we explain life's events. Say a kid pitches a great baseball game and the team wins. The optimistic way of understanding why this happened would explain the cause as something that is likely to recur and affect other circumstances, too: *Our team really works well together! We're going to have a great season!* The pessimistic way of explaining why something good happened would illustrate that the cause is just temporary, or specific to the situation: *It is a fluke we won today; the other team was missing their good players. That won't happen again.* We can help kids think optimistically by pointing out the reasons that good things will continue to occur. For example, pointing out that the pitcher's dedicated practice paid off is more optimistic than saying "You pitched a great game!" Practice hones skills for the long haul; pitching a good game might be just a fluke.

Optimistic thinking also comes from interpreting good events as something we made happen ourselves. Seeing success as a function of the pitcher's hard work is personal; a more pessimistic take on the situation would make the success impersonal: *The other team wasn't very good; anyone could have beat them.* That takes the success out of the pitcher's hands and gives credit to other people or circumstances.

The reverse is true when bad things happen. Say a kid trips on the sidewalk. The pessimist thinks, *I'm so clumsy. I'm always tripping everywhere, and now I look stupid.* The cause of her fall is permanent and personal; she sees clumsiness as a personality trait. The optimist thinks, *Dang! Someone outta fix that crack in the sidewalk!* The cause of her fall is impersonal and specific to that particular place in the sidewalk; she had nothing to do with it.

Not surprisingly, people who frequently blame themselves when things aren't going well are less happy than those who don't assign blame at all.

## The Growth Mind-Set, Praise, and Optimism

Thinking about the skills our kids need for optimism adds another dimension to how we should praise children, discussed in Chapter 2. Praise is important for kids, but it needs to be growth–mind-set praise— emphasizing effort and hard work— in order to make kids resilient and persistent in the face of challenges. The key is to keep our praise growth mind-set *and* optimistic. Growth–mind-set praise focuses on effort rather than innate ability. Optimistic praise points to the causes of good things as likely to occur again and specific to the person being praised. For example, praising my daughter's artwork, I could say, "I can tell you worked really hard on that painting, Fiona. Your passion for art shows."

I don't worry too much about being optimistic when I praise my kids; focusing on the growth mind-set is good enough. I do, however, avoid voicing pessimistic explanations that I may have for misfortune or misbehavior. Kids pick up on this, and we can teach our children to be pessimistic as easily as we can teach optimism. For example, say my daughter Molly hits her sister or says something nasty. A pessimistic reaction to this would be, "Molly, you are being mean. You are not going to have any friends at school if you behave that way." Assigning her the character flaw of being mean is personal, and it sounds like something I expect to be pervasive rather than temporary. Optimistic reaction: "You sure are having a hard time right now, Molly. I think you might be hungry. Please apologize to your sister, and let's go get you something to eat." This makes the bad behavior temporary and specific to the situation; she'll behave better once she's not hungry. Furthermore, the situation will be over with an apology, and it's nothing personal; it's more about her blood sugar than her personality.

## A Word About Genetics

But aren't some kids born as pessimists or as sunny optimists, as my doubter friends are always asking me? Of course! But genetics aren't everything; in fact, studies of identical twins reared apart tell us that our genes probably don't account for more than 25 percent of why we tend toward optimism. So we want to be careful before we label a child a born pessimist. Although genetics is our culture's most frequent explanation for why people are the way they are, this is a fixed–mind-set and a pessimistic way of thinking. Better to focus on teaching our kids the skills they will need to overcome pessimistic tendencies, as well as the skills they'll need to lead joyful lives as adults. If you've got a determined pessimist in your midst, I'd recommend Seligman's book *The Optimistic Child*. It's got a whole section on changing a pessimist into an optimist.

# FIVE

■ ■ ■ ■ ■ ■

# Step 5: Raise Their Emotional Intelligence

*When you start to develop your powers of empathy and imagination, the whole world opens up to you.*
—SUSAN SARANDON

My critics—those who think that happiness is frivolous and not as important as, say, kindness or success—always ask me about negative emotions. *What about stress?* they ask. *Isn't it often motivating?* Or *I think anger can be a good thing; I don't want my kids to feel like they need to be happy all the time.*

Though this is a book about fostering positive emotions in our kids, it isn't about feeling happy all the time. Even the happiest of lives are full of unpleasantries such as pain, disappointment, failure, loss, and betrayal. Often the biggest difference between happy people and depressive ones is that the happy people know how to cope with painful situations and emotions, and they know how to bounce back from them.

Resilience in the face of difficulty requires a particular form of intelligence. Traditional smarts—book smarts or even street savvy—won't necessarily bring happiness, but social and emotional intelligence will. Here's how to increase your children's emotional intelligence, which is nothing less than the foundation of lasting happiness.

The good news is that, once again, emotional intelligence is a skill, not an inborn trait. For that reason, I like the term emotional literacy better than emotional intelligence. Talking about literacy reminds us that we are teaching our children the skills they need to become better at understanding their many and changing feelings. People are emotionally literate to the extent that they can read and understand emotions—their own and those of other people. Emotionally literate kids can recognize, interpret, and respond constructively to their own feelings and those of others.

Parents build their children's emotional literacy in two fundamental ways. First, they establish secure attachments with them—those sensitive and responsive relationships that give kids the support they need to explore the world. Second, they "emotion-coach" their kids so they build a large vocabulary of feelings that they feel capable of and comfortable dealing with. This chapter will teach you how to do both of these things.

Part of raising happy kids—those whose lives are filled with lots of different types of positive feelings—is teaching them how to express and cope with their negative emotions. Uncomfortable feelings such as anger, sadness, and anxiety aren't necessarily bad; they can alert us to situations that we need to get out of or change, and they can lead us to realize just how deeply our bonds to one another are. But negative emotions do need to be dealt with effectively (researchers say they need to be "regulated").

Psychologist John Gottman's research on emotional intelligence shows that children who can regulate their emotions are better at soothing themselves when they are upset, which means that they experience negative emotions such as fear and anger for a shorter period of time. They have fewer infectious illnesses and are better at focusing their attention. Such children understand and relate better to people and form stronger friendships.

Emotional literacy is also one of the best predictors of school performance and career success, better even than IQ. This is in part because emotionally literate children are better learners and have better relationships in the classroom. Emotional literacy fosters resilience and helps narrow academic achievement gaps, promoting gains in nearly every area of children's lives—most notably happiness and school success. So emotional literacy is definitely something we want our kids to develop. Here's how.

## Attachment Relationships: More Is More

*It is in the shelter of each other that the people live.*
                    —IRISH PROVERB

Emotional literacy is rooted in the parent-child bond. When parents and caregivers pay close attention and respond to the emotional cues that their children express, children learn to regulate their emotions better.

The emotional bonds between parents and caregivers and their kids are called "attachments," and parent-child attachments come in three dominant styles: avoidant, anxious, and secure. I don't need to tell you that the bond we want to form with our children is the secure one. There are vast benefits to secure attachment. "Securely attached" kids are

- healthier

- more confident in their explorations of the world, and better able to deal with challenging circumstances

- more achievement-oriented, independent, and persistent problem solvers

- more willing to ask for help and seek comfort when frustrated

- better liked by their teachers, maybe because they require less guidance and discipline

- less likely to be bullied or be bullies themselves

- better behaved and less impulsive at school

One reason that secure attachments are so significant is that they serve as the foundation for future relationships. Kids with secure attachments to their parents and other caregivers are better liked by their peers and tend to have more friends. Strong attachment relationships build emotional literacy, which in turn facilitates the formation of positive, supportive relationships with teachers, friends, and others in their community.

Attachment security is important throughout childhood and adolescence and can even typify romantic relationships in adulthood. Securely attached children have a better sense of themselves, better memories, more positive feelings about friendship, and a more developed sense of morality. Establishing secure connections has its benefits when it comes to discipline, too: securely attached toddlers are more compliant when their parents ask them to do something, and their parents' disciplinary techniques are more likely to be effective.

So how do we raise a securely attached child? Quite simply, our level of responsiveness determines how secure our children will be. To be a responsive parent or caregiver, we can do the following.

**Be sensitive** to our children's needs and be warm in our interactions with them. What do our children need, given the circumstances? This is a matter of being present and paying attention. We can demonstrate empathy and convey warmth by acknowledging their needs: "I can see that you are feeling very tired and need a nap. I get grouchy when I'm tired, too. Let's go home and lie down."

**Be responsive and consistent.** Knowing what our children need is one thing; fulfilling that need is quite another. When our kids are infants, responding to their needs is usually fairly straightforward (albeit tiring). We change their diapers, feed them, help them get to sleep. But as kids get older, their needs become more complex. Make no mistake: being responsive does not mean giving them whatever they want. Sometimes when our children want a later curfew, what they need is a more regular routine or firmer discipline. Parental responsiveness predicts in children greater sociability, self-discipline, positive behaviors toward others, and self-esteem. Consistency matters, too: attachment guru John Bowlby calls it the law of continuity: "The more stable and predictable the regime, the more secure a child's attachment tends to be; the more discontinuous and unpredictable . . . the more anxious."

**Be available and accessible** to our children, emotionally and physically. We may spend a lot of time with our children, but if we aren't emotionally available—that is, if we are preoccupied with our BlackBerry or lost in our own worries—the time together doesn't count for much. The same is true for when our intentions are good but we aren't around enough. Our deep desire to connect with our children doesn't pay off if we don't give our kids enough time to actually do the connecting.

**Encourage multiple attachments.** Although infants and toddlers who are securely attached to their mothers or their daytime caregivers are more mature and positive in their interactions with others, children who have secure attachments with mothers *and* their caregivers are the most emotionally literate of all (attachment to fathers wasn't tested in this study). Kids benefit the most from three secure relationships: with a mother, a father, and a daytime caregiver.

Recognize the importance of sibling and peer attachments. Siblings and friends are also important for children's security, even for children as young as fifteen months. For example, when infants and toddlers are transferred to new day-care settings—requiring them to establish new attachments with caregivers—they do better when they are transferred with close friends than if they are transferred alone. Similarly, siblings can be important attachment figures by providing closeness, comfort, and security.

### Emotion Coaching: One of the Most Important Parenting Practices in the History of the Universe

*When we honestly ask ourselves which person in our lives means the most to us, we often find that it is those who, instead of giving advice, solutions, or cures, have chosen rather to share our pain and touch our wounds with a gentle and tender hand.*

—HENRI NOUWEN

At this point, many parents are probably thinking I've just reported on the science of the blazingly obvious: kids do better when their parents are sensitive and loving, consistent, and positively involved. We know this instinctively.

Here's something that may not be so instinctive: though love, dependability, and sensitivity do create secure attachments, they are not enough to foster emotional intelligence in children. Secure attachments are an essential foundation for emotional literacy, but parents also need to "emotion-coach" their kids, teaching them to cope with emotions such as anger, anxiety, and fear. Just as secure attachments create the safe environment in which children can be coached, emotion coaching helps build and maintain secure attachments while developing loyalty and affection between parents and children; the two things build on each other. Parents who are effective emotion coaches have a heightened sensitivity to their children's emotions, in part because they see these emotional expressions—even anger and frustration—as opportunities to connect with and teach their children. They listen empathetically, helping children to explore and validate their feelings. And they don't stop there: they teach their children to verbally label their emotions, and then they set limits ("It is not okay to hit your sister") while helping to problem-solve.

**Really? Do I Really Need to Become an Emotion Coach?** I know, I know: it sounds as though it's going to be a lot of work, and you're already coaching Little League. According to John Gottman, one of my all-time favorite researchers, emotion coaching is *the* key to raising happy, resilient, and well-adjusted kids. His research shows that it is not enough to be a warm, engaged, and loving parent. Warmth and attention foster certain aspects of emotional literacy, but they don't necessarily teach kids how to deal with negative feelings such as sadness and frustration. Emotion coaching does. The reality, of course, is that life inevitably involves pain and suffering, disappointment and failure, loss and betrayal. Much as we would like to, we cannot protect our children from these things. We can, however, teach them to cope with the difficult and often painful emotions that arise out of life's less happy moments.

Ironically, when we accept that our children are going to experience pain and resolve to coach them through it, their pain dissipates more quickly. Emotion-coached kids tend to experience fewer negative and more positive feelings. And for kids in households with parental conflict or divorce, Gottman has found that emotion coaching is the only thing that buffers them from emotional trauma and negative risk factors, such as trouble at school and problems with peers.

Gottman teaches parents how to become effective emotion coaches in his book and video *Raising an Emotionally Intelligent Child*. The three steps below are adapted from Gottman's plan; I can't recommend his book highly enough to parents looking for further reading. Not only has Gottman's emotion-coaching strategy helped me manage the emotions of my strong-willed children, it helps me manage my own emotions when I am around other adults, especially adults with whom I have strong emotional ties and therefore frequent conversations where emotions can run high. (Those of you who have been through a divorce know what I'm talking about here.)

The first step to coping with negative emotions (in yourself, your children, or your mother-in-law) is to figure out what they are feeling and to accept those feelings. Even if we don't accept the bad behavior that often accompanies negative emotions, we still want to send the message that all feelings are okay, even the worst ones. Negative feelings such as jealousy and fear and greed are invitations to grow, to understand ourselves better, and to become better people. When we see these "undesirable" emotions in our children, consider it an opportunity to learn more about their inner world and—importantly—to teach them how to deal with negative emotions now and in the future.

To become an effective emotion coach, we need to empathize with our children so that we can help them label their unpleasant emotions. The goal is to validate their emotions so that they learn to understand and trust what they are feeling. When we don't understand our emotions, we can't cope with them or the situation effectively, all of which leads to self-doubt and a loss of self-esteem. Often, especially with little kids, bad feelings are accompanied by bad behavior; think of the preschooler who gets frustrated and angry and then hits her friend. It is important for kids to realize that their feelings are not the problem; their poor behavior is. So ignore the misbehavior for now until you've accomplished Step 1: Label and Validate the Feelings at Hand.

## 1: Label and Validate the Feelings at Hand

Before we can accurately label and then validate our children's feelings, we need to empathize with them—first to understand what it is they are feeling, and then to communicate to them what we understand. This is simple but not always easy.

Empathizing does not mean taking a stab in the dark at what must be causing the feelings and then launching full force into problem solving. It also doesn't mean that we should try to relieve them of their pain by distracting them from their negative emotions. Or that we should reframe an uncomfortable situation by finding humor in it at the expense of our child. I'm often guilty of these three not-empathizing reactions to my children's negative emotions. Although Molly in particular can throw some spectacular fits, I am very effective at disarming her anger, if I do say so myself, through distraction, bribe, and indirect threat:

**Molly,** shouting: "I hate you! You are the meanest mommy in the world!"

**Me:** "Hey, Molly, did you say you wanted a giant stuffed dolphin for Christmas? I heard that Santa's elves can make that. Do you think Santa is listening to you right now?"

**Molly,** sniffling, in a strained, sweet voice: "Really? Fiona says that if I get a dolphin and I name it Phinn, she won't call it Finnley like that boy in her class."

I'm also quite good at assuming I know what is wrong—when I really don't—and barreling on from there. I've been known to say things that will often disarm her, such as, "Hey, Molly, you seem super-tired and in need of a snack. Let's get your blood sugar up and go read on the couch together." Even if I'm right that her emotions are being fueled by hunger and exhaustion, and even if I make it better by giving her a little extra love, I still haven't really communicated that I understand what she is feeling or why. Before solving the problem, I need to validate and label her feelings.

Occasionally, I also make the situation worse for Molly by allowing myself a good belly laugh at her expense. When she's screaming and carrying on, her threats can be quite funny (such as "Mommy, if you don't let me go to AnnaBelle's house, *I will never hug you again*"), and sometimes I'm tempted to just laugh. Humor is my default state because it feels so good, especially when tension is running high. But in this case, laughter would be mean and destructive. I can only imagine how I would feel if I were angry with my own mother and she started laughing at me.

The problem with these sometimes temporarily effective responses is that they don't validate Molly's feelings—which are very real to her—or help her understand them better. The key to this first step is to imagine ourselves in our kids' shoes and feel their pain. That is real empathy. Say Molly is feeling bad because she got into some trouble at school for talking too much in class (no idea where she might have gotten that tendency). Kids frequently displace negative emotions onto their loving siblings, parents, and caregivers, meaning that while Molly might be mad at herself, a classmate, or her teacher, it would be normal for her to displace that emotion onto me and Fiona when she gets home. So when I tell her she can't have a playdate with AnnaBelle right that second, it provokes an angry fury, during which she throws her backpack against the wall that I've asked her to hang it on and calls her sister a "stupid head" whom she would never want to play with "in a million years."

Instead of dealing with the bad behavior right away (time out!) or defusing her anger using the not-empathizing methods above, this is a terrific opportunity to accomplish the first step in emotion coaching: validating and labeling the negative emotions.

### EMPATHIZE, LABEL, AND VALIDATE

**Me:** "Molly, you are acting very angry and frustrated. Are you feeling small right now?" [I know that Molly often exhibits *big* emotions when she feels small.]

**Molly:** "Yes, I'm feeling small." (Her rage softens.)
**Me:** "Is there anything else that you are feeling?"
**Molly:** "I am SO SO SO MAD AT YOU."
**Me:** "You are mad at me, *very* mad at me. Tell me about that. Are you also feeling disappointed because I won't let you have a playdate right now?"
**Molly:** "YES!! I want to have a playdate right NOW."
**Me:** "You seem sad." (Crawling into my lap, Molly whimpers a little and rests her head on my shoulder.)

I've now helped Molly identify and label several feelings: angry, small, frustrated, disappointed, sad. I have also validated how Molly has been feeling; she knows I think it is okay to have all those "bad" feelings. Interestingly, now she is calm, tired—clearly needing a snack and a cuddle.

Sometimes, however, there very much needs to be a cooling-off period between the expression of feelings on the child's part and the identification of the feeling by us. One reader of my blog described how this process would go without the cooling-off period.

**Parent:** "Son, I can see that you are very angry and frustrated. Is there anything else you are feeling?"
**Son** (at the top of his voice while glaring): "I AM NOT ANGRY!!! I AM NOT FRUSTRATED!!!"
**Parent:** "What is it you're feeling?"
**Son** (while red in the face and wild eyed): "I AM HAPPY!!!"

On the other hand, when she calmly asks him to go sit on the couch, leaving him alone there for a few minutes to calm down, and *then* goes to talk to him, the conversation is more like this:

**Parent:** "It seemed like you were a little angry when you came in a minute ago." (Note the understatement.)
**Son:** "Yeah . . ."
**Parent:** "You also seem a bit sad . . ."

Son crawls into her lap, and Mom can go on to label emotions. Although we are using time-outs in these situations, they are designed to get kids calm enough that they won't resist anything and everything we do. We're not using them to punish bad behavior. Kids often start out so angry and negative that they will turn down ice cream if we are the ones to suggest it.

However long it takes, the key is to eventually label and validate our kids' emotions. The larger our children's emotion vocabulary, the easier it is to label emotions just before kids blow up into massive outbursts. Often when kids feel understood, they don't need to have a tantrum to be heard. Refer to the "Try This" section on page 100 to work on building your child's feelings vocabulary before you really need it.

### Step 2: Deal with the Bad Behavior (if applicable)

At this point, I just want to move on and forget about the backpack throwing and name calling. But it is important to set limits so that kids learn how to behave well even in the face of strong, negative emotions. (Also see Chapter 7, which is all about discipline and how to teach kids to regulate themselves.) I tell Molly that she needs to go to her room and have a five-minute time-out, and I make it clear that these behaviors are not okay: "It is okay to feel angry and frustrated, but it is never okay to throw things or call people mean names. When the timer goes off, please apologize to your sister and come have a snack."

Ten minutes after the initial incident, I am sitting with Molly while she eats. Time for Step 3.

### Step 3: Problem-Solve

Now is the time to explore a little further and to help Molly figure out how to handle the situation better in the future. After we've labeled and validated the emotions arising out of the problem, we can turn to the problem itself: "Molly, did anything happen at school today that is also making you feel bad?"

At this point, Molly tells me all about the scene at school where she had to sit at a table by herself because she was too disruptive during reading. I relate to how bad it would feel for my hypersocial and teacher-pleasing child to be isolated from her friends and to have disappointed her teacher, so it was easy for me to empathize. We talk about how sad and lonely she felt doing her work alone when the other kids were working together, and how embarrassed she felt by being singled out. We also talk about how she felt hungry and exhausted when she came home from school.

I do *not* tell her how she *ought* to feel ("Molly, I hope you feel bad for throwing your backpack against the wall"), because that would make her distrust what she did feel (the backpack throwing might well have felt good). The goal is to put her in touch with her emotions, good or bad. So even during the problem solving, I label and validate more of her feelings: lonely, embarrassed, hungry, tired.

Next, brainstorm together possible ways to solve a problem or prevent it from happening again. The more we parents can stay in our role as coaches—holding back all of our terrific (bossy!) ideas and letting kids come up with their own—the better. The best ideas come from the kids themselves, when they explore the problem from their own perspective and knowledge. Since Molly knows best when it is especially hard to stop chatting in class, she is the one who will come up with the most effective way to prevent it from happening again. Similarly, when we brainstorm different things she can do when she feels angry (instead of backpack throwing, for example), she is more likely to try the solutions if she thinks them up. She decides that the next time she comes home from school feeling frustrated and disappointed, she'll walk the dog around the block while she eats her snack until she feels better.

That's all there is to it! First, label and validate the emotions you see. Second, deal with misbehavior if you need to. Finally, help your child solve the problem. You are now a bona fide emotion coach. Here are a few other things to keep in mind.

- The goal is not to protect children from feeling bad but rather to help them understand what they are feeling and to cope with that. Resist the impulse to try to downplay negative emotions ("There is no reason to be afraid of that") or to deny what they are feeling ("You aren't scared; you've done this before"). This teaches kids to distrust their own feelings ("I feel frightened, but my mom says I'm not") and may also make them feel bad about their emotions ("I don't want to feel scared, and Mom doesn't want me to feel scared, but I do").

- The more time you spend emotion-coaching your children, the more they will see you as an ally, and the more they will trust you to help in the future. When we take the time to understand what

our children are feeling, they feel supported and they learn that
their feelings are valid and worthy of respect.

- Negative emotions are opportunities for growth and learning. This
  is difficult to remember when a child's angry outbursts are publicly
  embarrassing and we just want them to quit it. Or when their
  outbursts seem like a challenge to our authority, or simply because
  it is *so hard* to see someone we love in pain. Over the long run,
  however, the more we embrace difficult emotions as constructive
  teaching moments, the less time our kids will spend in these
  uncomfortable states.

## MANUFACTURING HAPPINESS

*There wouldn't be such a thing as counterfeit gold if there were no
real gold somewhere.*

—Sufi proverb

Another thing we can do to build emotional literacy in our kids—in addition to creating secure attachments and emotion-coaching our children—
is to teach them how to conjure up their own positive emotions when they
need them. Or—and sometimes this is easier at first—we can whip up
some good feelings ourselves to pass on to our children.

### Smile and the World Smiles with You

*A human being is a part of the whole, called by us, "universe," a part
limited in time and space. He experiences himself, his thoughts and
feelings as something separated from the rest—a kind of optical
delusion of his consciousness.*

—Albert Einstein

Why does an angry child so easily make us angry ourselves? Because we
have "mirror neurons" in our brains, and they cause us to catch the negative emotions of others like a nasty flu. Neuroscience has shown us that
our brains are designed to be in sync with those around us. Einstein was
right when he said that our separate sense of ourselves is a delusion of our
consciousness. Our mirror neurons sense what others are feeling and induce those same feelings in our own bodies.

When we are exposed to happy faces, we unconsciously smile; when we are exposed to sad faces, we frown. What is surprising is how instantaneous the response tends to be. In one study, researchers flashed pictures of happy or sad faces for a microsecond on a screen, so quickly that participants didn't know that they had seen a face. Researchers then put up a neutral image, such as a chair. Despite the fact that participants didn't register seeing a face, they had involuntary emotional reactions and in most cases weren't even aware that they were moving their facial muscles.

It isn't just that we can't help but perceive others' emotions, or make our faces mimic the expressions of others. We actually experience other people's feelings as though they were our own. Just hearing a barfing sound activates some of the same brain areas that would light up if we were actually experiencing disgust. Similarly, hearing someone laugh activates a region of our own brain that would light up if we were laughing ourselves. Good feelings are infectious, and so are negative ones.

This seems like good news with regard to happy feelings and bad news when our children are acting out. But it is actually good news on both fronts, because what we need most to be good emotion coaches is empathy, and it turns out that we are hardwired for it. So when our children are feeling bad, we can tune in to how it is making *us* feel, and use that to help us get through that important first step in emotion coaching: labeling and validating our kids' feelings. It can be especially validating—certainly it is good modeling—to acknowledge out loud how we are feeling as we acknowledge our children's feelings.

## Fake It Till You Make It

There is something else at work here: facial expressions themselves actually make us feel the corresponding emotion. If you wrinkle your nose and narrow your eyes as if you were angry, your body will release adrenaline and your heart rate may speed up as if you were actually angry.

The same thing is true for positive emotions. This means that sometimes we should smile even if we don't feel like it. As forced as that sounds, there is science to back up the notion that this will, in fact, make us feel happier. Facial expression alone, without first feeling the corresponding emotion, is enough to create discernible changes in our autonomic nervous system. Force a smile—lift up those pretty lips, as my grandmother used to say—and crinkle your eyes, and your body will release feel-good brain chemicals into your system. You can even just hold a pencil between your teeth—thereby activating your smile muscles—and you will likely find that your heart rate goes down and you start to feel calmer, happier. (The study shows that you'll also find things funnier for a while.) I've found the pencil-clenching trick works, but it makes me drool.

I'm not advocating that we force ourselves or our children to smile, or feel happy, when we're in the thick of bad feelings. As stated before, negative feelings are wonderful learning opportunities. When kids are feeling crummy, we need to emotion-coach them so that they learn to deal with their negative emotions. We can't fool them anyway; research shows that we aren't very good at hiding how we are feeling. We exhibit microexpressions that people might not know they are registering but that trigger our mirror neurons. So trying to suppress negative emotions when we are talking with someone about something upsetting—such as instances when we don't want to trouble someone else with our own distress—actually increases the stress levels of both people more than if we had shared our distress in the first place. It also reduces rapport and inhibits the connection between two people.

But after an episode of negative feelings (and perhaps backpack throwing) is over, we can have emotional hangovers that feel good to alleviate. After Molly's tantrum, we were all ready to share a few laughs. We label and validate negative emotions, deal with bad behavior, problem-solve, and then we move on. Knowing that if I smiled Molly would be likely to feel happier, or if I prompted her sister to giggle Molly would probably feel as though she is laughing herself, turns out to be a good parenting trick for creating a happy mood.

When we induce happiness this way, our positive emotions undo some of the physiological damage caused by stressful emotions. In other words, smiling triggers positive physiological changes in ourselves and those around us because it halts damage done by any negative emotions that might have come before it. Smiling boosts our immune system, reduces our stress, lowers our blood pressure, and makes people like us more. This is at least in part because good feelings have what positivity researcher Barbara Fredrickson calls the "undoing effect." Emotions—both positive and negative—have biological and physiological effects. Positive emotions "undo" the physiological response of negative ones, calming the heart rate and reducing levels of stress-related hormones in our bodies. They turn off, or tone down, our fight-or-flight response.

## Getting the Ratios Right

Hopefully you'll come away from this chapter realizing that even though what we ultimately want for our kids is happiness, negative feelings are important, too, particularly for building emotional literacy. So why would we want to "manufacture happiness," as this section suggests?

Because to be really happy in life—to flourish, as Fredrickson calls it—we need to experience three or more positive feelings for every negative one. Actually, we need to experience at least 2.9013 positive feelings for every negative one, which I mention only to impress upon you that this is a mathematical (and psychological) fact demonstrated in several extremely sophisticated scientific studies. There is a definite tipping point, according to Fredrickson, just as there is a definite point when ice melts into water. People whose positive emotion ratios are lower than 3:1 languish, as the researchers call it. Their performance at work suffers, they are more likely to be depressed (and not recover), their marriages are more likely to fail—and they definitely aren't happy. Their behavior becomes predictable to psychologists, and not in a good way: languishing people become rigid. They tend to feel burdened by life. People whose ratios fall below 3:1 may still experience positive emotions and happiness, but those positive emotions aren't as influential as they would be in greater quantities: they become inert. So our grand and well-meaning efforts to foster gratitude and the growth mind-set and emotional literacy—all in the service of happiness—will be futile if our kids aren't getting enough of these good things.

Fortunately, something remarkable happens when our ratio of positive to negative feelings passes that 3:1 mark. We flourish. Though social scientists classify only 20 percent of the population as flourishing, these people feel happy and resilient, even when facing great difficulty. They are high-functioning individuals who score well on things such as self-acceptance, purpose in life, environmental mastery, positive relationships with others, personal growth, creativity, and openness. They feel good and they *do* good, so to speak: they are highly engaged with their friends, their work, their families, and their communities.

This ratio—called the Losada line, after the mathematician who discovered it—holds true in groups, too. John Gottman has shown that unless a married couple can maintain a ratio of five positive comments or interactions to every negative one, their marriage is more likely to end.

(Those who get divorced typically have slightly fewer positive interactions than negative ones.)

Similarly, high-performance teams have a ratio of almost six positive "utterances" to one negative. Your family can be a "high-performance team," too, by keeping your interactions more positive than negative. A good tip to come out of this research is to make sure that more of your comments to your kids are other-focused rather than self-focused. First ask your kids how *they* feel before you tell them how *you* feel. And make sure that you are more often asking questions than defending your own point of view.

Researchers conclude that because negative emotions and experiences affect us more dramatically than positive ones do—feelings of being frightened, for example, generally stay with us for much longer than having a good laugh—we need to have more positive experiences and feelings to thrive. We also know that there is an upper limit to the number of positive feelings a person can take. Specifically, a ratio above 11.6 positive experiences or feelings to one negative can, ironically, turn a person sour. This is not something that I would worry about, though: if you jump too high, you might also bump your head on a cloud!

## TRY THIS

### Put on Some Happy Tunes and Dance Around

Another idea to file under science of the blazingly obvious is the now-proven fact that certain types of music induce positive moods. I've found that when I need the undoing effect of happiness after a particularly difficult afternoon with my kids, all I need to do is put on some music that makes them happy. (The trick is to find something that makes them happy but doesn't annoy me. Putting *High School Musical* songs on repeat makes them exuberant but makes *me* want to hurl myself off a cliff.) In my early twenties my friends and I would put on a few songs, always the same ones, to dance around to when we got home from work. All that unself-conscious dancing and singing made us high-spirited even after the roughest day at our entry-level jobs. Now neuroscientists have shown that while mentally fatiguing activities such as thinking and creating induce physiological signs of stress, music reduces these signs (such as the cortisol levels in our saliva).

The other well-studied effect of the dance party, as we call it in my household, comes from getting exercise. Physical activity is even better at inducing good moods than happy music, and it is crucial to the way we think and feel. Exercise prepares our brains to learn, improves our mood and attention, and lowers stress and anxiety. Put the two things together—music and exercise—and we've got a recipe for happy kids.

## THE SCIENCE OF HAPPY ENDINGS

We humans love happy endings. People generally rate a memory of a negative event as more pleasant if it is followed by a positive event—a happy ending—than if it wasn't followed by something better. How we evaluate how we felt about something can be predicted based on two points: the point when our emotions peaked in intensity, and how we felt when things were ending. This is what Barbara Fredrickson calls the "peak-and-end rule." In other words, during one frame in time (such as a whole day, or a picnic at your cousin Al's house, or a ten-minute interaction with a belligerent store-clerk), we tend to evaluate our experience as a whole based primarily on these two points of reference: the most emotionally intense point, and the ending.

For example, study participants were asked to put their hands in a bucket of fifty-nine-degree water for one minute (the "negative event"). Then people were asked to do it again for a longer period of time, but this time after the initial minute the water was warmed to a still-not-balmy sixty-one degrees (the happy ending—not exactly a Cinderella story). Here is what I think is so interesting: 69 percent of these participants said that if they had to do it again, they'd choose the *longer* trial with the better ending; they also had more favorable memories of the attempt with the "happier" ending.

Here is what I take away from these sorts of experiments. How long an event lasts doesn't affect how we remember it. So getting over negative emotions quickly is not as important as ending on a more positive note. Better to take my time to learn about—to label and validate—Molly's tantruming feelings so that she learns something than to rush through difficult emotions so that we all feel better sooner. Kids will make future decisions about their behavior based on how an incident *ends*. Negative "peaks" can be countered with happy endings to diminish the effects of the negative experience. As parents, we can pay particular attention to small acts of warming up the water, so to speak.

If our kids experience something really negative during the day, we can influence their memory of that day in a couple of ways using the peak-and-end rule. First, we can take a stab at giving them a different, and positive, peak. With my younger kids, a dance party (as described above) or an exuberant half hour spent roughhousing will do this; the joy they feel generally eclipses whatever was previously bothering them. Second, we can focus on ending the day on a positive note. I do this by asking my kids just before they drift off to dreamland to tell me about three good things that happened that day (see Chapter 8). This savoring evokes lots of positive emotions. Sometimes we laugh again about something funny that happened; often we feel profound gratitude for a fun moment with a friend. The savoring gives every day its own happy ending.

## TRY THIS

### Build Your Family Feelings Vocabulary

(*adapted from* EQ and Your Child, *by Eileen Healy*)

If we are to bolster our children's emotional literacy, we need to give them a vocabulary with which to describe their emotions. One way to do that is to simply start keeping a list of feelings to talk about. When children hear adults talk about their feelings, they learn how to talk about their own emotions.

### Create a Family Feelings List

This will help kids (and grown-ups) become aware of their own and other family members' emotions.

1.  Write "Family Feelings List" at the top of a large piece of paper.

2.  Brainstorm feelings and emotions that you and your kids have felt. The idea is to generate a list of lots of feelings, not to edit or

decide what is or isn't an emotion. Vague descriptions such as "left out" are fine.

3. Post the list in a place where anyone can add to it anytime, and revisit it regularly.

4. Start talking about the emotions on the Family Feelings List. At dinner or during a family meeting, take turns telling one another about a time when you each had a particular feeling on the list. Before you begin, make sure that everyone understands that no one is allowed to criticize, judge, or lecture about what is shared.

5. Let kids put check marks by the emotions on the list when they feel them, assigning each family member a different color. This will help kids realize that other family members sometimes feel the same way they do, dissipating the sense of isolation that sometimes accompanies negative emotions.

6. Decide on a feeling for everyone to watch for the following day. Next time, have everyone share their observations of that emotion. How did it make your body feel? What did the person's face look like?

### Narrate Your Own Emotions

Whenever you have a chance, name out loud how you are feeling. This doesn't have to be just negative feelings; any emotions will do. Here are some examples.

- I am so happy that the sun is out.

- I feel frustrated when the store lines are so long.

- I am hungry. I wish I had eaten more for lunch.

- I am so excited to go hiking tomorrow.

- I feel disappointed with myself when I forget to call people back.

- I feel so thankful and appreciative when Dad folds all of the laundry!

# SIX

■ ■ ■ ■ ■ ■

# Step 6: Form Happiness Habits

*As an irrigator guides water to his fields, as an archer aims an arrow, as a carpenter carves wood, the wise shape their lives.*

—Buddha

## HAPPINESS ON AUTOPILOT

It was a morning like any other morning. Fiona had been asking repeatedly, despite my definitive nos, to have a piece of the Halloween candy she'd been hiding for three months and accidentally happened upon. Molly was so deep in her pretend play with her stuffed animal, Toto, that I couldn't get her to follow even the simplest of instructions. Their father, Mike, and I had recently separated, and I was a single parent trying to figure out how to get the kids out the door and off to school. With only twenty-five minutes to drop off both kids before my first meeting started, I was going to be late. Possibly very late.

"Please put on your shoes, Molly. Look at me. Please put on your shoes."

"Fiona, did you brush your teeth? Is your homework in the blue folder?"

"*Molly.* Please put on your shoes. They're by the door."

I went upstairs to pack up my computer and became distracted by an e-mail. While I typed a reply, I screamed down to the kids, "I really need you both to get in the car!" I did not hear the pitter-patter of feet toward the front door, or car doors opening, so I went back downstairs. Agitated and balancing my briefcase, Molly's lunch box, and a travel cup of coffee,

I guided the girls toward the door. It was like trying to herd cats. When we were almost out the door, I realized I had forgotten to put on deodorant. I thought about heading back upstairs to put some on, but I saw that Molly still didn't have her shoes on. "*Molly!* How many times do I have to ask you? Put on your shoes or I'll take away Toto *forever!*" She didn't even look up at me. I grabbed her arm and sat her down on the bottom step. She resisted my hand around her arm and yelled defiantly, right in my face: "You are hurting my body!" I wanted to scream. "This is what happens when I have to put on your shoes. You have to wear these." I pushed her least favorite shoes toward her, the ones I actually spent some money on but she never wore. I was not using a kind voice. "If you want to wear your ruby slippers, tomorrow you need to put on your shoes yourself without me having to beg you to do it." She started to cry—hard. I was tired. Also, I was so anxious about how late I always run that I felt as if my heart might explode. I was not feeling happy. Molly ripped off the shoes that I had just put on her and threw one clear across the room. She wasn't happy either.

At some point that morning, it occurred to me that I knew better. The core premise of this book is that happiness is a skill set that parents can teach to their kids. If we want to be happy, and if we want our children to be happy, we have to learn how to turn the skills presented in this book, and the positive skills we already have, into automatic habits. But mornings such as that one made it clear that I had *also* been teaching my kids habits that foster negative emotions rather than positive ones. For example, clearly both kids had the annoying habit of waiting until the tenth time I'd asked them to do something before they did it. This was a frustration-fostering habit on my end and, because I often threw in a few random threats for added motivation, a fear-fostering habit on their end.

Most of us have some routines with our children that just aren't working but we continue to replay day in and day out anyway. For my friend Riley, nightly homework battles with her eighth grader leave her depleted and frustrated and her son distant and grouchy. How do we break such frustration-fostering habits? How do we instill happiness habits in their place? The research has much to say about this.

## THE ELEPHANT AND THE RIDER

As Jonathan Haidt artfully describes in *The Happiness Hypothesis,* our brain functions fall into two categories. *Automatic* processes are ruled by the older parts of our brain, the parts that lend animals their sophisticated automatic abilities, such as birds that navigate by star positions and ants that cooperate to run fungus farms. Automatic processes allow us to drive our cars on "autopilot," to react to a threat with that infamous flight-or-fight response, to laugh at a joke without first thinking through why it is funny. *Controlled* processes require language and conscious thought, and are pretty much unique to humans.

Haidt uses the metaphor of an elephant (the automatic processor) with a tiny rider (the controlled processor). As much as we might want the rider to direct the elephant, she is merely the elephant's closest advisor and, at best, guide. The elephant is in charge and usually goes where she is used to going, stopping for things that pack a reward (food, love) and running from things that signal danger. The rider can provide direction, but only when the elephant doesn't have conflicting desires of her own. "An emotionally intelligent person," writes Haidt, "has a skilled rider who knows how to distract and coax the elephant without having to engage in a direct contest of the wills."

Habits fall into the elephant's domain: they are automatic processes that we don't have to think about anymore. When we drive to work on the same roads every day, we don't have to think about how we are going to get there or that we need to slow for crossing children. It's automatic.

So if we want to help our children develop habits that foster positive emotions, we need to use our effort to train the elephant, not convince the rider. This is no small task.

### Why Rewards Are Rewarding

Rewarding children is controversial. Most researchers agree that it isn't a good way to motivate behavior over the long run. The same goes for my habit of threatening the kids with "consequences" (as in "Do that again and there will be no computer games for a week"). The problem with rewards and punishments is that they can teach children that love is conditional: they are loved only when they do what we want them to. Furthermore, happy people tend to be inspired by something within themselves rather than goaded by material rewards.

Some behaviors do reap their own intrinsic rewards. We tend to feel happier when we practice expressing gratitude, for example, so we wouldn't need a gold star to want to do it again. But there are a lot of things that are not fun. One big key to happiness is making the everyday unfun things in life into automatic routines, so that we don't have to fight the urge not to do them day in and day out.

Understandably, my kids are usually more intrinsically motivated to keep playing with their paper dolls than they are to empty the dishwasher. The only thing that housework has going for it from an intrinsic motivation standpoint is teamwork: kids want to feel a part of the family, so when we play up the teamwork aspect of getting things done together, that helps. But let's be real: when Molly is deep in pretend play and I ask her to please put her shoes on because we are running late, I need her to just do it. I need her to be in the habit of doing what I ask the first time or, better yet, to have a routine in place so that I don't even have to ask. For that, parents and teachers often use rewards. Good, juicy, rewarding rewards.

New habits are formed by training the elephant with a powerful reward called dopamine, an important chemical in the pleasure system of our brain. When we receive a reward or engage in certain activities (such as eating and, for adults, having sex and taking certain drugs), dopamine is released, creating feelings of enjoyment and an accompanying desire to repeat the activity. When a reward is consistently associated with a behavior, dopamine helps make the behavior an automatic process. Animals, kids, grown-ups: we all learn to repeat behaviors that lead to really good rewards. Consistency is key; the elephant makes a little note to self when a behavior isn't rewarded. This makes the elephant much harder to train.

Unlike dopamine-triggering rewards, "aversive stimuli" (for example, being yelled at) actually have the opposite effect, motivating the elephant to avoid these experiences, toward "the pleasure of avoiding the aversive stimuli." In other words, when I yell and threaten and am otherwise aversive, I actually motivate my kids to ignore me entirely; I'm motivating them to avoid listening to me when I make a request. It would be easier if it were the opposite and Molly would just put her shoes on to avoid being yelled at, but alas, negative stimuli rarely motivate positive behavior.

The good thing about dopamine is that it is all about the motivation and not so much about the activity. So my kids don't have to enjoy emptying the dishwasher; they just need to feel rewarded for doing it.

## Punished by Rewards?

Knowing that rewards can be motivating to kids in the short run, I used to (okay, so I sometimes still do) bribe my children. Constantly. "First one in the car gets to choose the music!" "Get your jammies on in less than two minutes and I'll read you an extra book!" I also threaten them, which is sort of the opposite of bribing them: "Fiona, if you kick the back of my car seat one more time, no playdates for a *month!*"

I know, of course, that bribing and threatening are not happiness habits, but they *are* effective ways to motivate and reward that elephant—in the short term. Life is full of undesirable but important tasks; most of us don't feel a fire in our soul to put away the laundry, but we do it anyway. Social scientists have studied this a lot. They call self-motivation "intrinsic" drive—the desire to do something purely because of the pleasure we derive from the activity itself. We also do things for "extrinsic" reasons—not for the process or the activity but for the outcome or reward. Kids often do their homework for the grade or the approval of their teacher rather than for the fun of learning something new.

Intrinsic motivation makes for greater happiness and success, particularly when it comes to academic life—a huge part of childhood. Self-motivated kids achieve more, perceive themselves to be more competent, and are less anxious. Extrinsically motivated kids are more prone to depression. While intrinsic motivation is a form of joy, extrinsic motivation can lead to unhappiness fueled by fear of failure or disappointment. Because girls are often more attuned to their external appearance and environment than boys are, girls tend to be more extrinsically motivated and thus are more likely to be depressed.

And despite the often dramatic short-term effect of rewards—the kid who leaps off the couch to walk the dog when ice cream is offered upon his return—rewards can have a detrimental effect over the medium and long term. Although rewards get kids to comply with externally imposed requests and rules, ultimately we want kids to become self-motivated without our external goading. Orienting kids toward external rewards can cause them to lose touch with their own feelings and their own intrinsic motivation. When kids find an activity or a task that they inherently like doing, such as reading or helping another kid, external rewards have an undermining effect. Rewards make kids like doing the activity less, and decrease the likelihood that they will engage in the activity again when given the choice. (This negative impact of rewards is stronger with children than with adults, by the way.)

But what about when the task is *not* something kids want to do for the sheer joy of it? To reward or not to reward, that is the question, particularly when it comes to the boring or difficult stuff in life. We don't have to prod kids to learn to walk or ride a bike or drive a car. But as kids get older, tasks get more complex, and to achieve mastery in those realms that brings them joy—developing a knack for the present participle so that they can speak Spanish, working at calculus long enough to find joy in mathematical insight—they need the self-motivation and stick-to-itiveness that will allow them to grow and learn. Ironically, self-motivation is largely a learned skill—meaning that we parents teach kids the proficiencies they need to maintain motivation, and that self-motivation is something that kids need to practice to get better at. All of Chapter 7 deals with teaching kids self-discipline, but this chapter will jump-start this process by making those uninteresting or difficult things in life—that initially take tremendous motivation—into automatic habits.

So where does that leave us? The elephant still needs motivating in the short term; it needs that short-term feel-good reward. The key, it turns out, is to make sure the rewards themselves are intrinsic.

## How to Motivate the Elephant, Specifically

A specific encouragement is the best way to motivate kids because it leads to a built-in reward: a naturally good feeling about themselves and their behavior after they perform even uninteresting tasks. That good feeling is itself the reward.

I bet that encouragement is not the big, fat, juicy reward you thought I was talking about, or the iTunes gift card that your tweener was hoping for. But keeping kids in touch with and motivated by their own feelings works better, and leads to greater happiness, even when it comes to emptying the dishwasher.

Here is how to support your kids' autonomy—their intrinsic motivation—when you're asking them to do tedious (but necessary) tasks. I had to make up a mnemonic device for myself so I could remember all three components at first: I call it ERNing, or motivating kids through empathy, reason, and noncontrolling language. Before, I was motivating them to *earn* a reward; now I motivate them with ERN encouragement.

I'm happy to report that this science-tested encouragement is now rolling off my tongue almost as easily as "If you brush your teeth now, I'll give you an extra star on your chart for being so speedy."

## ERNING AND LEARNING

1.  Show empathy before you finish making your request. This step was life changing—okay, maybe just habit changing—for my family. One night I wanted Fiona to brush her teeth, and I'd asked her several times already. Then I thought: oh yeah, express empathy. I said, "Fiona, I know you don't really want to, but you need to go brush your teeth right now." When there was no response, I realized that I didn't know why she was resisting, so I couldn't empathize. I simply asked her, "Fiona, why don't you want to go brush your teeth?" Her response was that she didn't want to go downstairs to use the sink by herself (there were no lights on, and it had gotten dark), and she wanted to be with me. So I said, "I can understand why you don't want to go downstairs in the dark, and I want to be with you, too. But I need you to go brush your teeth." To which she replied, "If you understand, why don't you just come with me?" I did not reply that I was trying to save all of about two minutes by having her brush her teeth alone while I did something else; I just went with her. And she brushed her teeth gleefully. Seriously. Since then I've realized that when I'm more attuned to my kids' experiences, things go much more smoothly for all involved. I don't make requests that I know will be heartily resisted or ignored for reasonable reasons, which translates to less fruitless begging and yelling. Empathy also leads me to respect what they are already doing, so I give them more warnings—"in ten minutes you'll need to clean up"—before I actually lay down the law. This prevents frustration all around.

2.  Offer meaningful rationales. Why are you asking your kids to do that seemingly unimportant task? I am getting into the habit of offering positive rationales such as, "Please go brush your teeth so they feel clean and healthy today." This is much more motivating to them than some version of "Please do it because I've asked you to do it a hundred times."

3.  Imply that they have a choice rather than using "controlling language." Shocking but true: my bossiness does not motivate my kids. It *is* a lot easier to just tell my kids what I need them to do,

as in, "Please empty the dishwasher. Now." Less controlling language would be "What I propose is . . ." or "If you choose to," or "It would be extremely helpful if you . . ." At first I thought, well, that isn't going to work—my kids will definitely reject the task if given a choice such as this, and the reality is that they really don't have a choice. Anything short of my usual bossiness seemed inauthentic. But then I realized that I didn't want to be that bossy woman, and also I had nothing to lose: they were already rejecting the tasks, repeatedly. Most kids know that they will end up doing most of what we ask them to do; it isn't an option not to brush their teeth or not do their homework. But when we avoid using directives and controlling language ("You should do . . ." or "What you have to do now . . ."), they have a lot less to resist, and thus offer a lot less resistance.

Here is a plus: when we encourage kids to do a blindingly boring task with empathy, rationale, and noncontrolling language, they feel happier when they are performing the task than they would if we'd offered them a material reward. That happiness they feel *is* the reward. Moreover, in one study, kids who were asked to do something tedious but were motivated using the ERN method were no less likely to perform the task the next time around than those who were offered material rewards instead. And kids who were motivated with empathy, rationale, and choice learned that just because something is boring and unfun doesn't mean that it isn't important.

In sum, rewards work in the short term because they provide us with a nice feel-good dopamine hit. Unfortunately, rewards tend to have a negative effect on kids' motivation over the long term. The solution is to motivate kids to do those not-so-fun things that are necessary in life with the particular kind of ERN encouragement described above. That way, their brains deliver those feel-good chemicals in response to their feelings of mastery and autonomy (intrinsic motivation) rather than in response to receiving a material reward (extrinsic motivation).

## Stages of Change

*What we plant in the soil of contemplation, we shall reap in the harvest of action.*

—MEISTER ECKHART

Change rarely happens all at once. It happens in stages. People who successfully create a new, healthy habit as part of their New Year's resolution, or who kick a difficult habit such as smoking, do it one step at a time. Psychologists James Prochaska and Carlo DiClemente have been observing and describing the various stages of change for decades, and they've learned that if you start trying to impose change when you or your kids are in the wrong stage, the new habit won't stick.

Prochaska's and DiClemente's research suggests that breaking an old habit (such as quitting whining) and successfully beginning a new one in its place (using your normal voice to ask for what you want) usually takes longer than we think it will—about three to six months rather than the twenty-one days that seems to be in popular parlance. Although it feels as though it will take forever, it is worth the effort.

All those daily struggles with kids can be made into happiness habits. Think about the well-run preschool where kids automatically put their sweaters in their cubbyholes, put their shoes on after nap time, and put a puzzle away before beginning a new one. It takes some serious focus and discipline, but it is well worth it. I used the plan described below to get Molly into the habit of putting her shoes on automatically before leaving the house in the morning and, more recently, to improve our dinnertime experience.

A few months ago, I noticed that our dinnertime was getting a bit unruly. The kids were getting up a lot or lying down on the cushions when seated at the banquet, playing with their food, using potty talk, et cetera. There were a lot of time-outs, and dinner was starting to be a drag. So I decided to embark on changing our dinnertime habits.

### Stage 1: Precontemplation

This is the stage where no one is thinking about changing. For my kids, it ended one bright morning in March. At breakfast I said, "Isn't this nice? Everyone is seated and eating politely. Dinner doesn't feel this nice. Mommy is tired of having to beg you people to use your manners at dinnertime."

### Stage 2: Contemplation

That same morning—not in the heat of problem behavior but when we were all calm, rested, and focused—we talked about why I wanted to work on improving our dinnertime experience. I asked them to contemplate why they might want to change, too. We talked about what they like about dinnertime, how it feels to get a time-out and have to leave the table, and what a "successful dinnertime" would look like to us. This became our big, overarching goal. A successful dinnertime, to us, would be one where (1) we all got dinner on the table as a team, (2) we had fun together eating and talking (no time-outs), and (3) we all cleaned up as a team without anyone (me) having to nag.

## Stage 3: Preparation

This stage is a transition from thinking about changing to beginning the new habit. I had to really plan—reorganize my whole late-afternoon routine, in fact—just to think about how to support their behavior change. It doesn't seem as though offering empathy, rationale, and choice is that difficult—and it isn't—but it was so different from what I was doing that I had to think hard about what was triggering my use of very, uh, controlling language. I knew that if I didn't leave enough time, I would start saying things such as, "Molly, please set the table *right now* or I'll take that book away from you" rather than "I know you'd rather read that book—I would too. But I propose that you help us get the dinner on the table. Fiona and I are working together as a team to make dinner so we can eat before we all get too grouchy. What would you like to do to help?"

I also knew from experience that kids would be resistant to helping with dinner and then sitting down nicely to eat it if they hadn't had any downtime between getting home from their after-school activities and having to launch into setting the table. So I had to plan to arrive home from work a full half hour earlier to make this happen. As I said, part of the preparation meant rearranging my late afternoon.

Another key part of the preparation is what I call a placebo effect: if you think it will work, it will. To any optimistic reader of Rhonda Byrne's *The Secret*, this is a no-brainer. Just believing that you are capable of changing your bad habits into good ones predicts success, according to research on people who successfully maintain their New Year's resolutions. So do whatever you can to help your kids believe that they are capable of making the change.

You can use an old sales trick: ask "intent questions." Corporate researchers know that just answering a question about what you intend to do (or buy) makes you automatically more likely to do it. If you've been seeing a lot of green Toyota Priuses around, and you like that car, and someone asks you what car you are going to buy next, you're likely to say a green Toyota Prius. Then you'll be more likely to go out and buy a green Toyota Prius than if no one had asked you in the first place.

How this translates for us: we need to ask our kids intent questions. *What are you going to do when the timer goes off? How can you make dinnertime successful tonight?*

### Stage 4: Action

*The vision must be followed by the venture. It is not enough to stare up the steps—we must step up the stairs.*

—VANCE HAVNER

Going cold turkey on giving up bad habits such as whining and begging is unrealistic, so divide your grand end goal into lots of smaller ones. I knew that no amount of ERN encouragement would get my kids to set the table, help with dinner, sit nicely through it, and then help clean up. We needed to start with one small behavior at a time.

The important thing is that at each step you and your kids succeed. This means breaking your big goal into an action plan made up of tiny turtle steps that eventually get you there. In life, I am more of a hare than a turtle, so this approach is hard for me. However, I frequently find success by taking direction and encouragement from another sociology Ph.D. and science translator, Martha Beck.

The key, according to Beck, is at each step of the way to "play halvsies until your goal is ridiculously easy to attain." I asked each kid what their first ridiculously easy turtle step would be. Molly said her first step would be to set the table. Since this wasn't ridiculously easy for her—usually I had to beg and cajole—we started playing halvsies until the turtle step was tiny: with one reminder, she would simply get out the place mats and arrange them on the table.

Fiona wanted her first turtle step to be "acting as polite as a princess" through dinner. By the time we got done playing halvsies, her first step was to eliminate playing with her food (this is a kid who likes to draw in the butter with her fingers). I wanted her turtle step to be framed positively so that her behavior would be guided by a positive ideal rather than a reminder of what she was not to do. So her first turtle step was to simply use her utensils at dinner when appropriate. She thought this first step was so ridiculously easy that it became a bit of a stand-up comedy routine for her. She'd sit herself down, proper as a princess, and announce in a faux-British accent: "I am now going to eat with my fork." Molly, too, found pleasure in the simplicity of taking her super-easy turtle step, presenting a table with place mats on it with a big "ta-daaaa."

My first turtle step was simply to remember to look at the Happiness Habits Tracker sheets (one for each of us) that we had posted on our fridge, with our main goal written out at the top and the turtle steps listed below. The key for me is the discipline of sticking to it, which is especially hard on the nights when I'm going out for dinner or to the gym, and another adult, such as the kids' dad, is taking over. On those nights, I'll say something such as "Who's going to put the broccoli in the microwave?" and then I'll get distracted by my iPhone. Or I'll make the request and then maybe mention something about Santa Claus watching them before I go upstairs to get dressed. Since these behaviors are not a part of our new happiness habit, the tracker helps me remember my main role in habit formation.

## THE PLAN, ONE WEEK AT A TIME

Once you have sprung into action, it is important to recognize and clearly keep track of successes. Each little positive change, or each turtle step taken, wins the kids a dose of growth–mind-set praise. Chapter 3 goes into what exactly growth–mind-set praise is and why it is so motivating for kids. But generally speaking, growth–mind-set praise is specific and oriented toward their effort—the factor that was in their control: "Nice work washing the strawberries without me even having to ask. I appreciate your effort." Positive behaviors also win them independence; if they get the table set, they can move on to the next task of their choice without being assigned one. Using the salad spinner is a popular choice.

To keep track of successes, I created a handy worksheet that you can print out and hang on your fridge. (See the Happiness Habit Tracker at the end of this chapter, or print it out from christinecarter.com.) You and your kids put your big overall goal at the top, and then each person chooses one ridiculously easy turtle step per week. The understanding is that if you take your turtle step, you get to color in an X. If you get X's every day (or every weekday, or each day the habit is relevant), you get to choose a new turtle step. For Molly, her next turtle step was place mats *and* napkins. For Fiona, it was using her utensils *and* not blowing bubbles in her milk. And so on. If you or the kids don't take your turtle step each day, play halvsies again for the following week: try making the turtle step even easier.

I know, this seems slow and rather painstaking. It would be easier if the kids would just do what we ask the first time we ask—if they had good habits in the first place. But remember two things. First, you are teaching your kids skills—breaking and forming habits—that will serve them for a lifetime. When they need to get in the habit of exercising or not biting their fingernails, or if they want to begin a meditation practice, they'll have the tools and will know how it is done. Second, even though the turtle steps are slow and absurdly small, they are the beginning of big change. Before we started our Happiness Habit Tracker at dinnertime, I would have to nag and beg Molly to set the table. Once we started with the place mat turtle step, Molly at least *began* setting the table without a lot of hassle; this often led to her willing and cheerful help in other ways that I wasn't seeing before.

If establishing a new Happiness Habit seems too labor intensive, remind yourself of all the ways that your existing habits aren't working. Usually, this approach takes a lot less energy than dealing with the misbehavior or bad habit you are trying to correct, such as asking Molly numerous times to put her shoes on (and then consoling her when she begins crying because I lost my patience and started yelling). The good thing is that eventually there is an end to this intense focus. That is the whole idea: whatever you are working on becomes automatic. The elephant does it without any instruction from the rider.

The following pages summarize a few other science points that lead to successful habit formation; I suggest you leave nothing to chance and try them all.

## Stimulus Removal

Another way to up the odds of success is to remove distractions and temptations. People trying to quit smoking cannot leave cigarettes lying around to taunt them. If I wanted Molly to get dressed without having to beg her, at first I needed to make sure our cat wasn't in the room or she'd pet the cat instead of getting dressed. The same thing went for me: when I decided that a first turtle step was to support my kids while they established a new habit, I couldn't also be texting dating advice to my brother, even though that was more fun and interesting than peeling the potatoes.

## Making It Public

People who have social support for their new habits—friends who help one another keep exercising, for example—make more lasting changes. Just making a goal public can increase social support—and pressure—to succeed, which is one reason why New Year's resolutions can be effective. Wide support is important for making changes in different settings, so be sure to involve your children's other caregivers if they have them, and make sure your kids know that their caregivers are there to help them with this family goal.

## Pick Only One Goal, and Make It Specific

When I first got my kids working on their habits trackers, I was eager to eliminate every annoying thing they did. The possibilities seemed limitless. But we can't change more than one bad habit at a time, and neither can our kids. Research shows that the more New Year's resolutions we make, the less likely we are to keep them. So have your kids come up with one big goal, and make it specific. Kids are more likely to reach a goal such as forming a new habit when they know specifically what counts as a good performance. Vague goals such as "do your best" don't tell them exactly what they need to do to succeed.

The turtle steps outlined above—linked to that overarching specific goal—account for the fact that kids also do better when they have some early and easy successes. So make sure that those first turtle steps are ridiculously easy. And make sure that older kids see all the turtle steps as linked; together, the steps form the plan for how to reach their goals.

## The Difference Between Lapse and Relapse

These days we usually make dinner and clean up afterward together as a family, and we rarely have time-outs during our meal. Though I may have to gently remind them of something, I often do little more than make suggestions and ask questions, such as, "Fiona, what do you want to do to help with dinner—butter the bread? Pour the milk?" I asked that exact question the other day, and she said, "I'll do both, Mom." *Believe me*, this is a far cry from the nagging, begging, and bribing I had gotten into the habit of and the general not listening when I started making dinner that she had been in the habit of. Six weeks after we started using the worksheets, our new habits began to solidify, and we are all happier for it: I for less aggravation and they for having accomplished something we all agreed was important.

We had lots of lapsed behavior before we hit a groove that worked, so don't be discouraged if it doesn't go so well for you at first. Lapses are a one-time return to the behavior you are trying to change. I often had to remind Fiona not to play with her food; on those days she didn't get to put an X on their worksheet, and we emphasized that tomorrow is another day. Occasional failures are a normal part of the learning process.

A relapse, on the other hand, is a series of steps in the wrong direction, taking you back to the old behavior and away from the new one. One week we forgot to visit the worksheet altogether. Another week we forgot to set the next turtle-step goals on Sunday, which can set us up for relapse. Relapse is a whole process, not a single event.

*Context* is important when it comes to lapse and relapse. Sometimes a change in context is stimulus enough for a full-blown relapse. At the beginning of trying to get the kids into the habit of dressing and being

## WHO KNEW? NOW IT WILL BE EASIER TO BREAK OTHER HABITS

This is the "bonus points" section. It turns out that self-discipline—or self-regulation, as the psychologists call it—is like a muscle. The more you use it, the stronger it gets. One of the best things you can do to create a new habit is to exercise willpower or self-control in some area of your life, even though that area may have no relation to the new habit. For example, researchers at Case Western Reserve University asked college students to pay attention to their posture and improve it whenever they could. After two weeks of this, the students improved their scores on a self-control activity test. Self-control is like a muscle in that it fatigues. If you are trying not to smoke and someone repeatedly offers you a cigarette, you are more likely to give in with each offer. But self-control is also like a muscle in that it gets stronger across the board. Your kids will use a little willpower to make whatever changes your family is working on, and then the next happiness habit will come more easily.

ready to head out the door themselves, we spent the weekend in a hotel, and *holy cow* was the whole routine messed up. New behaviors are often strongly dependent on current context—the time of day that a behavior occurs, or the room that it is performed in, or an event that happens right beforehand. Preliminary research suggests that varying the contexts in which the new learning takes place may help us maintain the new behavior over the long term, but I'm here to report that changing context makes the task at hand more difficult in the short term. Be prepared.

Habits form with repetition and practice, and no one gets it right all the time. Change is hard; no need to be a perfectionist about it.

## TRY THIS

### Form a Happiness Habit

1. Decide on a habit you'd like to start—or end—with your children, and then contemplate the changes you need to make for it to happen. What bad habit would you like to replace with a happiness habit? What specifically does success look like? Do the kids think the bad habit is working for them? What advantages do they see to replacing it with a happiness habit?

2. Prepare for change.

   - Print out a worksheet for each member of your family (go to christinecarter.com and look for "Happiness Habit Tracker"). Write your end goal at the top of each worksheet.

   - Decide what day and time you will revisit the worksheet to set new turtle-step goals, and note these on your calendar. Set reminder alarms on your phone or computer calendar program if you have one.

   - Think about what changes you, the parent, will need to make in order for your children to succeed.

3. Pick the first turtle step. Break down your end goal into a first turtle step, and then play halvsies with it until the step is ridiculously easy. Write it down on the worksheet.

4. Stack the deck for success. Ask intent questions before the behavior is to be performed. Remove distractions, and make your goals public. Practice the ERN method of encouraging kids by offering empathy, rationale, and noncontrolling language.

5. Get to it. Spring into action. Make it happen. When it does, ensure that everyone marks the Xs on their worksheets. Soon you'll have a visible marker of your progress.

## HAPPINESS HABIT TRACKER

| SOCIAL SCIENCE FOR RAISING HAPPY KIDS | | | | | | |
|---|---|---|---|---|---|---|
| **Habits tracker for:** | | | | | | |
| **My New Habit:** | | | | | | |
| *What does it look like when you've achieved this goal?* | | | | | | |
| **Turtle Step 1:** | Sun | Mon | Tues | Wed | Thurs | Fri | Sat |
| | X | X | X | X | X | X | X |
| **Turtle Step 2:** | Sun | Mon | Tues | Wed | Thurs | Fri | Sat |
| | X | X | X | X | X | X | X |
| **Turtle Step 3:** | Sun | Mon | Tues | Wed | Thurs | Fri | Sat |
| | X | X | X | X | X | X | X |
| **Turtle Step 4:** | Sun | Mon | Tues | Wed | Thurs | Fri | Sat |
| | X | X | X | X | X | X | X |
| **Turtle Step 5:** | Sun | Mon | Tues | Wed | Thurs | Fri | Sat |
| | X | X | X | X | X | X | X |
| **Turtle Step 6:** | Sun | Mon | Tues | Wed | Thurs | Fri | Sat |
| | X | X | X | X | X | X | X |

■ ■ ■ ■ ■ ■

# SEVEN

# Step 7: Teach Self-Discipline

*Formula of my happiness: a Yes, a No, a straight line, a goal.*

—FRIEDRICH NIETZSCHE

Years ago, a researcher named Walter Mischel conducted a series of now-famous "marshmallow experiments" with four-year-olds. One at a time, he left the kids in a room with a marshmallow. He told them that if they could wait until he reentered the room, they would get two marshmallows. If they couldn't stand the waiting, though, they could go ahead and eat the one marshmallow.

Kids handled the task in different ways. Some couldn't wait even a minute to eat the one marshmallow, while others waited more than fifteen minutes to get two. The experiments garnered a lot of attention because they turned out to be predictive of future behavior. The kids who couldn't wait were more likely to become bullies in elementary school, get worse teacher and parental evaluations ten years later, and have drug or alcohol problems by age thirty-two. The kids who *were* able to wait went on to get higher Scholastic Aptitude Test (SAT) scores as teenagers.

Here's the thing: You can influence how long your child is able to—metaphorically speaking—wait to eat the marshmallow. This chapter is about two kinds of discipline: the external kind that you exercise over your kids—enforcing rules and setting limits—and the internal self-discipline that you can help them develop.

All of our attempts at imposing discipline on our children are, of course, intended to make them more *self*-disciplined. But kids today are much worse at self-discipline than kids in previous generations. Researchers have replicated studies first done in the 1940s that looked at children's self-discipline—or "self-regulation," as scientists call it. In these studies, the researchers asked their subjects, ages three, five, and seven, to do things that are hard for kids: to stand perfectly still, for example. In the 1940s studies, three-year-olds understandably couldn't do it at all, five-year-olds could stand still for a few minutes, and most seven-year-olds could do it for as long as they were asked to. But when scientists replicated this study in 2001, the five-year-olds also found it difficult to remain still for any time at all—they looked just like the three-year-olds in the 1940s studies—and the seven-year-olds barely reached the self-regulatory ability of the five-year-olds from the earlier experiments.

These results explain why my mother gets so frustrated with my kids at dinnertime when they can't seem to sit still for more than thirty seconds. My mom likes to compare my own behavior as a kid with that of my own kids, commenting, "You kids were active, but we expected you to sit through dinner, and you always did." I used to assume that this was in the same vein as refrains such as "We walked to school both ways uphill in the snow," but now I know that she is right: my brother and I probably *were* better self-regulators, making it possible for us to sit still through dinnertime.

These research findings are no small deal: the ability to self-regulate is an important key to success and happiness. Remember, preschoolers' ability to delay gratification—to wait for that second marshmallow—predicts intelligence, school success, and social skills in adolescence. This is at least in part because self-discipline facilitates learning and information processing. In addition, self-disciplined kids cope better with frustration and stress and tend to have a greater sense of social responsibility. In other words, self-discipline leads not just to school success and sitting nicely at the dinner table but to greater happiness, more friends, and increased community engagement.

On the other hand, kids with poor ability to regulate themselves have more problems with things such as substance abuse, aggression, and violence and are more likely to engage in risky sex.

Researchers talk about two systems in our brains that either enable or undermine our willpower. One system is hot and emotional and the other is cool and cognitive. The "hot," or "go," system is all about impulsivity. The basis of our emotions and fears and passions, our "go system" helps us process emotional information quickly and react fast when we are in danger. It also makes us grab that marshmallow instead of patiently waiting for the researcher to return. The go system reacts to external stimuli and is therefore literally under "stimulus control" rather than self-control.

The "cool," or "know," system is the seat of self-regulation and self-control. This "know system" is slow and strategic, taking the time to think and consider consequences. The go system is thought to exist at birth; the know system develops throughout childhood. Our ability to balance these systems—the go system that undermines self-control and the know system that empowers it—depends on a number of factors, one being how much we've practiced and honed that crucial skill: the ability to delay gratification.

Our modern environment also contributes to the decline in children's ability to self-regulate. Rapid technological advances enable faster, more instant gratification in numerous aspects of everyday life. This increases the stimuli activating our go system, and heightens the conflict between the go system and the know system. We are a go system society, demanding instant food twenty-four hours a day, instant knowledge (who goes to the library when there is Google and Wikipedia?), instant communication (constant Twitter updates from our friends, colleagues—even our politicians). Is it any wonder that our kids are indulging their go systems more than they are developing their know systems?

Stress is another factor that inhibits self-control. Many kids are under a good deal more stress now than in generations past. When we get stressed out and anxious, our ability to handle additional stressors, no matter how small, is diminished. If kids' cool, know systems are otherwise preoccupied with worries about book reports and their parents' unemployment, kids will find it harder to do anything that requires self-control. Anyone who has tried to quit smoking or stick to a diet knows how quickly stress can sabotage these efforts. Research shows that chronic stress in children often results in a lowered ability to delay gratification.

## FROM THE OUTSIDE IN: TEACHING SELF-DISCIPLINE

How can we reverse these trends and help our kids develop the self-control they need in life? There are dozens of ways to help kids develop self-control. The same researchers behind the marshmallow experiments have spent decades understanding what tips and techniques people can use to increase their willpower, all of which we can teach to our children. This research tells us a lot about how to discipline our kids so that our kids eventually learn to discipline themselves. Once we have mastered the best ways to influence our kids from an external standpoint, we can teach and help them practice tips and techniques that directly increase their willpower and ability to self-regulate.

Parents today are saying "no" a lot less frequently than they did in past generations—by one study's estimate, 50 percent less often. While our reasons for not wanting to say "no" vary, the research makes one thing clear: kids need their parents to set limits, but in a positive way. When parents are firm *and* kind, when they are involved without being invasive, researchers call this "authoritative parenting."

Four decades of research have consistently determined that authoritative parenting is good for kids' health and well-being. Not only does authoritative parenting help kids develop a healthy penchant for self-control—making them less likely to have problems with drugs, alcohol, or teen pregnancy—it makes them far more likely to excel on many other measures of well-being. For example, teenagers with authoritative parents do better in school, have greater self-confidence, and have more friends.

## TRY THIS

### How to Be an Authoritative Parent

**Don't be a pushover.** Say no, even if it is difficult for you. It is hard to see our kids unhappy, and it is difficult to endure the whining or tantruming that limit setting may provoke, especially after a long day at work when we have precious little time to spend with our kids. But few things are more important for their healthy development and well-being. We can't expect our kids to develop their own self-control if we don't first establish what falls in bounds and out of bounds for them.

**Be involved.** A big part of authoritative parenting is follow-through, supervision, and just generally being there. It isn't enough to make rules; we also need to enforce them. Kids need to perceive that their parents know where they are and who they are with—that their parents are keeping tabs on what they do with their free time. Though it is hard to be persistent in our limit setting, especially with kids who are always testing us, inconsistency is a deal breaker. When "no" today turns into "yes" tomorrow, it doesn't count for anything.

**But don't be controlling, even in a well-meaning way.** Especially when they get to be teenagers, kids need their parents to recognize that they are individuals in their own right, capable of living their own lives. Not being psychologically controlling means allowing kids to make their own mistakes (Chapter 3) so they can learn that they are capable of picking themselves up after falling. It also means encouraging kids to express their own individuality, even if it conflicts with our opinions as parents. Avoid answering kids' arguments with comments such as "You'll know better when you grow up."

In studies with toddlers, researchers have found that children of parents who issue commands and physically control their children are less able to delay gratification at age five compared to kids whose parents used "teaching-based" limit-setting strategies. Instead of using more forceful techniques, these authoritative—but not authoritarian—parents set limits for their exploring toddlers by using distractions and gentle guidance and reasoning. Probably as a result, their kids developed above-average abilities to delay gratification.

If you suspect that researchers would classify the way you say "no" to your kids as power based or controlling, try to back off a little and give your children some freedom to be themselves.

**Exude warmth.** As explained in Chapter 4, affectionate and attentive parenting creates secure attachments. Research shows that secure attachment relationships are associated with emotional and behavioral regulation in infancy. For example, in one study, children whose mothers were warmer and relied less on physically punitive discipline showed a greater ability to regulate their own behavior four years later, in middle childhood.

Another study found that six-year-olds with emotive moms were better able to delay gratification than peers with less expressive parents. So be a little gushy with your love; ironically, all that love and warmth will make your child more disciplined.

**Don't react to misbehavior; preempt it.** This is another obvious suggestion that research has borne out: a little effort up front goes a long way. In one study, mothers who engaged their preschoolers in "helping" with shopping or by otherwise giving them something to do (besides misbehave in the supermarket) ended up with kids who, you guessed it, misbehaved less. Not surprisingly, waiting for kids to misbehave and *then* correcting it resulted in toddlers who misbehaved more. This principle holds true across situations and ages. Even as adults, when we are in situations that prompt us to do tempting things that aren't good for us—overeating, for example—we do better when we actively engage in something constructive rather than waiting for the tempting stimulus to coax us over the edge. Preempting misbehavior in children or in ourselves requires self-discipline, but, like strengthening a muscle, it also helps build it.

One less obvious way to preempt undesirable behavior is to put the focus on possible positive outcomes instead of on preventing disaster. Research shows that parents who try to prevent bad behavior by detailing possible disastrous outcomes ("Jack! Get down from there! You're going to fall and break your neck!" or "If you don't finish your homework, you won't do well on the test") tend to have kids who are similarly *prevention oriented* in their self-control. Parents who habitually focus on positive outcomes, such as meeting goals and fulfilling aspirations ("Jack, come check this out. You can really climb high over here!" or "Finish your homework so you ace that test. UC Berkeley, here comes my son!") tend to have kids whose willpower is *promotion focused*; they regulate their behavior in order to reach their goals rather than prevent something bad from happening. To be promotion focused, emphasize that kids can make good things happen instead of always trying to keep bad things from happening.

## TECHNIQUES THAT COOL THE "GO SYSTEM" AND ENGAGE THE "KNOW SYSTEM"

The marshmallow experiments reveal lots of different strategies that kids can use to wait even longer for that second marshmallow. We parents can help kids practice these techniques and skills that build self-regulation. For example, we can do the following:

**Play games** that teach self-regulation. Initiate games with kids where they have to regulate their behavior. Simon Says and Freeze Tag are good examples because kids have to think (engaging their "know system") in order to *not* do something, thereby practicing self-control. Similarly, activities that require kids to follow directions a few steps ahead also help them learn to delay gratification. Cooking is a good example of this, or games where they need to follow directions or patterns to build something. But beware: this does not mean structuring their activities so tightly that *you* end up regulating them instead of letting *them* practice self-regulating.

Allowing kids ample time for free play is another good self-discipline builder, especially if they have enough time to engage in complex imaginative play. Chapters 8 and 9 describe this in more detail, but for now suffice it to say that unstructured and imaginative playtime builds executive function in kids, an important cognitive skill related to self-regulation. Martial arts, dance, music, and storytelling—fun activities that require sustained attention—build self-discipline by requiring kids to hold complex information in their mind. Kids exercise their self-control when they use the information they are holding in their mind (such as the next part of a choreographed dance) while at the same time resisting their first impulses or inclinations to do something else.

**Encourage self-talk.** Another reason why imaginative play is good for building self-regulation is that it often involves the kids' talking to themselves or their playmates in a way that directs their actions. They learn self-control by talking to themselves in order to guide their own behavior (rather than always relying on Mom or Dad to guide them). Encouraging kids to talk to themselves and listen to that "little voice in their head" facilitates the development of self-regulation. When my kids do something that they know is wrong, I often ask them, "Did you hear a voice in your head telling you not to say that mean thing?" Making them aware of the fact that they have a "know system" that will help them overrule their impulses (say, to hit their sister) is a first step.

**Teach them to distract themselves.** This is a willpower technique that is helpful in lengthening the amount of time that kids can wait for the second marshmallow. One way to do it is to obscure the temptation—to physically cover up the tempting marshmallow. When a reward is covered up, 75 percent of kids in one study were able to wait a full fifteen minutes for the second marshmallow; none of the kids was able to wait this long when the reward was visible. The key thing about this effective parental distraction, though, was that the kids in one study who developed good self-control had mothers who didn't distract them by commanding them to pay attention to something besides the prohibited object; they actively engaged their child in something else.

Internal distraction strategies are also important to practice. Giving kids other things to think about helps keep them from going for that marshmallow right in front of them—and helps them sit still through a fancy dinner. In one study, researchers told kids to "think of anything that is fun" or to "think about singing songs or playing with toys," and the kids were able to wait for a reward for an average of twelve minutes, compared with less than a minute when they weren't instructed to distract themselves in this way. The key here is to refrain from suggesting that they *not* think about something. Saying, "Don't think of the marshmallow, think of . . ." will sabotage this technique. Our mind works in funny ways, and telling someone not to think of, say, a polar bear virtually guarantees that they will think of it.

Children do better with distractions that are physically present, even when they wouldn't ordinarily be interested in the distraction. Giving kids (from preschoolers to twelve-year-olds) a slinky to play with increased the amount of time they were able to delay going for that marshmallow to fifteen minutes—even if they wouldn't be interested in playing with the slinky under different circumstances.

**Reduce their stress.** Many parents of teenagers are concerned about how much stress their children seem to be under these days. Stress— particularly chronic stress—has a negative impact on our "know systems," making us more impulsive and less able to meet our goals. Research shows that living in high-stress environments corresponds with a poor ability to delay gratification. Ironically, worry and anxiety about grades and schoolwork make kids less likely to be able to delay gratification (studying instead of talking on the phone, for example) in order to get their schoolwork done.

**Turn off the boob tube.** Television and other forms of "screen time" may not be evil (see page 167, "Is Television the Root of All Evil?"), but they definitely take up time that could be spent playing. Many researchers believe that the reason kids today are so much worse at delaying gratification than they were in the 1940s is that they spend much more time in front of the television and computer, neither of which helps develop their willpower or control their impulses. In other words, there is an opportunity cost to television: it doesn't promote the things kids need for healthy development when many alternatives, such as playing outside, do.

**Have realistic expectations.** Self-regulation is hard, and kids aren't born with the tools they need to begin practicing it. Their go system is well developed at birth, but their know system matures well after birth (and possibly after adolescence). So as our brain develops, we can become increasingly better at self-control, but it is unrealistic to think that, even with a lot of practice, young children will exhibit stellar impulse control. In fact, it is virtually impossible for children younger than four to delay gratification on their own. By age five most kids are able to understand, for example, that thinking about a treat will only make it harder to wait to have it, and they are able to begin to use self-distraction techniques. Self-regulation develops rapidly with practice between the ages of six and twelve, and by sixth grade kids are generally developmentally ready to employ sophisticated techniques to delay gratification.

## Is a Light Spanking Ever Okay?

Sometimes the discipline techniques described in this chapter are easy—gushing love all over a cuddly child rarely seems hard, for example—but sometimes they seem Herculean. The other day I was in the grocery store with both kids, and believe you me, I wasn't preempting bad behavior by engaging the kids in fun math activities, as their school newsletter recently suggested. Like most other parents there, I was just trying to get my shopping done so I could get dinner on the table and their homework started before it was past everyone's bedtimes. Fiona was making me crazy: putting food in the cart that she knew I'd never buy for her, trying to ride on the back of the cart, taunting her sister, generally messing with me in every way that she could think of. I engaged in what is known in my family as the "grocery store grab," perfected by my own mother: a hard squeeze just above the elbow and a whispered threat that she better knock it off or she'll never get to watch TV again. Ever. I know that the grocery store grab isn't on the list of well-proven and effective parenting behaviors, but is it so bad every once in a while?

Like being psychologically controlling, punitive parenting wreaks havoc on children's ability to discipline themselves. Although the spare-the-rod-spoil-the-child generation made a big case for keeping kids in line through force—such as deprivation of privileges and corporal punishment—social science has built a clear body of evidence that shows that these techniques are ultimately ineffective and certainly undesirable for those interested in raising happy children. Although I am still not able to refrain from the occasional grocery store grab, I of all people should know that it doesn't work. On the particular occasion described above, Fiona yelled, *"You are hurting my body! Why would a mother hurt her child's body?"* She did not, suffice it to say, become a compliant and delightful shopping companion.

Besides being appalling for my public image as a parenting expert, the grocery store grab is a terrible way to teach children discipline. When parental expectations for behavior are conveyed to children in threatening or punitive ways, kids are likely to become angry, anxious, or frightened. This over-arousal shifts the focus from what the parent wants, or is trying to teach, to how the child is responding to the parent's message. This shift in focus reduces the likelihood that the parent's punishment will be effective or that the child being punished will understand and try to fulfill his or her parent's wishes.

Besides being ineffective over the long term, punishment—physically punitive practices such as spanking as well as threatening behaviors such as yelling, grabbing, and verbal coercion—tends to be damaging to kids. Lots of studies have found associations between harsh parenting and higher rates of defiance, behavior problems, and depression and anxiety in teenagers, not to mention kids' diminished ability to control their behavior and their emotions.

In other words, there is a big difference between true discipline and punishment. The word discipline has the same Latin root as the word disciple, meaning "process of learning." Disciples and people with self-discipline are people who are ready to learn. The word punishment, on the other hand, refers to pain, suffering, or loss inflicted on a person. Disciplining our children—and teaching them to discipline themselves—makes them ready to learn: curious, open, centered. Punishment does the reverse, drawing kids' focus not to what they can learn from a given situation, but to the pain they are feeling from it. The next time I'm tempted to control my kids with the grocery store grab, I'll ask myself: Will this help them learn self-discipline? Or help them be ready to learn anything at all?

## TRY THIS

### Beyond Bribes, Threats, and Dangling Carrots

Alphie Kohn, king of don't reward or punish your kids, offers some research-based suggestions for getting kids to do what we want without "gold stars, incentive plans, A's, praise, and other bribes" in his book *Punished by Rewards*. For years, one of my worst parenting habits has been my constant subtle bribing—all that "if you do X, you'll get Y" cajoling. Here are three things to try instead.

1. Pick your battles. If you are having a hard time rationalizing your request, maybe it isn't important enough. If you can't justify the limit you are imposing (for example, you are worried about their safety: "I don't want you to stay out that late at night because I don't think it is safe"), maybe it isn't a battle you should be fighting. Remember that it is always okay to rethink your request when you meet a lot of resistance. Is the resistance justified or not? Never relent out of exhaustion, but if you realize that you've made a mistake, admit it and let the request go.

2. Use a light touch. Think in terms of creating structure and limits rather than in terms of control. There is a world of difference between setting limits—establishing the structure you need to for discipline—and bossing kids around (as I am prone to do). It is fine to make rules and follow through with them: no hitting, bedtime is 8:00 p.m., and so on. That is structure.

   Researchers consistently find that using the lightest touch possible to set such limits, though, is usually the most effective. As Kohn says, "Don't move a child roughly if you can move her gently; don't move her gently if you can tell her to move; don't tell her if you can ask her."

   This means that we don't turn up the heat in response to resistance. When kids don't do what you tell them to, you'll get better results if you don't holler, hit, threaten, or punish them—in that particular instance *and* when you ask them to do something in the future.

3. Appeal to kids' reason. Instead of approaching misbehavior with an impulse to punish (or, as we euphemistically say in our household, "give consequences"), we can respond with the approach that something has gone wrong that we need to problem-solve around or, at the very least, explain. Offering an explanation for why misbehavior is misbehavior appeals to kids' ability to reason ("The reason why we don't use mean names is . . .") rather than our own power as parents ("Because I said so"). In many cases, reasoning will lead to discussion rather than argument. Invite kids to participate in the discussion—they may have something valuable to add about how to keep themselves from making the same mistake—rather than expecting them to listen silently while you lecture them.

# EIGHT

■ ■ ■ ■ ■

# Step 8:
# Enjoy the Present Moment

*People usually consider walking on water or in thin air a
miracle. But I think the real miracle is not to walk either
on water or in thin air, but to walk on earth. Every day
we are engaged in a miracle which we don't even
recognize: a blue sky, white clouds, green leaves, the
black, curious eyes of a child—our own two eyes. All is a
miracle.*

—THICH NHAT HANH

The biggest parenting epiphany of my life came during a silent retreat I impulsively decided to attend in January. I was at my wit's
end. I had just spent the holidays with my soon-to-be-ex-husband and his
mother and stepfather, and although we all got along fine, I was feeling
emotionally drained and sad that I don't have a "perfect" family. School
and homework and busy mornings had started up again. Schlepping the
kids to before-school Spanish was making me just late enough for work
that I arrived each day a bit unnerved. My balancing act included my day
job at UC Berkeley's Greater Good Science Center, and writing my blog
*Half Full,* writing this book, teaching parenting classes, regular speaking
engagements, and various consulting projects that help me pay the bills.
It was beginning to feel as though there would never be enough time to
get it all done. As soon as I was finally able to settle into my work, I'd have
only a few minutes before I would need to start tracking the kids' pick-ups
from their after-school activities. Is it Heather's day or mine to pick up the
kids from knitting? Was Mike picking up the kids from my parents? Or
was this a drama day? Or wait, is Fiona at Margaret's?

Racing from one thing to the next counted as exercise; wolfing down my food while quizzing the kids about their day was our family time. Do the laundry, plan a playdate, schedule a doctor's appointment, go to the grocery store, pay the bills, empty the dishwasher—daily life was an endless list of hastily done chores.

Weekends were often worse, as undone work, chores, errands, and hundreds of unread e-mails nagged at me. Because I was distracted, even playing with the kids started to feel like a grind. *Everything* felt boring and tedious. "All you want to do is work," Molly said to me one day when she was trying to get me to pretend to sip a make-believe latte for the umpteenth time and I wasn't paying attention. I was crushed. She was wrong: I *wanted* to be there, playing with her. But she was also right: I *wasn't* really there with her. I was fantasizing about absconding to my office with the phone and e-mail off, writing. Ironically, I felt relief from the madness of my busy life when reading happiness studies and writing about raising happy kids.

So when I was offered a space on a silent retreat for scientists studying happiness and well-being, a loud voice in my head told me to just do it. Seven days without phones or e-mail, without work, without reading or even writing. Or talking to anyone. My friends bet that I wouldn't make it seven hours, much less seven days. I had never been away from my children for more than four days, and I couldn't fathom even a day without talking with them. But I also knew I needed to go: if there were any way for me to center myself despite the chaos, this was it.

As I sat in meditation hour upon hour, day after day, I mostly felt nothing but pure bliss. No one was more surprised about this than I was; it is very unusual for a first long retreat to be immediately blissful. Why wasn't I bored? Agitated? Itching to accomplish something? The second night it occurred to me: if I could always live in the present moment like this, no part of life would ever be a struggle. Or a grind. If sitting in a dark room with my eyes closed directing my attention only to feeling my breath and beating heart wasn't boring, *nothing* could be boring. No amount of laundry, certainly not even a billion imaginary lattes.

This chapter is about three skills that can enable us to be super-busy and deeply happy at the same time: the ability to really experience the present moment through play, flow, and mindfulness. Kids do this naturally when they "just play," but we grown-ups tend to screw things up when we schedule every waking moment of their day with lessons and Little League. We live in the present moment anytime we savor our experiences, and—as when I would hide away and write—when we experience flow, that state of consciousness when time seems to stand still. Mindfulness—living in the present moment, sometimes expressed as play or savoring or flow but also to be practiced when we are edgy and tense, or experiencing any sort of emotional state that can be noticed—is a serious practice, steeped in Buddhist tradition and studied rigorously by neuroscientists. I know that most parents can't sneak off into the California hills for a week to rebalance themselves as I did, but I hope that this chapter will plant some seeds that will enable you to better recognize that even in life's toughest moments, each day with children is filled with small miracles.

## PRACTICE MINDFULNESS, EVEN IF YOU AREN'T A HIPPIE

*Whatever you are doing, ask yourself, "What's the state of my mind?"*
—DALAI LAMA

Life has become very stressful for many kids and their super-busy parents. This increased stress can result in anger and anxiety. It also hurts students' school performance because it disrupts their thinking and interferes with their learning. Because emotional stress can cripple our ability to learn and remember, it is particularly important for parents to find a way to reduce stress in their kids' lives and teach them to better cope with it.

Neuroscientists in Wisconsin and psychologists in North Carolina are finding scientific evidence for an incredibly simple (and inexpensive!) way to counter the stress of modern life. Kids at play understand experientially something that Buddhists have long understood: the "power of now," of being fully in the present moment. Also called mindfulness, this state of being attentive and aware of what is happening in the now has important benefits for our well-being, including our ability to cope with stress.

Mindful people tend to be more self-confident, outgoing, and grateful. They are less stressed out, neurotic, anxious, and depressed, perhaps because they experience fewer negative and unpleasant emotions in general. Mindfulness is also associated with

- More intense and frequent pleasant and positive emotions

- Heightened self-knowledge, which is a key component of self-control

- Greater empathy and attunement with others

Kids who learn to be "fully present"—who learn to practice mindfulness—tend to perform better in school because they focus and deal with stressful situations with greater ease. One study showed that kids who practiced mindful breathing (see Try This: Teach Your Kids to Meditate, page 135) in the classroom were more able to relax and made better decisions when faced with conflict. They were more focused, and when they did get off track, they were better at redirecting themselves back to the task at hand. They were also less anxious before taking tests.

Mindfulness cultivates emotional balance. When our emotions aren't active—as when we cope with stress by shutting down—life seems to lack meaning. This can make us feel dull or depressed. But when our emotions are overactive, getting too big and dramatic (this happens to me and the kids when we get overtired), life feels chaotic and overwhelming. Practicing mindfulness helps us find that elusive balance between chaos and boredom, between high drama and stuffing it all down.

Perhaps one of the biggest benefits to mindfulness—especially for kids who might err on the side of impulsiveness—is that it helps us gain the ability to pause before we act. This simple pause can help us consider options that we may not have appreciated had we acted more reflexively. This enables us to remain flexible, creative, and productive.

## But What Is Mindfulness?

Like gratitude, altruism, emotional literacy, and strong social ties, mindfulness is part of the happiness Holy Grail. Jon Kabat-Zinn, the scientist who first "translated" Buddhist practices of mindfulness into a secular program for people with chronic pain and stress, defines mindfulness as the "awareness that emerges through paying attention on purpose, in the present moment, and nonjudgmentally to the unfolding of experiences moment by moment." Kabat-Zinn's program, Mindfulness-Based Stress Reduction (MBSR), serves as the foundation of most of the science around mindfulness.

You can try being mindful right here, right now. What are you feeling in your body right now? What themes do your thoughts keep returning to—can you notice and label them? Are you experiencing any emotion? Tension? Calm?

Mindfulness is not necessarily a lack of emotion or a state of total calm. I can be feeling sad—even crying—and pay mindful attention to that experience. Nor is mindfulness necessarily the suppression of thought or an altered state of consciousness. In fact, mindfulness is often a running conversation with ourselves, describing our experiences as they are happening: *I am crying so hard I can feel my eyes swelling up. My stomach feels upset. I can hear the kids upstairs. I hear a bird. I'm thinking about my mom again. I'm going to bring my attention to my breath. I'm breathing in. I'm breathing out.* Notice the lack of judgment that is part of Kabat-Zinn's definition: I'm reporting what is, not chastising myself for feeling sad.

Mindfulness is the opposite of being on autopilot. As discussed in Chapter 6, there are some things we *want* ourselves and our kids to be in the habit of doing without much thought. But everything we do habitually can also be done mindfully. All we have to do is bring our attention and awareness to it. When we let ourselves spend too much time on autopilot, we hear our kids without really listening to them; we watch them but don't really see them; we talk without being aware of what we are saying. We are not present, so to speak: our attention is far in the future, perhaps planning for the weekend, or stuck in the past, worrying about something that happened earlier.

We are mindful when our attention is focused on what we are experiencing—both internally and externally, in real time, right now. Can you notice how each moment is born, experienced, and then passes away? I often try to practice eating mindfully. I'll take a bite and notice how the food tastes and smells, how it feels in my mouth. When I swallow, I notice that I'm no longer tasting—that this particular moment of eating has passed.

### TRY THIS

## Teach Your Kids to Meditate. Seriously.

We can cultivate mindfulness with our kids anytime and anywhere just by calling our attention to the present moment. Although I didn't fully understand the power of mindfulness until I'd had some instruction in it, the basic concept isn't rocket science. Try these simple exercises to get started. (If you want to go deeper, find an eight-week MBSR program or a meditation class. In my experience, the benefit to taking a class isn't so much the additional instruction—which you can get from any of the many good books on mindfulness and meditation—but the structure that it provides to help make mindfulness a regular habit.)

## The Raisin Meditation

Most MBSR courses begin with this simple way of practicing being present in an intense way. Here's how to do it.

1. Give each of your kids three raisins. If you don't have raisins, try popcorn.

2. Read this script in a slow, calm voice.

> Let's look at these raisins and pretend that we've never in our whole lives seen a raisin.
>
> Pick up one raisin.
>
> Think about how it feels between your fingers.
>
> Notice its colors.
>
> Notice any thoughts you might be having about the raisin.
>
> Notice if you are having any thoughts or feelings of liking or disliking raisins.
>
> Lift the raisin to your nose and smell it for a while.
>
> Now slowly bring the raisin to your lips, trying to notice everything you are thinking and feeling and smelling.
>
> Notice your arm moving your hand to position the raisin correctly.
>
> Notice your mouth salivating as your mind and body anticipate eating the raisin.
>
> Take the raisin into your mouth and chew it slowly, experiencing its taste.
>
> Hold it in your mouth.
>
> When you feel ready to swallow, notice if your body automatically wants to swallow the raisin.
>
> When you are ready, pick up the second raisin and just eat it as you normally would if you weren't learning to practice mindfulness. When you are finished, practice mindfulness again with the third raisin, eating it as you did the first.

After you do this raisin exercise, try to transfer that intense and mindful attention to the present moment in whatever you are doing, and encourage your children to do the same—showering, commuting, grocery shopping, eating dinner—or perhaps when your daughter asks you to drink 101 pretend lattes. Mindfulness can be practiced anywhere, anytime.

## Mindfulness Meditation

Practicing mindfulness meditation on a daily basis will deliver concrete benefits for adults and kids. Meditation can be a challenge because it is a practice that requires discipline. Think of it as a new skill that you need to practice a little bit each day. This daily practice is a simple skill that you can do anywhere, with little time or preparation. Here are some instructions for a basic mindfulness meditation, which you can use for yourself or teach your children. I enjoy meditating with my children: no other activity grounds us so fully in less than five minutes.

1. Sit in a chair or on a cushion or pillow on the floor. Find a position that is comfortable for you where your back is straight but relaxed. It is fine to support your back in a chair, or to lie down. (I try not to lie down when I meditate, because I fall asleep.)

2. Rest your hands in your lap, close your eyes, and take a few deep breaths.

3. Bring your attention to your breath, focusing completely on the physical sensation of breathing. How does it feel when cool air enters your nose and then warm air is exhaled? Be curious. How does it feel when your abdomen expands and contracts when you breathe and exhale?

This can be done for a minute or an hour. Decide on a period of time that is realistic and enjoyable for you and your kids. Start slowly and build up to longer periods of time. The most important thing is establishing a routine: for most people, five minutes every day is more effective than an hour-long meditation once a month. Here are some more things to keep in mind.

- If your mind wanders or you notice that you aren't paying attention to your breath anymore, simply return your attention to your breath. No need to worry about your wandering mind or to judge yourself; simply note what you were thinking about, and move your attention back to your breath. This *is* the meditation: focus on breathing, mind wanders, notice that mind was wandering, note and accept thoughts, bring attention back to the breath . . . again and again and again.

- Younger kids might never before have paid attention to their breathing, and it might feel weird to them (and you!). No need to try to change your breathing at all—to hold it, or to deepen it, or to speed it up or slow it down. Just notice how your body breathes without your help.

- Counting their breaths can help remind kids to stay focused. If your mind wanders and you lose track of where you are, just note what you were thinking about and return to counting your breaths, beginning again at "one."

- You may be surprised at how much practice it takes to remain focused on your breath. However, I find that even the meditations where my mind is wandering constantly are hugely beneficial.

- Use this focus on breathing in your daily life, and encourage your children to do the same. Whenever I am feeling anxious, overwhelmed, or angry—and also before I start a new project and when I first wake up in the morning—I take five deep breaths, paying as close attention to them as possible.

## Parenting Mindfully

Mindfulness not only helps your kids cope with the stressors of modern life, it helps you become a better parent. Possibly a much better parent. In fact, if mindfulness is the only thing that you remember from reading this book, the science indicates that your kids will be better behaved because of it. You don't even have to teach it to your kids.

You read that right. A group of social workers and psychologists in Virginia have made a fascinating discovery: practicing mindfulness doesn't just lead to decreased stress and increased pleasure in parenting, it brings profound benefits to kids. Parents who practiced mindful parenting for a year were dramatically more satisfied with their parenting skills and their interactions with their children, even though no new parenting practices beyond just being mindful had been taught to them. Over the course of the year-long study, the behavior of these mindful parents' kids also changed for the better: they got along better with their siblings and were less aggressive, and their social skills improved. And all their parents did was practice mindfulness.

So how do we parent mindfully? The short answer is that it takes constant practice. I am well trained in mindfulness practices, but I still struggle. Here's an example of real-life unmindful parenting. This morning everyone woke up late, and Fiona wasn't listening to me at all. When I asked her to get dressed, she started doing Mad Libs word games instead. I called from the other room, "Did you feed the dog?" which prompted her to find the cat, who was outside. Without taking note of the situation, I became more and more irritated with her. Raccoons had gotten into our house during the night, and the mad chasing to get them out had left us all tired and cranky. I wasn't ready for work myself and was beginning to worry about impending deadlines.

I started to bark orders. "Fiona! Get dressed!" And then I let loose a doozy: "Fiona! What is up with you? It's like you're three years old, not eight! Do I need to come in there and dress you myself?" For the record, I've never found insulting my children to be particularly effective, and it didn't work this time either. Fiona flew into a rage, screaming things such as "I'm not going to listen to you if you use mean words!" which did not exactly make me feel more calm about the situation.

If I could rewind the morning and begin more mindfully, things would have been entirely different. All I needed to do was take stock of the situation. Notice my feelings of anxiety and exhaustion. Notice that Fiona's exhaustion was also making her distractible and emotional. Notice that no matter how speedy we had been, I still would not have been able to get to work on time. Accepting this situation nonjudgmentally—rather than futilely trying to force it to be something other than what it was, or chastising myself for sleeping through the alarm—would have left me open to more productive and positive alternatives. I might even have been able to help Fiona be more mindful by putting her in touch with how her tiredness was making her more distractible. Then I could have ushered her along in a more supportive way, by showing empathy, offering her a meaningful rationale, and giving her choices (see Chapter 6 for more about this).

For me, the keys to mindful parenting are as follows: first, notice what is happening (and what you're feeling and thinking) and, second, accept what is going on without judgment. If you want to become a more mindful parent—and reap the benefits that come along with it—I highly recommend Myla and Jon Kabat-Zinn's book on this subject, *Everyday Blessings: The Inner Work of Mindful Parenting*. I particularly like the epilogue: seven intentions and twelve exercises for mindful parenting.

## Let Kids Just Play

Most kids already practice mindfulness—fully enjoying the present moment—when they play. But kids today spend less time just playing, both indoors and out. Many instead devote a considerable amount of time to organized activities such as athletics and structured after-school programs; others spend a lot of time on computers. All told, over the last two decades children have lost eight hours per week of free, unstructured, and spontaneous play.

Does it matter? Are kids better off in piano lessons if it means they spend less time playing in the backyard? Researchers believe that this dramatic drop in unstructured playtime is in part responsible for slowing kids' cognitive and emotional development. In Chapter 7 we saw that children's capacity for self-regulation—their ability to control their emotions and behavior and resist impulses—is much worse today than it was sixty years ago. In the study where today's five-year-olds had the self-regulation capability of a three-year-old in the 1940s, the critical factor seems to have been not discipline but play.

Researchers hypothesized that kids would be able to control their behavior better—in this case, standing still—when they were *playing* at standing still rather than arbitrarily standing still. In the original study, kids were asked to pretend they were guards protecting a factory. This little bit of imaginary play did, in fact, increase five- and six-year-old kids' ability to stand still—from three minutes to nine minutes.

But in a study replicated fifty years later by Russian psychologist E. O. Smirnova, not only was kids' overall ability to follow directions cut in half for children of all ages, but pretending to be security guards at a bank no longer helped five- and six-year-olds stand still. Researchers concluded that the decline in the amount of time kids "practiced playing"—remember, they were less skilled at pretend play—was responsible for this decline in their ability to self-regulate.

Clearly the benefits of play are great—more far-reaching than just helping kids blow off steam or get a little physical exercise. In addition to helping kids learn to self-regulate, child-led, unstructured play (with or without adults) promotes intellectual, physical, social, and emotional well-being. Unstructured play helps children learn how to work in groups, to share, negotiate, resolve conflicts, regulate their emotions and behavior, and speak up for themselves. "Neuroscientists, developmental biologists, psychologists, social scientists, and researchers from every point of the scientific compass now know that play is a profound biological process," says Stuart Brown, leading play researcher in the United States. Play "shapes the brain and makes animals smarter and more adaptable," he says. It fosters empathy in kids, and lies at the very heart of creativity and innovation. And the ability to play has a profound effect on our happiness.

Because play is so good for us, we needn't feel guilty for doing it. It isn't a waste of time when we grown-ups do it, and it certainly isn't a waste when children do it. Play is a catalyst that makes us more productive and happier in everything we do. And it is critical for children's brain development. So we driven parents need to curb our impulses to sacrifice good old-fashioned play in favor of preschool academics and structured sports.

In fact, starting academic instruction earlier does not necessarily lead to greater success, and it might even hinder it. In one study, children attending academic preschools showed no advantage in reading or math achievement over kids who went to play-based preschools, but they did have higher levels of test anxiety. As you will see in Chapter 9, these academically pushed kids were less creative and had more negative attitudes toward school than did the kids in play-based preschool.

The good news is that while children do need time and space to "practice playing," they know innately how to play. Grown-ups need to respect kids' play as a built-in mechanism for becoming more socially intelligent, more creative, and happier. We parents, on the other hand, may need to relearn what was once second nature. Here are three things to keep in mind when playing with your kids.

- *Let kids lead.* When we find ourselves saying things such as "I like the game you're playing, but why don't you let Sarah be the girl and you be the daddy?" we are probably dominating too much. Don't correct your kids when they are playing unless they are being unkind. If you notice yourself frowning, sighing, or rolling your eyes when your children aren't playing the way you want them to, take a step back and let them run the show.

- *Don't play with your kids in ways that bore you.* Spend time with your kids doing things that *you* enjoy (while still letting your kids lead). I love to roughhouse with my children, but I don't enjoy participating in their pretend play as much, so I mostly skip doing that part to avoid sending the message that they shouldn't like it either. It is perfectly fine for parents to back off a little and let children play on their own or with other children, especially once they are four to five years old. Kids learn to entertain themselves this way, and to get along with other children. The most important thing is that they know that you value and support their play—and your own.

- *Pretend play is particularly beneficial, so make sure kids have ample time for it.* Children with imaginary friends are not crazy or troubled; they are actually less shy than other children and more likely to smile and laugh in social situations. Projecting personalities and having make-believe interactions with stuffies, toys, or imaginary companions is a healthy way for kids to develop the skills they need to focus their attention and get along with other children. Dramatic pretend play with two or more children stimulates social and intellectual growth, which in turn affects a child's success in school.

The more complex the imaginative play, the better. Make sure that kids have enough time: a half hour is the minimum. Play that lasts several hours is better. Encourage kids to use symbolic props—sticks for fairy wands and boxes for cars or houses—rather than prefab toys. Older children can be encouraged to participate in drama classes and clubs. But remember: ballet class isn't the same as making up a dance with friends in the backyard.

### TRY THIS

### Five Ways to Teach Creativity

In addition to imaginative play for healthy development, kids need creativity. Many people assume that creativity is an inborn talent that their kids either do or do not have—that just as all children are not equally intelligent, all children are not equally creative. Actually, creativity is more of a skill than an inborn talent, and it is a skill that parents can help their kids develop.

Because it is key to success in nearly everything we do, creativity is a fundamental component of health and happiness and a core skill to practice with kids. Creativity is not limited to artistic and musical expression;

it is also essential for science, math, and even social and emotional intelligence. Creative people are more flexible and better problem solvers, which makes them more able to adapt to technological advances and deal with change, as well as benefit from new opportunities.

Many researchers believe that we have fundamentally changed the experience of childhood in a way that impairs creative development. Toy and entertainment companies feed kids an endless stream of prefab characters, images, props, and plot lines that make imaginative play unnecessary and even outmoded. Children no longer need to imagine that a stick is a sword in a game or story they've invented. They can act out scripted *Star Wars* scenes with plastic toy light sabers in costumes designed for the role they are playing.

Here are some ideas for fostering creativity in your kids.

1. Make your home a petri dish for creativity. At dinnertime, for example, brainstorm activities for the upcoming weekend, encouraging the kids to come up with things they've never done before. Resist pointing out which ideas aren't possible or deciding which ideas are best. The focus should be on the process, generating (versus evaluating) new ideas.

   Another way to nurture a creative atmosphere at home is to encourage kids to take risks, make mistakes, and fail. Yes, fail. In her book *Mindset,* Stanford researcher Carol Dweck shows that kids who are afraid of failure and judgment curb their own creative thought. Share the mistakes you've made recently so the kids get the idea that it's okay to flub up.

2. Allow kids the freedom and autonomy to explore their ideas. For me, this means not always being so bossy. External constraints— making kids color within the lines, so to speak—can reduce creative thinking. In one study, when researchers first showed kids how to make a plane or a truck with Legos, kids showed less creativity on their own than when they were let loose to make whatever they wanted with the same Lego set.

3. Encourage kids to read for pleasure and participate in the arts rather than watch TV. Studies by children's health researcher Dimitri Christakis have found that TV viewing before the age of three can harm language development and attention span later in life. Studies by Dutch researcher T. H. van der Voort suggest that

watching TV might dampen kids' creative imagination, and violent TV shows are associated with a decrease in fantasy play and an increase in aggressiveness. Less screen time means more time for creative activities, such as rehearsing a play, learning to draw, or reading every book by a favorite author.

4. Resist the temptation to reward kids for their creativity. A study led by child development researcher Melissa Groves found that incentives interfere with the creative process, reducing the flexibility of children's thinking. Instead of trying to motivate kids with rewards and incentives, we parents sometimes need to back off so that kids can work on the creative activities that they're intrinsically motivated to do.

5. Try to stop caring how much your kids achieve. I think this is one of the greatest challenges we parents face in today's ultracompetitive world. But Dweck's research is clear: kids gain confidence from an emphasis on process rather than product. This can be hard advice to follow when our kids come home from school with just the end product of an art project. But whether they're working at home or at school, we can emphasize the creative process by asking questions. How did you make that? Are you finished? What did you like about that activity? Did you have fun?

## SAVORING THE PRESENT, REPLAYING THE PAST

*Life is not a dress rehearsal. Every day, you should have
at least one exquisite moment.*

— SALLY KARIOTH

At night before bed, I ask my kids to tell me about three good things that happened during the day. What went well during their day, and why? Although I'm generally fishing for details about their time away from me (and encouraging them to practice gratitude), they almost always say that "right now" is one of their good things. They don't say "right now" because they are too lazy to think of something else, but because taking the time to enjoy the present moment really *is* a good thing and they know this.

One day Molly was sitting on my lap braiding my hair, and she looked up at me and said, "Oh, Mommy, this is definitely going to be one of my three good things." What had started as a daily gratitude practice had taught Molly to do what researchers call "savoring": literally slowing down to smell the roses. Savoring the present moment this way can make the part of our brain that registers positive emotions more active, can help us cope better under stress, and can strengthen our immune system. Being in the habit of savoring is related to "intense and frequent happiness."

Practicing mindfulness, playing, and savoring—stopping to notice something that feels good—are all ways of practicing the growth mindset discussed in Chapter 3. They make life about the process and not the end result. Enjoying the present moment teaches kids not to postpone happiness.

Because savoring extends and intensifies how much we enjoy something, it is a fun happiness skill for parents to model. When we celebrate or take pride in our kids, we are savoring. When we inspire a second or third fit of laughter by telling a funny story, or we rekindle joy by reminiscing about a happy time, we are savoring. (Our family does this by recounting funny movie scenes.) When we relish simple pleasures, such as a shared meal or new growth in our garden, we are savoring. While often easier said than done, simply slowing down to notice what we enjoy about raising our children, or what we are enjoying right now, is enough.

Another, less intuitive way to savor an experience is to remind ourselves—or our kids—that nothing lasts forever. This is a bittersweet way to savor life's joys: reminding ourselves to capture the moment while we still have it. Yesterday I was sitting on a park bench with my two kids sharing an ice cream cone, each of us trying to catch the drips and giggling while we tried to outdo one another by taking absurdly large bites. I knew that the whole experience—so full of happiness—would be over before we knew it, and I mentioned this to the kids: "Isn't this fun? This is going to be one of my three good things tonight. I wish it would last forever, but I can see that this ice cream cone is going to be gone in a blink." Fiona, who has clearly been listening to my Buddhist musings, said, "That's okay, Mom. Everything is temporary." Usually I invoke this notion (the Buddhist Law of Impermanence) when a toy breaks or a flower dies; Fiona reminded me that acknowledging the fleeting nature of a pleasant moment can intensify positive feelings.

Here are some other ways to practice savoring the moment:

- Imagine that a specific event is the last time you'll ever experience it. The other day watching the sun go down behind San Francisco,

I said to the kids (who were starting to get restless), "What if this were the very last sunset you ever saw in your entire life. What would you want to remember about it?" We then took turns pointing out what we found most beautiful and poignant, enjoying and engaged in the rapidly changing landscape. This helps us realize that savoring is not simply experiencing a positive feeling; it is more like perceiving that feeling through the eyes of an inquiring journalist in the present moment, and then reporting these perceptions to ourselves and those around us.

■ Practice being grateful. Gratitude is a good way of savoring (see Chapter 4 for more on how to foster gratitude in kids). In fact, one of the reasons that gratitude may bring so much happiness is that it prevents us from taking happy experiences for granted.

■ Avoid multitasking. Research shows that when we are trying to do more than one thing at a time, we have difficulty savoring any positive experiences or feelings. I've noticed this when I'm trying to get something done (such as responding to e-mail on my iPhone) at the same time that I'm hanging out with my kids. It isn't just that I can't fully enjoy playing with them at the park; it's that the multitasking actually prevents me from enjoying or playing with them at all. This multitasking also drains any pleasure that I might have derived from e-mail as well. In the interest of efficiency, I delete joke e-mails without reading them, saving thirty seconds but missing the opportunity to laugh.

■ Practice labeling positive feelings. While we usually think to emotion-coach our kids (see Chapter 5) when they are down, there are benefits to noticing and explicitly labeling positive moods as well: emotion-coaching during pleasurable moments enhances kids' ability to savor. (One reason why women are typically better than men at savoring is that they tend to be more aware of how they are feeling.) Have kids tell you exactly how they are feeling when they seem happy, just as you would have them do when you're trying to emotion-coach before a tantrum begins. Are they feeling affectionate, mellow, energized, uplifted, excited, powerful, comfortable? Is the situation particularly fun, fulfilling, heartwarming, or inspiring?

- Share your positive feelings and experiences with others, and encourage your kids to do the same. There is a strong relationship between expressing positive feelings to others and greater enjoyment of positive events. Sharing can amplify our positive feelings. Grandparents are often willing receivers of this sort of sharing. Fiona and Molly's grandmother in Maryland relished hearing about that ice-cream-cone-eating contest, for example, and the kids are happier for having told her.

- Remind kids how long they've waited. This is another way of recognizing that the positive things in life can be fleeting, and often we wait a long time for a particularly positive thing to happen. I do this most nights when I cuddle with my kids before bedtime by telling them that I had been waiting the whole day for that special time with them. I also find this to be a particularly wonderful way of savoring a relationship that is important to me but for whatever reason is irritating me a little bit. I recognize that one reason I am so happy right now is that I have great friends, and that at another time in my life I would have given anything to have the friends and family I do.

Savoring is about doubling our pleasure. While savoring might also intensify our positive feelings in a given situation, the more important thing is to prolong the positive situation, because the duration of our positive feelings and experiences, rather than their intensity, is a better predictor of our overall happiness.

## HELPING KIDS GET INTO FLOW

With all this talk about mindfulness and play, I'd be remiss not to spend some time talking about "flow"—that blissful state when we are so engrossed in doing something we love that time seems to stand still. I love how Mihaly Csikszentmihalyi, the world's foremost expert on "flow," describes it.

[A] person in flow is completely focused . . . Self-consciousness disappears, yet one feels stronger than usual. When a person's entire being is stretched in the full functioning of body and mind, whatever one does becomes worth doing for its own sake; living becomes its own justification.

For adults, this can happen when we get so absorbed in our work that we forget to eat or when we are "in the zone" on the athletic field. The sign for me that I'm deep in flow is when I start to heat up water for tea, and then the cup sits in the microwave all morning because I got going on something and never even heard the beep, or missed the caffeine. Flow is a form of mindfulness in that it is an intense experiential involvement in moment-to-moment activity; it is the merging of action and awareness. When we are "flowing," we are functioning at our very best.

Kids experience flow all the time, too. Play is that flow state we most often associate with childhood. When Molly and her best friends Kate and Anna get totally lost in their pretend play, that's flow. They are all opinionated (some would say obstinate), so joint imaginative play is not always easy for them. In a way, the three of them playing together is the ideal developmental challenge: they have to constantly negotiate one another's needs in order to keep the play going. Not easy, but possible. That's a key aspect of flow: the challenge cannot be too difficult, which would lead to frustration and anxiety, or too easy, which would lead to boredom and loss of engagement.

This is why the happiness that kids reap from their play far surpasses what they'd get out of watching TV, which takes no effort or skill whatsoever. And this is one of the important lessons in the childhood roots of adult happiness: kids learn to achieve flow when parents enable them to participate in the activities likely to produce it—namely, those things that challenge them and provide them with some immediate feedback.

Like play, flow contributes significantly to kids' growth and development. Experiencing flow prompts kids to seek out the challenges they need to build skills. Frequent flow experiences undergird qualities such as hope and perseverance—both critical to kids' success and happiness—as they learn that their efforts can lead to meaning and mastery. Further, flow helps kids take pleasure in solitude, so they can concentrate more on the skills they need to learn in order to perform well, and less on how their performance appears to others.

Here are some ways to help kids achieve flow:

■ Teach them the skills they need to master an activity. When challenges begin to exceed kids' skills, they first become vigilant, and then anxious. If you notice anxiety, step in and help so that they can get back in the flow.

- Help them find the next challenge. As kids gain mastery over an activity, it can become less interesting for them. Helping kids balance their skills with challenges can keep them engaged.

- Teach kids that there is more to finding flow than going with the flow, so to speak. Kids need to be self-disciplined enough to maintain their attention and efforts through periods of self-doubt and boredom.

- Parenting style can also foster flow. Authoritative parents (as opposed to authoritarian, remember!)—those who combine rules and high expectations with opportunities for choice and self-expression—provide more opportunities for their kids to experience flow. The key here is to be encouraging *and* firm, remembering that supporting kids' efforts sometimes means not letting them quit when the going gets tough. Kids with parents who support *and* challenge them spend more time each day in flow. Kids with parents who are challenging without also being warm and supportive tend to report that their day is filled with drudgery. And kids with parents who are supportive but not challenging tend to spend more time each day goofing off doing activities that might be enjoyable but aren't productive.

Like play and mindfulness, flow is all about the process—engagement with the present moment—without too much concern about the end result.

# NINE

■ ■ ■ ■ ■ ■

# Step 9: Rig Their Environment for Happiness

*Throughout history, people of all cultures have assumed that environment influences behavior. More than two thousand years ago, Hippocrates' observation that our well-being is affected by our settings was established as a cornerstone of Western medicine. Now modern science is confirming that our actions, thoughts, and feelings are indeed shaped not just by our genes and neurochemistry, history and relationships, but also by our surroundings.*
—WINIFRED GALLAGHER

My dear friend Dana recently pulled her second grader out of the local public school—a good one for Oakland, California, but still a little rough around the edges—and enrolled him in a Catholic school. Her logic was that he was beginning to hang out with kids who were encouraging his attention-seeking misbehaviors, and this would increasingly become a problem. As she put it, she wanted the "range of normal" to be narrower, to decrease the odds that he'd end up an underachieving substance abuser.

What parent hasn't felt that fear, that desire to control who our kids associate with? We worry that if our kids are exposed to "bad" kids or "bad" neighborhoods, they'll fall in with the wrong crowds and we'll lose them forever. We worry that we don't have any control; we seek to recover our control by rigging their environment. Does this work? Can we rig our kids' environment for happiness?

This question is a complicated one, for sure. As a sociologist, I have long studied what makes certain social structures—families, schools, businesses—more likely to foster certain emotions and inhibit others. Why do some companies elicit such creativity and joy from their employees while others turn out Dilbert-like sarcasm and minimal productivity? Why do some schools seem to foster gratitude and community while others fester in materialistic entitlement and cynicism? This book is about how we can create families that cultivate positive emotions in our children; this chapter addresses some of the big happiness factors outside of our families. What kind of child care and schooling increase the odds that our children are happy? Do kids really need all the latest and greatest technologies and lessons? How much should we protect our children? Ultimately, how much control over their environment do we really have?

To be writing (and reading) a chapter such as this is a privilege; not everyone is lucky enough to have even an ounce of control over their environment. Many families simply do not have the resources to pull a child out of public school, as my friend did, or have the same child-care choices that others have. But even when our resources are restricted, often we can cobble together some choices for ourselves and our children. And when we do have the socioeconomic resources needed to be able to make these big decisions about our children's environment and culture, we need to understand them in order to create a society that is better—happier—for all children.

## BUILDING RAT PARK

My favorite metaphor for how we can create social structures that foster well-being comes from a series of studies designed by drug-addiction researcher Bruce Alexander. In the late 1970s, Alexander had grown suspicious of the research that seemed to "prove" beyond a doubt that drug addiction is a hardwired neurological phenomenon and not something else, something environmental. As Alexander watched rats maniacally press levers that would deliver narcotics straight into their veins, he couldn't help but think that if he were a rat trapped in a cage, he would push the lever, too—not so much because of the drugs but because of his unfortunate circumstances. Hooked up to the drugs through surgically implanted catheters, trapped in boxes, isolated from their colonies, deprived of every activity that comes naturally to rats—playing, fighting, foraging, mating—all they had to do was push a lever to get high. *No wonder they so readily became slaves to narcotics.*

Alexander wondered: would rats become addicted to drugs if their circumstances weren't so dire? To find out, he built what he calls "Rat Park": heaven on Earth for rats. He reunited his lab rats with their friends and families in enclosures two hundred times the size of a normal laboratory cage, and outfitted them with everything a rat could desire: cedar shavings, boxes and tin cans to play with and hide in, places to climb and nest, and good food. He then offered them both plain water and water laced with morphine. The overwhelming majority of Rat Park residents drank the plain water. When he added sugar to the drug-laden water, more drank the morphine-laced water than the water without the sugar, but still, most rats preferred their water drug free. Only when Alexander neutralized the effects of the morphine by adding naloxone did the rats start drinking more from the water-sugar-morphine bottles: rats like candy water, but they don't want to get high.

Here is another startling thing: when Alexander put rats that were already addicted to morphine into Rat Park and offered them both plain and morphine-laced water, many more of these rats switched to the plain water than did their caged counterparts. Without lectures about how plain water would be better for them, without knowing that drug addiction is self-defeating, and without support groups, Rat Park rodents willingly endured excruciating withdrawal effects in order to stay sober.

Turns out drug addiction isn't so much hardwiring as it is environmental—and not just for rats. Studies with human subjects also show that environment matters a lot in predicting whether someone will choose heroin over Kool-Aid.

Alexander's studies make me think of Dana pulling her son out of public school. Rat Park adds to my conviction that she was right to think that environment matters, though less for the "bad" elements to which her son might be exposed (the narrower "range of normal") than for the environmental factors that influence kids' happiness.

Given the choice, what kind of park should we create for our children, and how much stuff should we put in it? Although the analogy might make you cringe, I think that we humans aren't so different from our rodent friends (we do share 95 percent of our genes with them, after all). What makes for a good Rat Park may also make for a good Kid Park. Like rats, kids mostly need the time and space to socialize and play, work out their fights, and maybe do a little foraging. They need places to hide and climb and nest. They need to be with their friends and families in colonies. They need nutritious food.

This chapter addresses three big things that can make kids' environments seem more like Rat Parks than rat cages. The first thing is their early child care, including preschool. Although parents don't always have full control over the variables related to their children's care, choosing child care and preschool are among the first and most important decisions that parents make regarding their children's environments, and there is a mountain of research that can inform these decisions. The second environmental factor to be addressed is the culture that permeates the air we breathe, particularly as it relates to pervasive materialism. The last feature of Kid Park, as I like to think of it, slightly reverses all this thinking by discussing how much control we want to have in creating idealized environments for kids.

## CAN CHILD CARE CAUSE BEHAVIOR PROBLEMS?

We sociologists and our pals the psychologists have collected a lot of empirical data about the risks and benefits of child care, and the popular press has probably made sure that you're informed in one way or another. It seems as though every time a new study is released, the results conflict with the last study, or they amplify bad news without giving us any useful alternatives. A few years ago, I remember reading in *Newsweek* about a new study on how child care affects children's cognitive development. I promptly got a half-dozen panicky calls from my friends. *What if I can't afford a nanny? What if I can't afford not to work? Are my kids going to be disadvantaged? Would it be better if I stayed home?*

I myself have chosen what turned out to be potentially terrible child care—not once, but twice. A litany of mistakes led to each of these poor choices, which I share with you in detail so that you can learn from them. I figured out my mistakes before too long and was able to correct them, though not before I reviewed hundreds of studies to try to figure out what my ideal should be and how to get there.

Bad child care choice number one: hiring—and paying through the nose for—a terrible nanny. I was in graduate school when Fiona was an infant, and I was overwhelmed with the double whammy of being a new mother and a first-year grad student. Forget reading Marx in a fog of sleep deprivation, my problem-solving resources were tied up just trying to keep Fiona fed. (She had a weird palate that made feeding slow and difficult. The low point was when our dog ate my nipple shield.) My first thought was to leave Fiona with my mom while I was in class, which would have been convenient because we lived with my parents at that point. When it turned out that my mom preferred the grandmother role over the nanny role, I thought it would be ideal if my high school friend, Ryan, who had also been Fiona's labor and delivery nurse, babysat. I knew she loved babies. But Ryan thought I was kidding. Clearly I hadn't thought through the key details. How was I going to pay her the hourly rate (three times what nannies make) that she was making as a nurse? Was she supposed to schedule her hospital hours around my classes? I realized I would have to put my precious bundle of profound specialness into the care of a *total stranger*.

My first mistake: waiting until I needed child care to think about it seriously, much less look for it. Knowing nothing, I scanned craigslist for a nanny. I interviewed only one candidate in person, and she seemed so good that I hired her before I even saw her interact with a child or a baby. Jessica had an interesting background: she wrote screenplays, was a National Public Radio producer, had her master of fine arts degree, and told a great story about why she wanted to become a nanny (mostly having to do with missing that time when her own children were babies and she wanted to stay at home with them but couldn't). Three weeks into the whole ordeal, I began to suspect that Jessica might be mentally ill, or at least seriously unstable. Fortunately, I was able to find alternate child care before anything bad happened. My succession of mistakes: not knowing what to look for in child care or a nanny, not interviewing a range of experienced people with long track records and relevant references, not observing her care for infants and children.

I have learned a lot since the Jessica incident. For starters, there is a huge body of science that stemmed from researchers arguing with one another over the risks and benefits of nonmaternal child care. Jay Belsky, a British psychologist famous for his work on the importance of the mother-child bond, lit the fuse in what became the "day-care wars" among researchers: he showed empirically that "early, extensive, and continuous" child care comes with risks. This topic has been so incendiary that millions of dollars have been spent trying to assess just how kids benefit— and suffer—when their infancy, toddler, and preschool years are spent in the care of someone other than their mother.

As a result, we have good, solid, research-based answers to the first questions raised by Belsky's work a decade ago. Here is what we have learned.

1. The quality of child-care situations matters a lot less than we used to think. Obviously, poor-quality care is not a good experience on many levels for your kids. If you can afford to, avoid it. Kids *do* benefit from more attentive, responsive, and stimulating care at virtually any age, and suffer developmentally when put in poorer-quality care (care where the caregivers aren't particularly warm, for example, or the child-to-teacher ratio is high). Surprisingly, however, these benefits and developmental costs disappear completely by the time kids are in the fifth grade, and sometimes sooner, depending on the particular cost or benefit. High-quality care makes your child more likely to have higher standardized math, reading, and memory scores, but only through the third grade. By the time kids are about eleven, the only lasting academic benefit of high-quality care is relatively higher vocabulary scores.

   When it comes to happiness, the most important thing about the quality of child care is how it compares with parenting. Infants are more likely to develop insecure attachments to their mothers when the quality of their day care is low *and* their mothers are insensitive. More harmonious interactions and more secure attachments between infants and mothers are likely when babies have high-quality care during the day, even when their mothers are not very sensitive. This is important because, as we know from Chapter 5, attachment relationships between infants and their parents are predictive of later happiness and well-being. But even here, by the time those infants in low-quality care with insensitive mothers are three years old, the effects of the low-quality care (though not the insensitive parenting) seem to vanish.

   The reason that day care and preschool quality matter less than we might imagine is that other things matter a lot more. The effects of child-care quality are small in magnitude when compared to parenting practices, for example.

   All this is not to say that quality is not important; it is, and you should strive to provide your kids with the highest-quality child care that you can afford and find. We can say, however, that if your kids don't get into that fancy preschool, if you can't afford a nanny, or if there isn't an exceptional day care close enough to your home, as long as the care is not abusive, the kids will not be scarred for life.

2. The type of care you put your child in has different effects—some good, some bad. The best research compares center-based child care to home-based child care (family day care, nannies who care for children from multiple families) to relative care, such as a dad or an aunt or a grandmother. (I know, shocking that researchers put dads in the same camp as grandmothers—I'm outraged, too.) I get a lot of questions about nannies: are they so much better than day care that they are worth the much higher cost? Although we don't know for sure—since so few families can afford private nannies, they don't often get counted in this research—I suspect that nanny care is similar to relative care in some respects, at least when it comes to cognitive (intelligence) and behavioral outcomes. Researchers in the biggest and best studies also take into consideration that kids often have multiple types of care situations. For example, a child might be cared for by a parent until going to preschool for half a day at age three. Or the child might be in full-time family day care until two and a half, and then full-day preschool until kindergarten.

Here is what we have learned from all this science: child-care centers have far-reaching developmental consequences on children when compared with other kinds of care. So the answer to this section's header question is yes: center-based child care can make behavior problems more likely. Although kids who are put in center-based care early in life tend to have greater language development until they start kindergarten, these short-term benefits do not, in my mind, outweigh the costs. The only effect that seems to last—at least as long as researchers have tracked kids, which right now is from birth through the end of elementary school—is the increased likelihood that kids will have acting-out types of behavior problems in kindergarten and beyond. Center-based child care increases the chances that kids will be more disobedient and more aggressive and have more conflict with their teachers. None of these things will bring kids lasting happiness.

3. The amount of time spent in child care matters a lot. There are a couple of components to this quantity question. The first is how early child care begins: does it begin at six weeks old or with preschool? The second component is how extensive the care is: how long is the child care or preschool day? How continuous the care

is also matters when assessing quantity. Early in life the risk that comes with a large quantity of nonmaternal child care depends on the quality of the parent-child relationship. When there are other sources of risk involved, such as having a mother low in sensitivity, a large amount of time spent in day care increases the odds that a child will develop an insecure attachment (see Chapter 5 for why this is a problem). In this example, any more than ten hours per week of day care when an infant is between the ages of three and fifteen months will increase the likelihood of an insecure attachment with a low-sensitivity mother—a mother who is less perceptive of and responsive to her child's needs. But that ten-hour threshold isn't relevant for sensitive mothers' children.

When researchers look at how mothers and children interact with one another (are the interactions harmonious or filled with conflict? Positive or negative?), more time in nonmaternal child care predicts less harmony through the first grade.

And like center-based child care, the sheer quantity of time spent in any type of nonmaternal care in the first four and a half years of life predicts elevated levels of aggressive and disobedient behavior. Unfortunately, there is no known threshold for the amount of time that is or isn't detrimental to kids. I would like to be able to give you solid guidelines, such as: if you keep their hours in child care under thirty-five hours a week, no effect will be evident. But I can't do that. We do know that the more time that kids spend in nonmaternal care relative to their peers, the more likely they will be rated by their teachers and caregivers as

- Talking, bragging, and arguing too much

- Disobedient and defiant, talking out of turn and talking back to staff, and otherwise disruptive in school

- Aggressive: more likely to get into fights; be cruel, bullying, or mean; and be destructive to their own belongings

These risks associated with spending a lot of time in child care— and they are just risks, not guarantees—hold even when researchers take into consideration factors such as a family's economic status, the parents' marital status, and the parents' education.

Besides these acting-out behavior problems, spending a lot of time in day care also predicts poorer academic work habits and less social competence in grade school.

But here is the good news again: these effects don't seem to last and are most pronounced for center- or group-based care. For kids who have spent a lot of time in nonmaternal care, behavioral problems are no longer evident by the time they reach the third grade, and the poorer academic work habits and inferior social competence disappear by the time they are sixth graders.

In sum, here are three things I take away from all this research.

1. Less is better. When possible, reduce the amount of time your youngins spend in paid care, especially as infants.

2. Especially try to reduce the amount of time kids under age three spend in center-based day care, as that is what seems to have the largest negative effects. Resist the temptation to dwell on the positive effects of center-based day care. Who cares how big your kid's vocabulary is if he's getting into fights and sassing the teacher?

3. The effects of child care are small compared to the other things that affect kids' success and happiness, and the negative effects that do occur rarely last past grade school. It is better to focus on improving your parenting practices, which you obviously already care about if you are reading this book, than on obsessing about the quality of your kids' day care. This is especially true if your child-care choices are limited.

## If I Have a Choice, What Should I Choose?

By the time Molly needed regular child care—Fiona was in preschool, and Molly had outgrown her nanny share—I thought I was a pro at selecting the right child-care environment. Which leads me to bad child-care choice number two: the Fancy-Pants Day-care Center (not its real name). Since I hadn't yet done all the above research, I didn't realize I should avoid center-based care if possible: I was focusing on how much cheaper it was going to be. I had heard through the grapevine that Fancy-Pants, a well-known day-care center in a tony neighborhood near us, had an opening. I went for a tour and was thoroughly impressed by the director's philosophy and the kids' activities. They didn't have a TV on the premises, and there was a large play structure and huge outdoor play space. Though there were a lot of kids, there were also a lot of caregivers. The facility, a large converted home, was beautiful and clean and downright homey. And they fed the kids a healthy, organic lunch and two snacks each day—one less chore for me in the morning.

At that point, I had learned that it was wise to do some observation and talk to a lot of other parents before making a choice. But I already knew a bunch of smart people who sent their kids there, which counted in my book as a good part of due diligence. And unless I gave the Fancy-Pants director a deposit then and there, she was going to offer the one spot to someone else. Feeling pressured and panicked that I might miss a golden opportunity, I pulled out my checkbook and presto, Molly was enrolled. That was my big mistake.

The day Molly started, which was the following Monday after I first set foot in Fancy-Pants, I stayed and observed for several hours. I noticed that the director's boyfriend hung around all day as an extra caregiver. I love to see paid male caregivers, and I mentioned this to the director. "Oh, he's not paid," she said. "He's not licensed. He's just a big help. Shh! Don't tell!" Giant red flag number one. Later that day, I saw the boyfriend take two kids off-site to a local park, which made me uncomfortable.

At dinner the following evening, Molly was trying to describe something exciting that had happened at Fancy-Pants in her limited eighteen-month-old language—something about swimming and TV and gold. We guessed that people were talking about the Olympics, since they were in session at the time. That night, I called the other parents I knew, and no one gave glowing references; they were too busy justifying why they sent their kids there, despite what they called the "creepy boyfriend."

Trying to assuage my mounting fears that I'd made a mistake and was about to lose a huge deposit, the next day I paid an unannounced visit, something I highly recommend. I entered through the back door without knocking. If I could do so unnoticed, this would be a red flag from a safety standpoint. Once inside, I asked a two-year-old if he knew where Molly was. He pointed to a door that I hadn't seen before. That door led downstairs to an area I hadn't been shown on the tour. Before a caregiver even saw me, I found Molly in a musty basement parked in front of a huge big-screen TV among a dozen other sleepy toddlers. Watching the Olympics.

The lesson in all this, of course, is not to make hasty decisions based on reputation alone. Child-care center directors can talk a good talk about their philosophy, but are their practices as good as their intentions? The only way to know is to be there and observe, and to talk to a lot of other parents about their experiences.

After basic safety and basic cleanliness, which you need to establish before going further, there are three primary things to focus on when choosing child care, whether it is family day care, a nanny, a center, or any other child-care setup. The first factor is the quality of the connections between the caregivers and the children. Are the kids forming strong attachments to their caregivers? Is the staff turnover extremely low— ideally, zero—so that kids don't get attached and then lose those relationships? Is the ratio of kids to caregivers low enough that each kid has at least one secure attachment to a caregiver, preferably more?

The second important thing is positivity. Does the environment foster lots of positive emotions? How warm are the caregivers? Are they nurturing and responsive to the children? Are the caregivers themselves happy? Do the caregivers use growth–mind-set praise (see Chapter 3)? Is their discipline structured but positive? In other words, do they preempt misbehavior rather than just react to it? Can they control the kids without using commands and threats? What are the kids doing? Are the activities positive and joyful, such as painting and dancing?

The third thing to consider when choosing child care is play. How much time do the children spend playing versus sitting in front of the television or attending to worksheets? It isn't that all structured activities are bad (circle times and music classes are important, too), but too much structured time isn't ideal (see "Why Play Is So Important" on page 161). If you are hiring a nanny, watch her with her current charges or on trial days with your kids. When you interview potential caregivers, ask them to brainstorm a list of ten or more activities in which they are likely to engage the kids. How many of those activities involve play?

Often parents feel as though they are choosing between apples and oranges with child care: should they choose the sparkling clean center with the ideal philosophy but huge kid-to-teacher ratio? Or the incredibly loving but uneducated family caregiver who cannot articulate her child-rearing beliefs? If you are facing such a decision, it is sometimes easy to be wooed by a good mission statement and organic snacks. But it is the more subtle things—the strength of the potential connections your children can form, the positivity of the environment and care, and how much time your children will be able to spend just playing—that are most important in rigging their environment for happiness.

## WHY PLAY IS SO IMPORTANT

In our achievement-oriented world, we often lose sight of just how important play is for young children. We all too quickly prioritize time spent learning letters over time in the sandbox. Taken to an extreme, that is a mistake, especially for children under five. Play contributes in a huge way to kids' cognitive, social, and psychological development and well-being. Consider these benefits of play.

- Better social skills. Kids at play are learning intensely. They are learning to share their toys and other resources with their siblings and playmates; to join and contribute to groups; to take turns; to negotiate conflict and differences; to cope with disappointment when other kids don't do what they want; and, perhaps most important, to express their needs and imaginations verbally. Child psychologists and education specialists have repeatedly found that kids who devote more time to complex pretend play before grade school age (versus kids who spend a lot of time in structured or caregiver-directed activities) are more likely to be cognitively and socially competent with peers and adults.
- Higher emotional intelligence. Children who engage in more pretend play with peers tend to demonstrate a greater understanding of other kids' emotions. Imaginary play helps kids embody—and therefore understand—the emotions and motivations of the characters they are playing; kids who do this a lot are more empathetic. In addition, rough-and-tumble play gives kids practice taking other children's perspectives and distinguishing between their friends' real and play-related expressions.
- School success. Increased emotional intelligence and social skills contribute dramatically to children's school success. Play increases the odds that kids will be persistent and stay engaged in difficult

classroom tasks, helping them become more involved learners. Play also helps kids improve their concentration, motivation, and problem solving—all of which are important for strong student performance. In addition, kids exercise logical thinking and diverse aspects of language when they play.

- Superior self-discipline. As detailed in Chapters 6 and 7, fantasy play helps kids develop the internal strength they need to control their own behavior.
- Greater creativity. Fantasy play expands kids' cognitive and behavioral repertoires, leading to more highly developed creativity, divergent thinking, and cooperative problem-solving skills.

For all these reasons, play is super-important in and of itself. It is not just a break from learning letters and numbers, but has an essential impact on children's development.

There are many different preschool philosophies and theories (for example, Reggio Emilia or Montessori) but because these different school styles tend to be executed differently, I suggest you evaluate a school according to how child-focused vs. academic it is. When it comes to preschool in particular, a play-based curriculum is especially beneficial for later engagement in school. Kids in child-focused schools, rather than in didactic programs that spend more time teaching academic skills directly, show more motivation at school. They also demonstrate more academic confidence, rating their own abilities more highly and expressing greater expectations for their own success in academic tasks. Kids in child- or play-based preschools show less dependency on adults for permission and approval, are more proud of their accomplishments, and worry less about school. Kids who attend preschools that allow some freedom to initiate activities and complete them without pressure to follow a particular formula, or to get "correct" answers, are more likely to choose more challenging activities and academic tasks than do their peers in didactic programs.

So while didactic preschool programs do improve kids' scores on reading (but not math) achievement tests, they can kill kids' love of learning. Didactic preschools are more likely to have poor social climates, and kids who go to them, ironically, emerge less likely to choose a basic academic skills task over another kind of activity. This suggests that they find learning about numbers and letters less interesting than do preschoolers in child-centered programs.

### TRY THIS

## Choose a Great Preschool

It takes researchers about three hours to assess a preschool program, so when you are looking for a preschool for your children, plan on visiting different programs and spending at least this much time. Do your homework first on the basics—licensing, safety records, other parents' experiences, and any other background information you can gather. Then here are some things to look for when you visit.

1. Are kids showing initiative in choosing their activities? Are they given a diverse set of activities and materials to choose from in a play-like environment?

2. How warm are the teachers? Are they nurturing, accepting, respectful, and responsive to the children?

3. How positive are the teachers in their discipline? Do they provide interesting activities and maintain control using positive approaches, such as communicating clear instructions and expectations and refraining from using commands and threats with the kids?

4. Are lots of art and materials for art available for the kids to use? Moreover, where is the art hung: at the kids' level, or the parents'? I've seen some pretty preschools that appeal to a lot of parents, but pretty isn't relevant here. Preschool isn't home: you should be able to spill paint on the floor and just wipe it up, hang stuff on the walls (and not worry about the gorgeous wallpaper), and have fun with the Play-Doh without someone asking you to watch out for the rug.

5. Are there areas for kids to look at books, play with blocks, and engage in lots of imaginative play? Look at the materials for pretend play: are they commercial or generic? Ideally, kids will need to use their own imagination to create something new, rather than reenacting something they saw on TV again and again.

Avoid preschools that seem to spend an inordinate amount of time teaching kids basic academic skills, especially if they are using commercially prepared worksheets. With preschoolers, academic instruction needs to be connected to meaningful activities or kids' everyday experiences. Cross off your list schools that put performance pressure on preschoolers. Avoid teachers who criticize wrong answers, use threats of punishment to "motivate" kids, or are intolerant of unconventional (but not disruptive) behavior. Similarly, nix preschools where teachers give external evaluations and rewards (such as grades and stickers for performance) or make social comparisons.

## IS OUR CULTURE A HAPPINESS HAZARD?

*A new dress doesn't get you anywhere; it's the life you're living in the dress, and the sort of life you had lived before, and what you will do in it later.*

—DIANA VREELAND

Child care is, of course, only one variable in our kids' environment. Researchers frequently dedicate entire careers to understanding how the many factors in our environment—and the cultures that color it—influence our success and well-being. One particularly noticeable feature of modern Western culture is its materialism: how much we celebrate wealth and the fancy stuff it brings. Our materialistic and commercial culture fuels an attitude that more money is better, that money will bring more friends and more cool stuff, and that all these possessions will make us happier and more fulfilled. This message, paid for by consumer product companies that want you to purchase their products and reinforced by celebrities who buy into it, is not lost on our kids. Eight-year-olds recognize the social status information conveyed in expensive houses and cars. By the time they are twelve, kids understand the subtle and symbolic meanings conveyed by brands and material goods.

What's wrong with materialism? For starters, materialism does not promote success in school, probably because highly materialistic kids spend lots of time shopping and watching TV and being influenced by advertising. They like school less and get poorer grades. But perhaps even more important, materialism is not a happiness habit. Materialistic tweeners and teenagers are more anxious and less happy and have poorer self-esteem. As you will see below, materialism and unhappiness run in a dangerous cycle: unhappiness makes kids more likely to be materialistic, but materialism furthers their discontent.

## What Makes Kids Materialistic?

Two things influence how materialistic kids are. The first is fairly obvious: consciously or not, we adults socialize kids to be materialistic. When parents—as well as peers and celebrity role models—model materialism, kids care more about wealth and luxury. When parents are materialistic, kids are likely to also be materialistic. Same thing with television viewing: the more TV kids watch, the more likely they are to be materialistic.

The less obvious reason why some people are more materialistic than others has to do with the degree to which our needs are being fulfilled. When people feel insecure or unfulfilled—because of poverty or because basic psychological needs such as safety, competence, connectedness, and autonomy aren't being met—they often try to quell their insecurity by striving for wealth and a lot of fancy stuff. Because of this, relatively poor teenagers ironically tend to be more materialistic than wealthy ones. And less nurturing and more emotionally cold mothers tend to have more materialistic offspring.

So materialism and the behaviors that go with it—desiring and buying brand-name clothes and luxury items—are symptoms of insecurity *and* a coping strategy used to alleviate feelings of self-doubt or bolster a poor self-image. But if what kids are really seeking is greater happiness and fulfillment, materialism is a terrible coping method. At best, it provides only short-term relief; in the long run it is likely to deepen feelings of insecurity.

One way to curb kids' materialism is to limit their exposure to advertising. Another way, it turns out, is to do the very things advocated in this book.

## Does Money Buy Happiness?

It is clear that materialism won't buy happiness, but does that mean that family income isn't important for children's well-being? There is a difference between being a super-consumer and having enough money to "rig our kids' environment." Although we live in a society rife with choices, the luxury choices are generally left for the wealthy. Does this matter for kids' happiness?

Despite the popular belief that money doesn't buy happiness, having a high income *is* correlated with many positive outcomes. Wealthier people tend to be healthier, both mentally and physically—and this is not just the poor versus all others; the wealthiest tier in one study was healthier than the second-highest income group. People with higher incomes experience fewer stressful life events and tend to receive lighter prison sentences for the same crimes. Accordingly, a lot of research in psychology, sociology, and economics shows that money actually *does* buy happiness.

For adults, higher income is dramatically correlated with higher happiness, but only up to about $50,000 a year, and then the association weakens. After our basic needs are accounted for, the correlation between income and happiness is surprisingly weak. Turns out that members of the Forbes 400—the richest people in America—are barely happier than the rest of us. For this reason, a great many scholars (and commentators and grandmothers) have concluded that money does not buy *very much* happiness. Given just how much richer the Forbes 400 are than most of us, if money bought happiness you'd expect that each one of them would be, well, a billion times happier than I am. But they aren't. Once our basic needs are met, financial resources seem to lose their hold on our happiness and well-being.

But the link between happiness and parental income is more important for children than it is for adults. In addition to being more dependent on significant material resources—such as child care and preschool—children are more sensitive to lapses in things such as housing, health care, and proper nutrition. Many are also sensitive to lapses in their parents' financial resources—in that stress caused by economic hardship can cause parenting practices to deteriorate, which in turn affects the emotional well-being of the child.

My own research shows that nearly 10 percent of all poor adolescents are unhappy, compared with less than 2 percent of upper-income teens. As family income increases, this percentage of unhappy teenagers steadily declines. So being poor can definitely increase the odds that a teenager will be unhappy. But the reverse is not always true: affluence doesn't necessarily mean ending up happy. When teens are grouped into happiness categories (unhappy, infrequently happy, sometimes happy, often happy), having a higher family income makes them less likely to be unhappy, although it simply pushes them into one of the middle categories rather than all the way into the "often happy" category.

Why does family income move the needle on unhappiness more than on happiness? Because kids have a lot of basic needs that cost a lot of money. When those needs aren't being met, the odds that the kids will be unhappy increase. The catch is that meeting those basic needs is not in itself sufficient for happiness. For example, take the basic need of having enough to eat. While not having enough to eat might make children profoundly unhappy, resolving this need—providing more food—will not necessarily make them happy; it will make them not so hungry. This book is about a second set of factors—happiness factors, such as secure attachments, lots of social connections, growth mind-sets, and plenty of time to play. When these happiness factors are met in addition to the kids' basic needs, the odds that kids will be "often happy" *do* increase, and dramatically.

## IS TELEVISION THE ROOT OF ALL EVIL?

When I was pregnant with Fiona, my friends—all childless themselves—thought it would be funny to write a parenting advice book for my husband and me. Obviously, no one knew that I would go on to routinely give parenting advice. They each wrote entries about the things they thought their own parents did well. My buddy Rick—who happens to be smart, funny, *and* kind—detailed all the ways that watching "too much TV" as a child benefited him in later life. Though I realized that a knowledge of 1970s popular culture could take a kid only so far, knowing Rick I was inclined to be unconcerned about letting my kids watch TV.

But then I found out that the American Academy of Pediatrics (AAP) adamantly recommends that parents not let their children watch any TV until they are at least two years old, not even if the tired mommy wants to take a shower. Being something of a rule follower, I made sure that Fiona didn't know the word for TV until her second birthday, when she promptly became a *Sesame Street* and *Blue's Clues* junkie. I conveniently forgot about the AAP recommendation with Molly; it seemed too hard to cut out TV altogether. Is that bad?

I certainly wasn't alone in letting my baby watch TV. American children spend two to five hours a day watching television, on average. Fifty-nine percent of children younger than two—who aren't supposed to be watching any television—watch an average of 1.3 hours daily.

It turns out that a large number of studies have reported harmful effects from children's television viewing, including worse performance in school, obesity, attention-span problems, aggression, sleep deprivation, requests for advertised foods, and eating fewer fruits and vegetables and more pizza, snack food, soda, and high-fat foods. Most—if not all—of these things are related to poor self-control. Even videos that claim to be beneficial, such as the Baby Einstein video series, aren't good and may be bad. In one study, for example, for every hour per day spent watching such videos, children understood an average of six to eight fewer words than did those of the same age who did not watch the videos—a 17 percent drop in vocabulary. Although earlier I did say that an impressive vocabulary isn't the most important thing in the world, in this case I think it is an indicator that screen time slows infant development.

On the other hand, video games don't necessarily deserve their bad rap. They can be a good way to socialize and connect with friends (especially for boys). And video games can facilitate, rather than discourage, physical play. Boys who play sports video games, for example, are much more likely to play those games in real life. They use the video games to master new moves, and then they go outside and practice.

### Eight Things to Keep in Mind When the Electronic Babysitter Is Getting a Lot of Play

1. Television brings little or no benefits, but it replaces activities that do make kids happier, healthier, and smarter. The more kids watch TV, the less time they spend with their parents and siblings, the less time they spend doing homework (for seven- to twelve-year-olds), and the less time they spend in creative play (especially in children younger than five). For very young children (less than three), time spent watching TV replaces activities that children need for proper brain development, particularly interaction with their caregivers.

2. Watching a lot of television makes kids more materialistic. Several studies have shown that television ads stimulate materialistic values among children of all ages. Researchers believe that commercials teach kids that they cannot attain beauty, success, and happiness without material possessions. Television viewing fre-

quency has also been shown to correlate with materialism levels: the more television kids watch, the more materialistic they become.

3. Research has shown that playing video games doesn't usually take time away from sports or other active pursuits, and that game-playing teens spend the same amount of time with family and friends as nongamers.

4. Infants and toddlers under two should not have any screen time. Early television exposure is associated with problems such as attention deficit disorder (ADD) and attention deficit/hyperactivity disorder (ADHD), and decreased intelligence later in childhood.

5. Computer use by children under the age of three is not recommended. However, some research shows that computer programs, when combined with activities that facilitate what the programs are trying to teach, can help three- to four-year-olds develop a range of skills, including long-term memory, manual dexterity, and verbal skills.

6. Not all screen time is equal. In our homes we can ban the 20 percent of video games that are rated as too violent or sexual for kids. There is a strong link between violent video game play and aggressive feelings and behaviors; violent video games trigger a part of the brain that drives people to act aggressively. And violent video game play measurably decreases helpful behaviors. Similarly, watching violent programming on TV is associated with a decrease in fantasy play among preschoolers and an increase in children's aggressiveness.

7. Parents who watch television with their children and reinforce the educational aspects of shows can improve the quality of the learning experience for their children. Unfortunately, most kids usually don't watch educational television with their parents. Families watch general-audience programs targeted to adults rather than children.

8. Although 68 percent of American kids have televisions in their rooms, children with a TV in their bedrooms are 1.3 times more likely to be overweight (even when physically active and/or participating in team sports).

I don't think that television is the root of all evil. I put my kids in front of heinous princess videos occasionally: how else would I stay sane? But television viewing is not a happiness habit. In fact, research demonstrates a strong link between happiness and *not* watching television. Sociologists show that happier people tend to watch considerably less television than unhappy people. We don't know whether TV makes people unhappy, or if already unhappy people watch more TV. But we do know that there are a lot of activities that *will* help our kids develop into happy, well-adjusted individuals. If our kids are watching TV, they aren't doing those things that could be making them happier in the long run. Looks as though my friend Rick, who probably watched TV every waking moment of his childhood but whose brain developed just fine, is an outlier. Our best bet is to turn off the boob tube and send the kids out to play.

## YOU'VE DONE YOUR BEST: NOW LET THEM GO PLAY

There is a flaw in the logic of this chapter. Not only *can't* we rig kids' entire environments, we shouldn't even try. There are some key environmental factors that we should influence if we can. Our kids' early care and the values that inform the culture around them are important and can have an effect on their happiness and well-being. But believing that we can place our kids in a happiness-padded bubble will ultimately undermine their well-being in dramatic ways.

We naturally want to protect kids from pain and difficulty, but when we do this we deprive them of the challenges that will help them grow intellectually and emotionally. At a recent talk given by the Dalai Lama at UC Berkeley, a graduating student asked for advice for navigating the road ahead. His Holiness answered, "You will need to get a job and find a partner. These are hard tasks. Even if you don't want it to be, life is difficult. You will have problems and challenges. But even though life is difficult, it is possible to be happy." His point: when we accept, rather than resist, the notion that life is difficult, we can deal with it better. In my own research I found that happiness can actually come *out* of difficulty, not just in spite of it. The only thing that the low-income kids in my study had that brought them happiness that the rich kids didn't have was challenge. Having adequate challenges in their lives was strongly related to happiness among adolescents. While the most advantaged teens in the study had many more of the other factors that led to happiness, they did not feel adequately challenged.

Our generation of parents has not embraced the notion that it is okay for our kids to experience difficulty, especially when it comes in the form of pain and sadness. We want to step in and solve our kids' problems at school and with their friends. Über-involved parents talk to principals to ensure that their children are properly understood and supported; we "help" with homework to an extreme; we orchestrate playdates that manipulate who our children's friends are and how those friendships are carried out. We guard against potentially mean dogs and creepy neighbors, unfair coaches, and too much responsibility. This has had a measurable effect on our kids' generation: compared to people raised in the 1960s, kids today perceive their lack of control. Jean Twenge, a psychologist and the author of *Generation Me,* has shown that young Americans increasingly believe that their lives are controlled by outside forces rather than their own efforts. Ironically (from the viewpoint of parents trying to rig their kids for success), Twenge finds that the implications of this belief are "almost uniformly negative": they are connected to poor school performance, helplessness, ineffective stress management, decreased self-control, and depression. We might be preventing pain and protecting their innocence, but we are also depriving our children of the chance to know what they are made of, to learn to cope with life's inevitable difficulties and sadnesses, to develop their grit.

It turns out that grit—the term researchers use when measuring stick-to-itiveness in the face of difficulty—is an important predictor of success. Want your kid to succeed in school? In a large study of college students, task commitment—the perseverance, endurance, and hard work that make a person "gritty"—turned out to be the most important factor in predicting success in many different arenas, including science, art, sports, and communications. Grit was more important than SAT scores, high school rank, and high school extracurricular involvement.

Grit is also a core component of lifelong happiness. When kids learn that they *can't* cope with life's difficulties—because mom or dad always seems so eager to make sure that they never occur, and because mom and dad are always solving kids' problems—the kids come to fear challenge. Mistakes become something to be avoided at all costs. This can create perfectionistic tendencies, which, as discussed in Chapter 3, are a particular form of unhappiness.

So while we *should* make the best decisions we can about our kids' early care and the environment they grow up in, we *shouldn't* assume that we can control everything in their Kid Park—or even that it would be a positive move to exclude "negative" things such as anguish, sadness, and frustration. Although we can put a great deal of care and thought into creating the best possible Kid Park we can for our kids, they are still going to face pain and difficulty. Even so—or perhaps because they are allowed to face their own challenges—their lives can be happy. Maybe even wildly happy. We want to rig their environment, yes, but also remember that it is the un-hyper-controlled environment, rich with the freedom and joy that come from long stretches of imaginative play, that create the most satisfying Kid Parks.

# TEN

■ ■ ■ ■ ■ ■

# Step 10:
# Eat Dinner Together

*Dining with one's friends and beloved family is certainly
one of life's primal and most innocent delights, one that
is both soul-satisfying and eternal.*

—JULIA CHILD

I can just hear the groaning now. *But we are way too busy to eat
dinner together.* Or *My kids are too little. They need to eat dinner
before we even get home from work.* Or *I'd love to eat dinner as a family, but
the kids have drama and soccer practice right in the middle of dinnertime.* I
know that this is a tough topic for families today; we often think about
time together the same way starving people think about food.

Having dinner as a family is the last and one of the most important
pieces of science-based advice I will give you for raising happy kids. Family mealtimes offer a concentrated dose of nurture and nourishment, two
of the greatest and most fundamental human needs. And, as you'll see
below, dinnertime is our best opportunity to actually implement the first
nine steps presented in this book.

The benefits of family mealtimes for kids are remarkable. Studies
show that kids who eat dinner with their families on a regular basis are
more emotionally stable and less likely to abuse drugs and alcohol. They
get better grades. They have fewer depressive symptoms, particularly
among adolescent girls. And they are less likely to become obese or have
an eating disorder. Family dinners even trump reading to your kids in
terms of preparing them for school. And these associations hold even after
researchers control for family connectedness, which means that the benefits of family meals go above and beyond being a close-knit family.

Lest you think I'm suggesting having the entire family gathered around a beautifully set table, complete with linens and several courses, here is what I mean by eating dinner together: kids regularly eat dinner with at least one adult five nights a week or more. They help with food preparation to the extent that they are able, and with table setting and clearing. The boob tube is off. There is no kids' table. You can do takeout or something simple and homemade; *what* you eat is frankly less important than *with whom you eat.* I know you may not want to eat your dinner so early, that you'd rather wait and have a grown-up dinner when your spouse gets home, after the kids are in bed. This chapter is about how and why to find a dinnertime routine that works for everyone.

So why is dinnertime such a powerful tool for raising happy kids? For starters, adults model important things during dinner, such as healthy eating, of course. And so many social skills are learned at the dinner table that I hardly know where to begin. The research shows compelling connections between language development and dinnertime, and language is the most important facet of social intelligence that we have.

For example, a team at the Harvard Graduate School of Education wanted to know where children learned the rare words that they had found were particularly good markers of literacy. Of the 2,000 words they were looking for, only 143 of them came from parents reading to their children. More than a thousand were learned at the dinner table—words such as oxygen, arboretum, sea horse, gusto, shrimp, bureaucrat, budget, and government. This is why dinner loses its power when we isolate kid meals from adult meals. My eight-year-old isn't able to teach my six-year-old all those rare words (though I'm sure she could teach her about 250 euphemisms for, oh, just about any bathroom word).

Manners are a more important social skill than we might think. Certain social norms teach kids about the emotions that make up a happy life. When I say, "Molly, please don't interrupt your sister," I am teaching her about reciprocity and empathy. When they watch me offer a guest the biggest piece of cake, they learn generosity. Simple acts of gratitude, such as saying thank you to someone for passing the salt, are happiness building blocks. Social skills, including language, are just that—skills that are built over time and better learned by example than explicit instruction. Kids develop any skill more readily if they learn it in a routine situation that feels safe, and the dinner table is an ideal familiar place—maybe the best place—to teach and learn certain skills.

## TRY THIS
### Model Healthy Eating

The most obvious thing that we grown-ups can model during family meal-times is healthy eating. Eating a variety of foods is important for health, and physical health is important for happiness. My kids would prefer to eat mac n' cheese (specifically the shells with white Cheddar) three meals a day; to say that they resist new foods would be a gross understatement. This hearty reluctance to try new foods is believed to be an evolutionary trait designed to keep our young from eating anything green or unripe, which makes it our job to encourage our children to eat lots of different kinds of foods.

Here's how: Kids learn to like new foods by watching adults and other kids eating them. The bad news is that it's all about repetition. Meaning your kid needs to watch you eat the food a lot—maybe daily, maybe for years.

Paul Rozin, an anthropologist, investigated how kids in Mexico learned to eat spicy foods. Most Mexican babies and toddlers initially dislike spicy foods, but they grow up watching adults eating them. Around the time they are five to six years old, they begin enjoying what we Americans would call "adult food." An interesting aspect of this study is that family dogs behave in the same way: pets that hang out near the table learn to eat spicy foods through their owners' modeling, while stray dogs that never eat with families but have equal access to spicy foods can't be trained to eat them.

I talk a good game about having my kids eat the same thing that the adults are eating, but walking that talk is more difficult. "My kids eat anything; don't fix them something different!" I say blithely when we're at friends' houses. Molly understands that adults love kids who eat anything, so, when faced with a plate of "new" food, she'll pretend to take a bite and then declare with gusto, "I love cucumber raviolis!" All the adults respond with ooh's and aah's and say things such as, "Golly, I wish Jack would eat spinach pudding!" Nine times out of ten, Molly hasn't actually tasted anything.

Second to eating, cooking is my favorite hobby. So it is a little disheartening when no one will eat my labor of love without first being bribed or cajoled. Still, what I should do is just expose them to the food (it's on their plate; I'm eating it) and leave it at that. The experts don't recommend the type of encouragement that I am prone to: "Fiona, if you take three bites of that *delicious* slow-cooked pozole your mother *worked so hard* to make, you can have two Girl Scout cookies for dessert." Nutritionist and psychologist Ellyn Satter gives us a good rule of thumb: "The parent is responsible for the *what, when and where* of feeding, and the child is responsible for the *how much and whether* of eating." Hard for me to do, but after about six months of always putting salad on my kids' plates and then letting them ignore it, they now (usually) eat their salad.

## MAKING CHOW TIME INTO A "RITUAL"

Another reason that family mealtimes have such powerful effects is that they can become a "ritual." Rituals, or any kind of routine that has symbolic or expressive meaning, are important for a happy life because they illustrate our values. Kids know intuitively that we celebrate or ritualize the things we believe are most important. I have little rituals that I do with the kids individually, such as talking about our "three good things" (see Chapter 8). But the only thing we do every day all together is eat.

When we make mealtime into a daily family ritual, we boost kids' happiness and well-being in two ways. First, we show them that they are a part of something larger than themselves—their family. As I detailed in Chapter 2, happiness research consistently shows that human happiness is all about meaningful social connections. Kids need to feel a part of their family on a daily basis, and dinnertime is a terrific way to accomplish this. When we sit together—often literally in a family circle—we make tangible that larger thing that kids are a part of. When we do it routinely, it becomes an extension of who kids are and how they see themselves: they feel embedded in something larger than themselves, and this gives them security.

The second way that ritualized family mealtimes can boost happiness is by evoking joy and many other positive emotions. Dinnertime can become a predictable time every day to feel happiness, love, gratitude, and a lot of other good things. The easiest way to make this happiness habit happen is to start (or continue) a family tradition of saying grace, even if you aren't religious. A blessing is an opportunity to habitually cultivate a whole range of positive emotions.

1. Usually you are expressing some sort of gratitude or appreciation for the food (my kids often spontaneously give thanks for bigger things, such as "being in this world"). Gratitude is a positive emotion about the past.

2. A blessing (or a toast or whatever) can at the same time be a moment of contentment—joy that comes from hearing a little girl or boy give thanks, gladness that comes from being together. Contentment, joy, gladness: these are positive emotions about the present.

3. Saying grace can also be an act of faith, which is a form of optimism and positive emotion about the future.

4. Joining hands around a table is an act of love. It says "I care enough about you to share this meal with you." Love is a positive emotion about others.

If a happy life is defined as one that is full of positive emotions, as I advocated in the Introduction, then a blessing at dinnertime is a powerful tool for cultivating happiness.

I am often asked if there are other equally beneficial things besides family mealtimes that might function in a similar way. A nighttime family prayer might work, encouraging all those positive emotions that go with grace. But reading probably wouldn't. What else could you do where you model those behaviors that lead to higher social and emotional intelligence, and teach good nutrition and social skills, plus emphasize family history and establish a strong sense of belonging? Perhaps storytelling in a circle, as a family. At breakfast.

## TRY THIS

### Create a Dinnertime Routine That Works

I know how difficult it can be to make family dinnertime work, even for believers like me. Last night I sat at the table with my two daughters eating a Trader Joe's frozen delight, thinking, this doesn't feel symbolically

meaningful. No one wanted to tell me about their day. I don't think anyone learned any new words. Grace happened, but everyone was curiously
thankful for the same things that they had been thankful for the night before. There was a lot of complaining about the food and wanting to leave
the table. But when I was putting the kids to bed, Fiona told me that dinnertime was one of the three best things about her day. Go figure.

Here are some things that might help you make dinnertime into a
powerful ritual for your kids.

1.  Happily ever after isn't necessary, but repetition is. There can be
    one adult, or two, or five, and they don't have to be married. Chil-
    dren of single-parent families who have regular dinnertime rou-
    tines reap the same benefits. This means that if you are married,
    you can tag-team. As long as there is one adult sitting down and
    eating with the kids, it works. And remember that the magic
    comes with the repetition, not the decision to do it. It is okay to
    have many mealtimes that seem more draining than magical.

2.  Be creative. Now that you understand what makes mealtimes
    powerful, go ahead and bend the rules. Maybe you have family
    breakfast rather than dinner. Maybe the kids have a heavy snack
    at 5:30 p.m. and then eat their "dinner" (even if it is a small
    amount of food) with you when you are able at 7:30 p.m. Maybe
    you have takeout every night: this would still serve the purpose.
    Or maybe one day a week you have family mealtime in a restau-
    rant. That's fine. Just stick with your routines and rituals as best
    you can. Remember it's the *with whom* that matters more than
    the *what* or even the *where*.

3.  Combine forces with other families. Do you live in a neighbor-
    hood with lots of people you'd love to know better? Invite them
    over for a potluck dinner on a weekly or near-weekly basis. As
    long as the adults and children eat together—rather than segre-
    gating themselves into kids' and adults' tables—kids will reap the
    benefits of family dinnertime.

4.  Say no to less important things, even if those things seem very im-
    portant to your kids. In our family this has meant trying not to
    participate in sports that practice during dinnertime, and not let-
    ting the kids sing in the children's choir of their choice. My

daughters think I am mean for setting these boundaries, but I know that the quality of all of our lives is enhanced because of them. This is a hard thing for many families. If you have a kid who has a sport four nights a week and it is keeping you from eating dinner as a family, you might want to rethink your schedule. Can you move your family dinner later during that season? Or can you divide and conquer with other parents? For example, my friend Maureen's nine-year-old son has baseball games several nights a week. On the nights when he has a baseball game that's going to get him home late, one parent eats with him after the game; the other parent eats earlier with his six-year-old sister. This works: the kids get special time with one parent, which can be particularly meaningful, too.

5. Running out of things to talk about? Start telling your kids about your family history. Talking about your shared past creates strong and secure emotional bonds and directly impacts how well families function. You don't even have to tell *positive* family stories. Not coincidentally, one study found that kids who knew a lot about their family history learned it at dinnertime.

6. For goodness' sake, say grace (see above if you're wondering why). If you don't believe in God, just say a general blessing or a toast, or use this as an opportunity to invent your own family tradition. When we have guests over, we all hold hands, go around the table, and each name one thing that we are grateful for. Yes, it can be awkward at first, but our friends have come to expect it, and the kids hold us to it. Last week our six-year-old neighbor Jilly said, "I'm thankful that I have everything I need" before dinner. It was so sweet and so heartfelt and so moving that it cut right through the awkwardness. A moment of silence—where everyone is practicing mindfulness (see Chapter 8) or thinking of what they are grateful for—is another good way to begin a meal, especially if it is followed by everyone sharing what they are grateful for.

7. Go family style. Think about what *the way* you eat together says about your family symbolically. This includes cooking dinner and cleaning up together afterward. For starters, serve food from family-style platters. Letting kids serve themselves from the bowls and platters on the table gives them back some control;

many parents I know make up their kids' plates in the kitchen and serve it to them as though they are in a restaurant.

In my family, we arrange ourselves at the table to literally create a family circle. And we try to get dinner on the table as a team. Everyone helps cook, even if this only means having Molly press start on the microwave and Fiona wash the lettuce. (We carry out this routine even when it involves nagging and takes longer, leaving everyone starving and cranky.) We clean up together, too, though again it is often tempting to let the kids leave the table while the adults hang around and talk. The idea is to model for our children the way to care for one another on a daily basis. Many parents I know *prefer* to do the cleanup themselves; it's easier, or they like the time they have with their spouse while they clean up. This is fine, as long as the kids also play a meaningful role. In my household, the kids clear their plates, scrape them, and load the dishwasher. I often need to reload the dishwasher, but at least the dishes are already in it, and the kids love this part of the job, especially if they get to put the soap in and push the buttons to start the machine. If the adults are finished eating when the kids are, the kids take sponges and wipe down the table (funny how they love this job). I inevitably end up spending more time in the kitchen washing the pots and putting food away, but at that point the kids have contributed to the whole meal. Symbolically speaking, I'm not the sole chef, server, busboy, and dishwasher: we've worked together as a team.

Sometimes it *is* easier to do the mom-as-waiter/personal chef routine. But when we wait on our children, the symbolic meaning is that they are passive actors who are entitled to our service rather than lucky and active participants in a larger whole.

If it still seems hard to imagine having dinner as a family five nights a week or more, remember that it *is* hard. You are not just coping with a private organizational nightmare, you are countering a big social problem. Our households have shrunk to such a degree that what used to be a community affair of people working together to get food on the table is now often just a single person's problem. Broad economic forces have contributed to the fact that many people are now at work when a generation ago they would have been eating dinner at home. Kids' athletic practices have been pushed right into the middle of dinnertime. Overcoming these obstacles is difficult, but it is important. As more and more people realize the importance of prioritizing family mealtimes, particularly people who have the power to change things, it will become easier.

## TAKE ON THE FIRST NINE STEPS AT DINNERTIME

As if all that weren't enough, I wrap up this book by giving you eight more reasons to have dinner as a family—and one reason not to. When do I most often put all nine steps to raising happy children into practice? Mealtimes, of course! Here's how it works.

**Step 1: Put on Your Own Oxygen Mask First.** These are the times when you *shouldn't* eat with your kids: when you've scheduled time for yourself or your spouse. If your favorite gym class is during dinnertime, take it! Go out to dinner with your buddies. Schedule that date night! *You* don't need to eat dinner every night with your children, but your children still need family mealtimes at least five nights a week. The way this works is that sometimes the family mealtimes—and similar routines and rituals—are carried out by someone other than you. Their favorite uncle, for example. Or the family that you are trading babysitting with. Or their other parent. Or a grandparent. Even if you go to the gym twice a week and have a date night every Saturday, your kids can still clock family mealtimes five nights a week or more with an adult who cares about them. And that's what it takes.

**Step 2: Build a Village.** Dinnertime is the ideal time to not only build the skills it takes to become someone who attracts a large village, but also to nurture the bonds in the village itself. We have friends and family members over for dinner so frequently that when no one is coming the kids and I look at each other and marvel at the relative quiet for a moment, and then they immediately start complaining that it is "just us." One of the functions of dinnertime is to help kids feel a part of something larger than themselves; give some thought to how large you want that something else to be. I include my parents and brother, as well as a handful of close family friends and neighbors.

This isn't as hard as it sounds. It isn't as though I'm adding "frequent entertaining" to my already full task list. When you invite your dinner guests to contribute to meal preparation and cleanup, I've found that cooking for eight or nine is just as easy as cooking for three or four. When people offer to bring something, always say yes to something substantive: a salad or vegetable rather than a bottle of wine. Have the kids set the table all together. If the kids want to make place cards or pick flowers for the table, great! But aside from the kids' expressions of enthusiasm, don't be fancy. Resist all Martha Stewart urges. In fact, the first time you do this, just order pizza. On school nights, skip dessert. And let everyone help clear the table and load the dishwasher while you put away the leftovers. The greatest time-saver and village builder about frequently having people over for dinner? People reciprocate. We eat dinner at someone *else's* house once a week.

**Step 3: Expect Effort and Enjoyment, Not Perfection.** Dinnertime is the ideal time to model growth–mind-set thinking. I like to use our dinner discussions to emphasize that it is A-OK to make mistakes. I do this by asking everyone about the mistakes they made that day, and by sharing my own (see page 58, Try This: One Mistake I Made Today . . . ). We also share our "high points" and "low points" at dinnertime. The day's accomplishments are met with growth–mind-set praise ("You did well on your spelling test because you practiced so hard yesterday. Way to go!"). And the day's failures are treated as opportunities from which to learn.

**Step 4: Choose Gratitude, Forgiveness, and Optimism.** Grace or a blessing will have everyone habitually expressing gratitude, if not also forgiveness and optimism. As your kids talk about their day at school, you can respond in a way that teaches and reinforces optimism (and helps you practice it yourself). One of the main ways that I do this is by giving others the benefit of the doubt. So if Fiona tells us about a girl who was ignoring her at school, I'll suggest alternate explanations that have nothing to do with Fiona (maybe she was lost in her thoughts and didn't even see Fiona). This stimulates optimistic thinking—bad things aren't taken personally and aren't likely to reoccur—and also empathy, which is a building block for forgiveness.

**Step 5: Raise Their Emotional Intelligence.** A lot of what occurs naturally at dinnertime will build your children's intelligence, emotional and otherwise. But dinnertime is also a terrific time to consciously build your family's "feelings vocabulary." Before you sit down for dinner, take a look at your Family Feelings List (page 100) and agree to a few feelings that you'll discuss. I usually start with something that I know my kids like to talk about ("Tell me about a time today when you felt silly") and then progress to more difficult concepts for my kids, such as having them talk about a time when they felt angry and embarrassed at the same time. How did your body feel? How did you behave when you were having that feeling? What do you want to do the next time you have those feelings?

**Step 6: Form Happiness Habits.** Dinnertime is a terrific happiness habit in the long run, but bad habits such as picky eating and potty talk at the table can ruin a good thing. Dinnertime habits are a great place to test-run the habit-creating skills you learned in Chapter 6, because it happens at roughly the same time every day. You can even bring your Happiness Habit Tracker (page 118) to the table and use dinnertime to track and set goals. (In our family, remembering to track our progress is the thing that most often trips us up.) The family can have one overarching dinnertime goal, such as *Eat dinner as a family five nights a week or more with pleasant conversation (no time-outs). The family works as a team to prepare for and clean up after the meal.* But everyone needs to have their own Happiness Habits Tracker. And remember, the turtle steps to get there need to be ridiculously easy.

**Step 7: Teach Self-Discipline.** Where better to routinely practice self-discipline than at the dinner table? Restaurants and other people's homes are ideal places to practice those techniques that cool the go-system and hone the know-system. Prepare for this by having a bag of tricks before you sit down in a restaurant; I now carry a Slinky and an activity book in my purse. And I have a little list of things to help distract kids during long waits, such as, "Imagine you are doing something fun. What are you doing?" We also play games, such as Simon Says, that help kids develop good self-control. Remember, the goal is to preempt misbehavior rather than just react to it.

**Step 8: Enjoy the Present Moment.** Dinnertime is a good time to savor the day's joys *and* the present moment. We can do this very deliberately. For example, start each meal with one minute of eating in silence mindfully, much as we did in the raisin meditation. This is settling and centering for the whole family, and a good way to set up your meal for success.

For me, food preparation is one of life's real joys, so I try to share this experience with my children. Cooking is a creative art and a science that requires planning and discipline. I try to foster creativity (see page 142) in my kids by including them in meal planning and preparation. My daughters learn how I get into the flow on Sunday afternoons, when I do most of our family's food preparations for the week. I explain to them that there has to be something new and different, something just challenging enough for me when I'm cooking, or I can't get into the flow: it's too boring to just make macaroni and cheese every week.

**Step 9: Rig Their Environment for Happiness.** At this point, I'm guessing that you can see that regular mealtimes are a core component of Kid Park. In addition, I've found that meals are one of the best times to get a read on what the rest of Kid Park looks like. I've done my best to rig their environment for happiness by choosing their school and care; at dinnertime I hear how things are going. I try to teach values that counter the materialistic drone of our culture, and I try to fill them up with love and all the things they need so that they aren't tempted to fill up on luxury items that won't make them happy (and that we can't afford). What they say at dinnertime tells me how good—or bad—Kid Park was today. Hearing about what they were grateful for and what the day's high points and low points were can be revealing. I can tell if they are too tired, or if they have already been sitting down for too long (and need more time for play). Most of all, I can tell where I'm succeeding. When Molly says she is thankful that she is who she is—the other day she said, "I'm thankful that I'm me"—or when Fiona has a half-dozen high points and draws a blank when I ask for her low point, I know that things in Kid Park are good.

There: you've done it. Covered all ten steps to raising happy kids, all in one twenty-minute meal. The thought actually makes me laugh out loud, maybe because I know that there are a few of you out there who will try. Could all of these things be accomplished in a single meal? In a week's worth of meals? Who knows; the point is not to do everything all at once, perfectly, but to do *something*. And even taking those small, turtle steps will turn into something big when they're taken 20 meals a month, or 240 meals over the course of a year. As I said in the Introduction, finding even one thing here that works for your family—just having dinner together is a feat in itself—can increase your children's happiness, and yours as well. Consciously practicing gratitude alone, for example, has been shown to make people measurably happier. If you do this, *and* you practice mindfulness, just imagine!

We are lucky to be engaged in this business of Raising Happiness. This work is not trivial; it is the foundation for a better world. We are lucky to have the opportunity to teach kids the skills they need to be kind and compassionate, confident and emotionally intelligent, socially connected and loving. What the world needs now is more of these children, these people. This is the way that our society and civilization will grow stronger and become more peaceful. In the words of Thich Nhat Hanh: "If in our daily life we can smile, if we can be peaceful and happy, not only we, but everyone will profit from it. This is the most basic kind of peace work."

# ACKNOWLEDGMENTS

■ ■ ■ ■ ■ ■

No words can really express how grateful I am to all the people who helped make this book possible, but in the spirit of practicing gratitude (see Chapter 4) I'm glad for the opportunity to try.

First, thank you to my parents, for being everything fundamental. Your great big safety net has made Fiona's, Molly's, and my happiness possible in countless practical and emotional ways. Big love and thanks also to my brother, Tim, for your support and for giving me a place to write.

I wouldn't be doing this work were it not for Dacher Keltner's coaching and support; thank you for being my mentor, my colleague, and my dear friend. Thanks also to Jason Marsh for your patience, and Alexandra Davidson for your enthusiastic and intelligent help. I couldn't have written this book or my blog without my tireless research assistants, especially Stephanie Harstrup and Caroline Wilmuth. Caroline, thank you for putting this book into action with Fiona and Molly and for the countless ways you've helped me this year. Deep thanks to Tom and Ruth Ann Hornaday, Lee Hwang, and those at the Herb Alpert Foundation who have made my work possible through their support of the Greater Good Science Center. Much gratitude to Liza Veto (and Alexandra again!) for reading all my rough drafts, and to Eileen Healy and Cassi Vieten for their thoughtful suggestions.

I have profound gratitude for all the people who sustain me and the kids with their big love and far-reaching support. My village is huge, and it's got really great people in it. Thanks to Mike McLaughlin for being such a kind and thoughtful soul, and to my friends for being such great sources of fun, play, and love this year. Kerryn LaDuc, Andrea Muchin, and Heather Haggarty, thanks for being there at the critical moments. Kelly Huber and Laura Beth Nielsen, you are the very *best* best friends anyone could imagine. Marissa Harrison, Sheryl O'Loughlin, and Katie

Keim, thank you for inspiring me; Kristen Malan, Ariel Trost, Jen Colten, Danielle Hawn Bluey, Charlie Marinelli, Alex Peterson, Tracy Clements, and Melissa Raymond, thank you for helping me keep it together and for bringing me so much joy. For all the ways you've been there for me or cared for me and the kids, thanks also to Elizabeth and Paul Simonetti, Stacy Merickel, Annie and Coley Cassidy, Catherine Teare, Lydia Adams, Lois Cottrell, Denise Lombard, Chad Olcott, Dave Crombie, Sara Lardner, Brett Arnott, Laurie Dalton White, John LaGatta, Deborah Efron, Jennifer Pringle, Grammy and Grampa Snuggles, and my cousins Kevin and Amy. Very, very special thanks to Monica Jane, to whom I could never adequately express my gratitude for the many important ways you've contributed to our family's happiness.

Finally, thanks to Jackie for believing in the project from the beginning and for connecting me to my fabulous agent, Andrea Barzvi, who then connected me to my wonderful editor, Marnie Cochran. I'm so grateful for all the ways the three of you have guided this book.

# NOTES

■ ■ ■ ■ ■ ■

## INTRODUCTION: THE ART AND SCIENCE OF RAISING HAPPY KIDS

ix  **Nearly half—maybe more:** For a scientific explanation of this written for a general audience, see Sonja Lyubomirsky, *The How of Happiness: A Scientific Approach to Getting the Life You Want* (New York: The Penguin Press, 2007).

ix  **That isn't to say that genetic makeup:** Daniel Goleman, *Social Intelligence: The New Science of Human Relationships* (New York: Bantam Dell, 2006), p. 151.

xi  **According to a series of studies commissioned:** These studies are reported on at: http://www.lpfch.org/newsroom/releases/parentpoll10_27_05.html.

xi  **We have reason to be concerned:** References and statistics about these correlations can be found at http://www.childtrendsdatabank.org/indicators/30FeelSador Hopeless.cfm.

xii **Mothers who are anxious:** E. P. Davis, et al., eds., *Prenatal Stress and Stress Physiology Influence Human Fetal and Infant Development, Placenta and Brain, Birth and Behavior, Health and Disease* (Cambridge, England: Cambridge University Press, 2006); M. E. Coussons-Read, M. L. Okun, and C. D. Nettles, "Psychosocial Stress Increases Inflammatory Markers and Alters Cytokine Production across Pregnancy," *Brain, Behavior, and Immunity* 21, no. 3 (Mar 2007); L. Bonari, et al., "Risks of Untreated Depression During Pregnancy," *Canadian Family Physician* 50 (Jan 2004).

xii **In addition, emotionally literate children:** John Gottman and Joan DeClaire, *Raising an Emotionally Intelligent Child* (New York: Simon & Schuster Paperbacks, 1997).

xii **Despite the popular notion that:** Christine Carter McLaughlin, *Buying Happiness: Family Income and Adolescent Subjective Well-Being,* (Doctoral Dissertation, University of California, Berkeley, 2007).

xii **One recent study shows that:** G. H. Brody, et al., "Parenting Moderates a Genetic Vulnerability Factor in Longitudinal Increases in Youths' Substance Use," *Journal of Consulting and Clinical Psychology* 77, no. 1 (Feb 2009).

xiii **Just by fostering gratitude in your:** See Chapter 4 for more about gratitude.

xiii **We parents have two solid decades:** Goleman, *Social Intelligence: The New Science of Human Relationships*.

xiii **On average, happy people are:** The benefits of happiness—and the scientific studies behind them—are clearly articulated in these three books: Lyubomirsky, *The How of Happiness: A Scientific Approach to Getting the Life You Want*; Barbara L. Fredrickson, *Positivity: Groundbreaking Research Reveals How to Embrace the Hidden Strength of Positive Emotions, Overcome Negativity, and Thrive* (New York: Crown Publishers, 2009); and Ed Diener and Robert Biswas-Diener, *Happiness: Unlocking the Mysteries of Psychological Wealth* (Malden, MA: Blackwell Publishing, 2008).

xiv **positive emotions help our bodies:** Fredrickson, *Positivity: Groundbreaking Research Reveals How to Embrace the Hidden Strength of Positive Emotions, Overcome Negativity, and Thrive*, p. 226. See also Lyubomirsky, *The How of Happiness: A Scientific Approach to Getting the Life You Want*.

190     Notes

xiv **It turns out that:** Shigehiro Oishi, Ed Diener, and Richard E. Lucas, "The Optimum Level of Well-Being: Can People Be Too Happy?" *Perspectives on Psychological Science* 2, no. 4 (2007).

xiv **But it also turns out that:** Fredrickson, *Positivity: Groundbreaking Research Reveals How to Embrace the Hidden Strength of Positive Emotions, Overcome Negativity, and Thrive.*

xvi **Diane Ackerman once remarked:** Jone Johnson Lewis, "Diane Ackerman Quotes," http://womenshistory.about.com/od/quotes/a/ackerman.htm.

STEP 1: PUT ON YOUR OWN OXYGEN MASK FIRST

5  **Extensive research has established:** For research on the link between parental depression, stress, and anxiety and children's outcomes, see S. B. Campbell, et al., "Trajectories of Maternal Depressive Symptoms, Maternal Sensitivity, and Children's Functioning at School Entry," *Developmental Psychology* 43, no. 5 (2007); Xin Feng, Daniel S. Shaw, and Jennifer S. Silk, "Developmental Trajectories of Anxiety Symptoms among Boys across Early and Middle Childhood," *Journal of Abnormal Psychology* 117, no. 1 (2008); Karen L. Franck and Cheryl Beuehler, "A Family Process Model of Marital Hostility, Parental Depressive Affect, and Early Adolescent Problem Behavior: The Roles of Triangulation and Parental Warmth," *Journal of Family Psychology* 21, no. 4 (2007); Xin Feng, et al., "Emotional Exchange in Mother-Child Dyads: Stability, Mutual Influence, and Associations with Maternal Depression and Child Problem Behavior," *Journal of Family Psychology* 21, no. 4 (2007); K. A. Moore, et al., "Depression among Moms: Prevalence, Predictors, and Acting out among Third-Grade Children" (Washington, DC: Child Trends, 2006).

6  **Children imitate their parents' emotions:** A. N. Meltzoff, "Imitation and Other Minds: The 'Like Me' Hypothesis," in *Perspectives on Imitation: From Cognitive Neuroscience to Social Science,* eds. S. Hurley and N. Chater (Cambridge, MA: MIT Press, 2005).

6  **If I model key happiness habits:** Bill E. Peterson, "Generativity and Successful Parenting: An Analysis of Young Adult Outcomes," *Journal of Personality* 74, no. 3 (2006).

6  **The researchers documented that the emotions:** C. Anderson, D. Keltner, and O. P. John, "Emotional Convergence between People over Time," *Journal of Personality and Social Psychology* 84, no. 5 (2003).

6  **Like those of roommates and lovers:** Ferran Casas, et al., "Does Subjective Well-Being Show a Relationship between Parents and Their Children?" *Journal of Happiness Studies* 9, no. 2 (2008).

6  **A political scientist from:** J. H. Fowler and N. A. Christakis, "Dynamic Spread of Happiness in a Large Social Network: Longitudinal Analysis over 20 Years in the Framingham Heart Study," *British Medical Journal* 337, no. a2338 (2008).

7  **Consider, for example, that:** Frank Fujita and Ed Diener, "Life Satisfaction Set Point: Stability and Change," *Journal of Personality and Social Psychology* 88, no. 1 (2005).

8  **People with a lot of:** Robert D. Putnam, *Bowling Alone: The Collapse and Revival of American Community* (New York: Simon & Schuster, 2001).

8  **Neuroscientists believe that:** Dacher Keltner, *Born to Be Good: The Science of a Meaningful Life* (New York: W. W. Norton & Company, 2009). (See Chapter 7 on Laughter for all the ways that laughter is good for you.)

8  **Have your kids or partner:** Ibid. (See Chapter 9 for more on the benefits of touch.)

9  **Want to turn your brain waves:** See Sharon Begley, *Train Your Mind, Change Your Brain* (New York: Random House, 2007), for a fascinating discussion of this science.

9  **As science writer Sharon Begley:** Begley, *Train Your Mind, Change Your Brain.*

9  **People who "practice gratitude" feel:** Robert A. Emmons and Michael E. McCullough, *The Psychology of Gratitude* (New York: Oxford University Press, 2004).

10  **Regular exercise will make you:** John J. Ratey and Eric Hagerman, *Spark* (New York: Little, Brown and Company, 2008).

10  **One experiment showed that:** Fredrickson, *Positivity: Groundbreaking Research*

*Reveals How to Embrace the Hidden Strength of Positive Emotions, Overcome Negativity, and Thrive*; M. G. Berman, J. Jonides, and S. Kaplan, "The Cognitive Benefits of Interacting with Nature," *Psychological Science* 19, no. 12 (2008).

10 **Materialistic people are more:** T. Kasser, "Frugality, Generosity, and Materialism in Children and Adolescents," in *What Do Children Need to Flourish? Conceptualizing and Measuring Indicators of Positive Development,* ed. K. A. Moore and L. H. Lippman (New York: Springer Science + Business Media, 2005).

11 **Research shows that more than half:** Suzanne Bianchi, John P. Robinson, and Melissa A. Milkie, *Changing Rhythms of American Family Life* (New York: Russell Sage Foundation, 2007).

11 **Married mothers now spend:** Liana C. Sayer, Suzanne M. Bianchi, and John P. Robinson, "Are Parents Investing Less in Children? Trends in Mothers' and Fathers' Time with Children," *American Journal of Sociology* 110, no. 1 (2004); another excellent resource for research on how families and domestic duties have changed over time is the Council on Contemporary Families: http://www.contemporaryfamilies.org/index.php.

11 **But if you improve your marriage:** C. P. Cowan and P. A. Cowan, *When Partners Become Parents: The Big Life Change for Couples* (Mahwah, NJ: Lawrence Erlbaum Associates, 2000).

11 **Research psychologist and prolific author:** Gottman has written several books on his research for a general audience, including the one he wrote with Nan Silver, *The Seven Principles for Making Marriage Work* (New York: Crown Publishers, 1999).

12 **The best predictor of a wife's marital satisfaction:** Alyson Shapiro, John Gottman, and Sybil Carrere, "The Baby and the Marriage: Identifying Factors That Buffer against Decline in Marital Satisfaction after the First Baby Arrives," *Journal of Family Psychology* 14, no. 1 (2000).

12 **In *The Seven Principles for*:** J. M. Gottman and Nan Silver, *The Seven Principles for Making Marriage Work.*

13 **Sex is less satisfying:** M. Dixon, N. Booth, and R. Powell, "Sex and Relationships Following Childbirth: A First Report from General Practice of 131 Couples," *British Journal of General Practice* 50, no. 452 (2000).

13 **How often we do it:** Susan H. Fischman, et al., "Changes in Sexual Relationships in Postpartum Couples," *Journal of Obstetric, Gynecologic, & Neonatal Nursing* 15, no. 1 (1986).

14 **"From a Darwinian, evolutionary:** Tara Parker-Pope, "Is It Love or Mental Illness? They're Closer Than You Think," *Wall Street Journal* (February 13, 2007).

14 **One of the most important:** Vaughn Call, Susan Sprecher, and Pepper Schwartz, "The Incidence and Frequency of Marital Sex in a National Sample," *Journal of Marriage and the Family* 57, no. 3 (1995).

14 **There are also some other gender differences:** Rachel Zimmerman, "Researchers Target Toll Kids Take on Parents' Sex Lives," *Wall Street Journal* (April 24, 2007).

14 **Another generalization:** Felicia de la Garza-Mercer, Andrew Christensen, and Brian Doss, "Sex and Affection in Heterosexual and Homosexual Couples: An Evolutionary Perspective," *Electronic Journal of Human Sexuality* 9 (2006), http://www.ejhs.org/volume9/Garza.htm.

15 **Studies show that women:** David P. Schmitt, et al., "Is There an Early-30s Peak in Female Sexual Desire? Cross-Sectional Evidence from the United States and Canada," *Canadian Journal of Human Sexuality* 11 (2002); Julie Y. Huang and John A. Bargh, "Peak of Desire: Activating the Mating Goal Changes Life-Stage Preferences across Living Kinds," *Psychological Science* 19, no. 6 (2008).

15 **Anyway, research shows that:** Call, Sprecher, and Schwartz, "The Incidence and Frequency of Marital Sex in a National Sample."

16 **As a society we tend to think:** Judith S. Wallerstein, *The Unexpected Legacy of Divorce: The 25 Year Landmark Study* (New York: Hyperion, 2001).

16 **Here is what I've gleaned:** P. A. Cowan and C. P. Cowan, "Strengthening Couples to Improve Children's Well-Being: What We Know Now," *Poverty Research News* 6, no. 3 (2002).

17   **It depends on how high-conflict:** Donna Ruane Morrison and Mary Jo Coiro, "Parental Conflict and Marital Disruption: Do Children Benefit When High-Conflict Marriages Are Dissolved?" *Journal of Marriage and the Family* 61, no. 3 (1999).

17   **A substantial body of research:** G. T. Harold, J. J. Aitken, and K. H. Shelton, "Inter-Parental Conflict and Children's Academic Attainment: A Longitudinal Analysis," *Journal of Child Psychology and Psychiatry* 48, no. 12 (2007); Marcie C. Geoeke-Morey, E. Mark Cummings, and Lauren M. Papp, "Children and Marital Conflict Resolution: Implications for Emotional Security and Adjustment," *Journal of Family Psychology* 21, no. 4 (2007); K. H. Shelton and G. T. Harold, "Marital Conflict and Children's Adjustment: The Mediating and Moderating Role of Children's Coping Strategies," *Social Development* 16, no. 3 (2007); E. M. Cummings, K. S. Simpson, and A. Wilson, "Children's Responses to Interadult Anger as a Function of Information About Resolution," *Developmental Psychology* 29, no. 6 (1993); E. M. Cummings, et al., "Children's Responses to Different Forms of Expression of Anger between Adults," *Child Development* 60, no. 6 (1989).

17   **Certain types of arguing:** John Gottman discusses Shapiro's work for a general audience at: http://www.edge.org/3rd_culture/gottman05/gottman05_index.html.

17   **how a couple argues:** This finding is from Alyson Shapiro's dissertation. John Gottman discusses it at: http://www.edge.org/3rd_culture/gottman05/gottman05_index.html.

17   **And if you aren't yet motivated:** S. J. T. Branje, W. H. J. Meeus, and M. D. Van Doorn, "Longitudinal Transmission of Conflict Resolution Styles from Marital Relationships to Adolescent-Parent Relationships," *Journal of Family Psychology* 21, no. 3 (2007).

19   **Eileen Healy, a family counselor:** Eileen D. Healy, *EQ and Your Child: 8 Proven Skills to Increase Your Child's Emotional Intelligence* (San Carlos, CA: Familypedia Publishing, 2005).

19   **Though these are seemingly:** Christina M. Rinaldi and Nina Howe, "Perceptions of Constructive and Destructive Conflict within and across Family Subsystems," *Infant and Child Development* 12 (2003).

## STEP 2: BUILD A VILLAGE

21   **Very happy people:** E. Diener and M. E. P. Seligman, "Very Happy People," *Psychological Science* 13, no. 1 (2002).

21   **Sharing positive events and feelings:** D. G. Myers, *The American Paradox: Spiritual Hunger in an Age of Plenty* (New Haven, CT: Yale University Press, 2000).

22   **Despite the fact that technology:** Putnam, *Bowling Alone: The Collapse and Revival of American Community.*

22   **Little is more important:** J. P. Shonkoff and D. Phillips, *From Neurons to Neighborhoods: The Science of Early Child Development* (Washington, DC: National Academy Press, 2000).

22   **How well children establish:** K. H. Rubin, W. Bukowski, et al., *Peer Interactions, Relationships, and Groups. Handbook of Child Psychology*, 5th ed., Vol. 3: *Social, Emotional, and Personality Development*, edited by W. Damon (New York: John Wiley & Sons, 1998).

22   **Children consistently rejected:** Shonkoff and Phillips, *From Neurons to Neighborhoods: The Science of Early Child Development.*

23   **When you talk to:** Goleman, *Social Intelligence: The New Science of Human Relationships.*

23   **When you establish rapport with another:** Linda Tickle-Degnen and Robert Rosenthal, "The Nature of Rapport and Its Nonverbal Correlates," *Psychological Inquiry* 1, no. 4 (1990).

24   **In one study, employees:** B. L. Fredrickson, "Why Positive Emotions Matter in Organizations: Lessons from the Broaden-and-Build Model," *Psychologist-Manager Journal* 4, no. 2 (2000).

24   **For example, when students:** F. J. Bernieri, "Coordinated Movement and Rapport in Teacher-Student Interactions," *Journal of Nonverbal Behavior* 12, no. 2 (1988); ———, "Interpersonal Sensitivity in Teacher-Student Interactions," *Personality and Social Psychology Bulletin* 17, no. 1 (1991).

24   **Scientists have shown that:** Goleman, *Social Intelligence: The New Science of Human Relationships.*

25   **Similarly, infants and toddlers:** Ibid.

25   **When confederates:** Ibid.

26   **Conflict between children:** D. W. Johnson, et al., "Effects of Conflict Resolution Training on Elementary School Students," *Journal of Social Psychology* 134, no. 6 (2001); D. Chen, "Preventing Violence by Promoting the Development of Competent Conflict Resolution Skills: Exploring Roles and Responsibilities," *Early Childhood Education Journal* 30, no. 4 (2003).

26   **Most kids shun conflict:** Chen, "Preventing Violence by Promoting the Development of Competent Conflict Resolution Skills: Exploring Roles and Responsibilities."

27   **Try This: Ten Steps:** Adapted in part from Johnson, et al., "Effects of Conflict Resolution Training on Elementary School Students"; C. Pearlman, "Finding the 'Win-Win': Nonviolent Communication Skills Help Kids—and Adults—Resolve Conflicts in Ways That Work for Everybody," *Children's Advocate* (2007), www.4children.org/news/1107hcone.htm; C. Miller, "Teaching the Skills of Peace: More Elementary and Preschools Are Going Beyond 'Conflict Resolution' to Teach Positive Social Behavior," *Children's Advocate* (2001), http://www.4children.org/news/501teach.htm.

28   **In one study, 40 percent of uncoached kids:** Chen, "Preventing Violence by Promoting the Development of Competent Conflict Resolution Skills: Exploring Roles and Responsibilities."

30   **For starters, helping others:** Stephen Post and Jill Neimark, *Why Good Things Happen to Good People* (New York: Broadway Books, 2007); Stephen G. Post, "Altruism, Happiness, and Health: It's Good to Be Good," *International Journal of Behavioral Medicine* 12, no. 2 (2005).

30   **People who volunteer:** Allan Luks, "Doing Good: Helper's High," *Psychology Today* 22, no. 10 (1988).

30   **Giving help to others:** Post and Neimark, *Why Good Things Happen to Good People,* p.7.

30   **it means that volunteering:** Doug Oman, Carl E. Thoresen, and Kay McMahon, "Volunteerism and Mortality among the Community-Dwelling Elderly," *Journal of Health Psychology* 4, no. 3 (1999).

30   **We feel so good:** Jorge Moll, et al., "Human Fronto-Mesolimbic Networks Guide Decisions About Charitable Donation," *Proceedings of the National Academy of Sciences of the United States of America* 103, no. 42 (2006).

31   **About half of the participants:** Post, "Altruism, Happiness, and Health: It's Good to Be Good."

31   **Volunteer work substantially:** Marc A. Musick and John Wilson, "Volunteering and Depression: The Role of Psychological and Social Resources in Different Age Groups," *Social Science & Medicine* 56 (2003).

31   **helping others and receiving help:** Carolyn E. Schwartz, et al., "Altruistic Social Interest Behaviors Are Associated with Better Mental Health," *Psychosomatic Medicine* 65 (2003).

31   **Adolescents who identify:** Zipora Magen, "Commitment Beyond Self and Adolescence," *Social Indicators Research* 37 (1996).

31   **Similarly, teens who:** Musick and Wilson, "Volunteering and Depression: The Role of Psychological and Social Resources in Different Age Groups."

31   **Generous behavior reduces:** Peter L. Benson, E. Gil Clary, and Peter C. Scales, "Altruism and Health: Is There a Link During Adolescence?" in *Altruism and Health: Perspectives from Empirical Research,* ed. Stephen G. Post (New York: Oxford University Press, 2007).

31   **Teens who volunteer:** Joseph P. Allen, et al., "Preventing Teen Pregnancy and Academic Failure: Experimental Evaluation of a Developmentally Based Approach," *Child Development* 64, no. 4 (1997).

31   **patients in one study:** Larry Scherwitz, et al., "Type A Behavior, Self Involvement, and Coronary Atherosclerosis," *Psychosomatic Medicine* 45, no. 1 (1983).

32   **"One of the healthiest:** Post and Neimark, *Why Good Things Happen to Good People*.

32   **Psychologist Barbara Fredrickson:** B. L. Fredrickson, et al., "The Undoing Effect of Positive Emotions," *Motivation and Emotion* 24, no. 4 (2000).

32   **One study showed:** Neal Krause, "Church-Based Social Support and Mortality," *Journal of Gerontology* 61B, no. 3 (2006); Neal Krause, Christopher G. Ellison, and Keith M. Wuff, "Church-Based Emotional Support, Negative Interaction, and Psychological Well-Being: Findings from a National Sample of Presbyterians," *Journal for the Scientific Study of Religion* 37, no. 4 (1998).

32   **In young children and adolescents:** Gustavo Carlo, et al., "Parenting Styles or Practices? Parenting, Sympathy, and Prosocial Behaviors among Adolescents," *Journal of Genetic Psychology* 168, no. 2 (2007).

32   **Boosting people's feelings of:** Mario Mikulincer, Phillip R. Shaver, and Dana Pereg, "Attachment Theory and Affect Regulation: The Dynamics, Development, and Cognitive Consequences of Attachment-Related Strategies," *Motivation and Emotion* 27, no. 2 (2003).

33   **Altruistic kids tend:** Norman Buckley, Linda S. Siegel, and Steven Ness, "Egocentrism, Empathy and Altruistic Behavior in Young Children," *Developmental Psychology* 5, no. 3 (1979).

33   **Kindness can be contagious:** Goleman, *Social Intelligence: The New Science of Human Relationships*.

33   **Research suggests that altruistic:** Martin L. Hoffman, "Altruistic Behavior and the Parent-Child Relationship," *Journal of Personality and Social Psychology* 31, no. 5 (1975); Peterson, "Generativity and Successful Parenting: An Analysis of Young Adult Outcomes."

33   **Similarly, preschoolers with nurturing:** Marian Radke Yarrow, Phyllis M. Scott, and Carolyn Zahn Waxler, "Learning Concern for Others," *Developmental Psychology* 8, no. 2 (1973).

33   **Empathetic preaching from:** Nancy Eisenberg-Berg and Elizabeth Geisheker, "Content of Preachings and Power of the Model/Preacher: The Effect on Children Generosity," *Developmental Psychology* 15, no. 2 (1979).

33   **Four- to thirteen-year-olds:** Geoffrey Maruyama, Scott C. Fraser, and Norman Miller, "Personal Responsibility and Altruism in Children," *Journal of Personality and Social Psychology* 42, no. 4 (1982).

34   **Just thinking about giving:** D. C. McClelland and C. Kirshnit, "The Effect of Motivational Arousal through Films on Salivary Immunoglobulin A," *Psychology & Health* 2, no. 1 (1988).

34   **Similarly, praying for others:** Krause, "Church-Based Social Support and Mortality."

34   **This research suggests that:** Felix Warneken and Michael Tomasello, "Extrinsic Rewards Undermine Altruisitic Tendencies in 20-Month-Olds," *Developmental Psychology* 44, no. 6 (2008).

34   **Parents who express positive:** Ariel Knafo and Robert Plomin, "Parental Discipline and Affection and Children's Prosocial Behavior: Genetic and Environmental Links," *Journal of Personality and Social Psychology* 90, no. 1 (2006); ———, "Prosocial Behavior from Early to Middle Childhood: Genetic and Environmental Influences on Stability and Change," *Developmental Psychology* 42, no. 5 (2006).

35   **Multiple sclerosis (MS) patients:** Carolyn E. Schwartz and Rabbi Meir Sendor, "Helping Others Helps Oneself: Response Shift Effects in Peer Support," *Social Science & Medicine* 48, no. 11 (1999).

35   **We can take a cue:** Stephen J. Suomi and Harry F. Harlow, "Social Rehabilitation

of Isolate-Reared Monkeys," *Developmental Psychology* 6, no. 3 (1972); H. F. Harlow and M. A. Novak, "Psychopathological Perspectives," *Perspectives in Biology and Medicine* 16, no. 3 (1973).

36 **One particularly impressive study:** Paul Wink and Michele Dilon, "Religiousness, Spirituality, and Psychological Functioning in Late Adulthood: Findings from a Longitudinal Study," *Psychology of Religion and Spirituality* 5, no. 1 (2008).

36 **Teenagers whose families were relatively harmonious:** Ibid.

37 **The work of positivity psychologist:** David P. Johnson, et al., "Loving-Kindness Meditation to Enhance Recovery from Negative Symptoms of Schizophrenia," *Journal of Clinical Psychology* 65, no. 5 (2009).

39 **Mothers serve as the exclusive:** E. Z. Tronick, S. Winn, and G. A. Morelli, "Multiple Caretaking in the Context of Human Evolution: Why Don't the Efe Know the Western Prescription to Child Care?" in *The Psychobiology of Attachment and Separation,* ed. M. Reite and T. Field (New York: Academic Press, 1985).

39 **Multitudes of studies show:** Harry McGurk, et al., "Controversy, Theory and Social Context in Contemporary Day Care Research," *Journal of Child Psychology and Psychiatry* 34, no. 1 (1993), p. 15.

39 **In general, kids with dads:** S. Allen and K. Daly, "The Effects of Father Involvement: An Updated Research Summary of the Evidence," in *Report by Centre for Families, Work & Well-Being* (University of Guelph, Guelph, Canada 2007).

41 **Family sociologists often:** Oriel Sullivan and Scott Coltrane, "Men's Changing Contribution to Housework and Child Care: A Discussion Paper on Changing Family Roles," in *11th Annual Conference of the Council on Contemporary Families* (Chicago, IL: University of Illinois, 2008).

41 **There are three things:** C. P. Cowan, et al., "An Approach to Preventing Coparenting Conflict and Divorce in Low-Income Families: Strengthening Couple Relationships and Fostering Fathers' Involvement," *Family Process* 46, no. 1 (2006).

42 **Mothers sometimes serve as "gatekeepers":** Sarah Schoppe-Sullivan, et al., "Maternal Gatekeeping, Coparenting Quality, and Fathering Behavior in Families with Infants," *Journal of Family Psychology* 22, no. 3 (2008).

42 **Unless the relationship between parents:** Paul R. Amato, Laura Spencer Loomis, and Alan Booth Source, "Parental Divorce, Marital Conflict, and Offspring Well-Being During Early Adulthood," *Social Forces* 73, no. 3 (1995).

43 **The best predictor of the quality:** A. M. Anderson, "Factors Influencing the Father-Infant Relationship," *Journal of Family Nursing* 2, no. 3 (1996).

43 **Participating in "leisure activities":** E. Flouri, "Fathering and Adolescents' Psychological Adjustment: The Role of Fathers' Involvement, Residence and Biology Status," *Child: Care, Health, and Development* 34, no. 2 (2007).

43 **The amount of child support received:** Allen and Daly, "The Effects of Father Involvement: An Updated Research Summary of the Evidence."

45 **Supportive, nurturing, and accepting?:** Ibid.; R. Palkovitz, "Reconstructing 'Involvement': Expanding Conceptualizations of Men's Caring in Contemporary Families," in *Generative Fathering: Beyond Deficit Perspectives,* ed. A. J. Hawkins and D. C. Dollahite (Thousand Oaks, CA: Sage, 1997).

STEP 3: EXPECT EFFORT AND ENJOYMENT, NOT PERFECTION

47 **Once mastered, the growth mind-set:** The best review of the science behind mind-sets, written for a general audience, is C. S. Dweck, *Mindset: The New Psychology of Success* (New York: Random House, 2006).

48 **Stanford psychologist Carol Dweck's research:** C. M. Mueller and C. S. Dweck, "Praise for Intelligence Can Undermine Children's Motivation and Performance," *Journal of Personality and Social Psychology* 75, no. 1 (1998).

48 **Unfortunately, when kids want:** C. S. Dweck and M. L. Kamins, "Person Versus Process Praise and Criticism: Implications for Contingent Self-Worth and Coping," *Developmental Psychology* 35, no. 3 (1999).

50   **Happier people earn more:** Julia K. Bowhm and Sonja Lyubomirsky, "Does Happiness Promote Career Success?" *Journal of Career Assessment* 16, no. 1 (2008).

50   **But happiness often precedes:** S. Lyubomirsky, L. A. King, and E. Diener, "The Benefits of Frequent Positive Affect: Does Happiness Lead to Success?" *Psychological Bulletin* 131 (2005).

50   **But researchers across a wide:** Michael J. A. Howe, Jane W. Davidson, and John A. Sloboda, "Innate Talents: Reality or Myth?" *Behavioral and Brain Sciences* 21 (1998).

50   **K. Anders Ericsson, a psychologist:** K. A. Ericsson, R. T. Krampe, and C. Tesch-Romer, "The Role of Deliberate Practice in the Acquisition of Expert Performance," *Psychological Review* 100, no. 3 (1993).

51   **"elite performers in many:** Quoted in Geoffrey Colvin, "What It Takes to Be Great," CNNmoney.com; http://money.cnn.com/magazines/fortune/fortune_archive/2006/10/30/8391794/index.htm.

51   **finally, great performers have:** A. Bandura, et al., "Self-Efficacy Beliefs as Shapers of Children's Aspirations and Career Trajectories," *Child Development* 72, no. 1 (2001); A. Bandura and D. H. Schunk, "Cultivating Competence, Self-Efficacy, and Intrinsic Interest through Proximal Self-Motivation," *Journal of Personality and Social Psychology* 41, no. 3 (1981).

51   **But knowing that it is practice:** A. Bandura and R. Wood, "Impact of Conceptions of Ability on Self-Regulatory Mechanisms and Complex Decision Making," *Journal of Personality and Social Psychology* 56, no. 3 (1989).

52   **Parents who overemphasize achievement:** Suniya S. Luthar and Bronwyn E. Becker, "Privileged but Pressured? A Study of Affluent Youth," *Child Development* 73, no. 5 (2002); Suniya S. Luthar, "The Culture of Affluence: Psychological Costs of Material Wealth," *Child Development* 74, no. 6 (2003); Suniya S. Luthar and K. D'Avanzo, "Contextual Factors in Substance Use: A Study of Suburban and Inner-City Adolescents," *Development and Psychopathology* 11 (1999); Suniya S. Luthar and S. Latendresse, "Children of the Affluent: Challenges to Well-Being," *American Psychological Society* 14, no. 1 (2005); Suniya S. Luthar and C. C. Sexton, "The High Price of Affluence," in *Advances in Child Development and Behavior,* ed. R. Kail (San Diego, CA: Academic Press, 2005).

53   **Carol Dweck's research team:** Dweck and Kamins, "Person Versus Process Praise and Criticism: Implications for Contingent Self-Worth and Coping."

53   **Dweck explains:** C. S. Dweck, "Caution—Praise Can Be Dangerous," in *Educational Psychology in Context: Readings for Future Teachers,* ed. Bruce A. Marlowe and Alan S. Canestrari (SAGE, 2005), p. 209. http://greatergood.berkeley.edu/goodwiki/index.php/Psy

55   **Instead of enjoying:** Kathleen Y. Kawamura, et al., "Perfectionism, Anxiety, and Depression: Are the Relationships Independent?" *Cognitive Therapy and Research* 25, no. 3 (2001); Petra H. Wirtz, et al., "Perfectionism and the Cortical Response to Psychosocial Stress in Men," *Psychosomatic Medicine* 69 (2007).

59   **One study showed that teenage:** Clay Risen, "Quitting Can Be Good for You," *New York Times* (December 19, 2007).

59   **One study showed that:** Gregory E. Miller and Carsten Wrosch, "You've Gotta Know When to Fold 'em: Goal Disengagement and Systemic Inflammation in Adolescence," *Psychological Science* 19, no. 9 (2007).

60   *The Power of Full Engagement* **authors:** J. Loehr and T. Schwartz, *The Power of Full Engagement* (New York: Free Press, 2003).

61   **According to perfectionism researcher:** Hara Estroff Marano, "Pitfalls of Perfectionism," *Psychology Today* magazine (2008); Randy O. Frost and Patricia A. Marten, "Perfectionism and Evaluative Threat," *Cognitive Therapy and Research* 14, no. 6 (1990); Randy O. Frost, et al., "Reactions to Mistakes among Subjects High and Low in Perfectionistic Concern over Mistakes," *Cognitive Therapy and Research* 19, no. 2 (1995).

62   **Barry Schwartz, the psychologist:** Barry Schwartz, *The Paradox of Choice: Why More Is Less* (New York: HarperCollins Publishers Inc., 2004).

STEP 4: CHOOSE GRATITUDE, FORGIVENESS, AND OPTIMISM

65 But fully 40 percent of: S. Lyubomirsky, *The How of Happiness: A Scientific Approach to Getting the Life You Want*, pp. 20–22; S. Lyubomirsky, L. A. King, and E. Diener, "Pursuing Happiness: The Architecture of Sustainable Change," *Review of General Psychology* 9, no. 2 (2005); K. M. Sheldon and S. Lyubomirsky, "Achieving Sustainable Gains in Happiness: Change Your Actions, Not Your Circumstances," *Journal of Happiness Studies* 7 (2006); Robert A. Emmons and Michael E. McCullough, "Counting Blessings Versus Burdens: An Experimental Investigation of Gratitude and Subjective Well-Being in Daily Life," *Journal of Personality and Social Psychology* 84, no. 2 (2003); C. Tkach and S. Lyubomirsky, "How Do People Pursue Happiness: Relating Personality, Happiness-Increasing Strategies, and Well-Being," *Journal of Happiness Studies* 7 (2006).

66 One gratitude researcher: Robert A. Emmons, "Pay It Forward," *Greater Good* (2007).

67 At night before bed: Martin E. P. Seligman, et al., "Positive Psychology Progress: Empirical Validation of Interventions," *American Psychologist* 60, no. 5 (2005).

68 Psychologists have tested: Emily L. Polak and Michael E. McCullough, "Is Gratitude an Alternative to Materialism?" *Journal of Happiness Studies* 7, no. 3 (2006); Martin E. P. Seligman, *Authentic Happiness: Using the New Positive Psychology to Realize Your Potential for Lasting Fulfillment* (New York: Simon & Schuster, 2002).

68 And adults who do this: Seligman, et al., "Positive Psychology Progress: Empirical Validation of Interventions."

68 If you think this sounds: Juliet Schor, *Born to Buy: The Commercialized Child and the New Consumer Culture* (New York: Simon & Schuster, 2004).

69 For example, scientists have found: Emmons and McCullough, *The Psychology of Gratitude*; Emmons, "Pay It Forward."

70 Savoring good experiences: see Chapter 8.

71 But important it is: G. Bono, M. E. McCullough, and L. M. Root, "Forgiveness, Feeling Connected to Others, and Well-Being: Two Longitudinal Studies," *Personality and Social Psychology Bulletin* 34, no. 2 (2008); M. E. McCullough, E. L. Worthington, and K. C. Rachal, "Interpersonal Forgiving in Close Relationships," *Journal of Personality and Social Psychology* 73, no. 2 (1997).

71 Researchers find that unforgiving people: Everett L. Worthington, "The New Science of Forgiveness," *Greater Good* (2004); Frederic Luskin, "The Choice to Forgive," *Greater Good* (2004); P. Koutsos, E. H. Wertheim, and J. Kornblum, "Paths to Interpersonal Forgiveness: The Roles of Personality, Disposition to Forgive and Contextual Factors in Predicting Forgiveness," *Personality and Individual Differences* 44, no. 2 (2008); Michael E. McCullough and Charlotte van Oyen Witvliet, "The Psychology of Forgiveness," in *Handbook of Positive Psychology*, eds. C. R Snyder and S. J. Lopez (New York: Oxford University Press, 2002); Michael E. McCullough, "Forgiveness: Who Does It and How Do They Do It?" *Current Directions in Psychological Science* 10, no. 6 (2002); Lyubomirsky, *The How of Happiness: A Scientific Approach to Getting the Life You Want*.

72 Avoidance is a common response: M. E. McCullough, G. Bono, and L. M. Root, "Rumination, Emotion, and Forgiveness: Three Longitudinal Studies," *Journal of Personality and Social Psychology* 92, no. 3 (2007); Lyubomirsky, *The How of Happiness: A Scientific Approach to Getting the Life You Want*.

72 Hostility harms our health: C. V. O. Witvliet, T. E. Ludwig, and K. L. Vander Laan, "Granting Forgiveness or Harboring Grudges: Implications for Emotion, Physiology, and Health," *Psychological Science* 12, no. 2 (2001).

73 The best way to activate: Luskin, "The Choice to Forgive."

73 In a study of Protestants: Ibid.

74 Having a smile, a laugh: Lyubomirsky, *The How of Happiness: A Scientific Approach to Getting the Life You Want*.

74 Fred Luskin, the director of: Luskin, "The Choice to Forgive"; Frederic Luskin, *Forgive for Good* (New York: HarperCollins, 2003).

76  **Here are some exercises:** Aaron Lazare, "Making Peace through Apology," *Greater Good* (2004).
77  **According to Aaron Lazare:** Ibid.; ———, *On Apology* (New York: Oxford University Press, 2005).
78  **Compared to pessimistic people:** Seligman, *Authentic Happiness: Using the New Positive Psychology to Realize Your Potential for Lasting Fulfillment*; L. Y. Abramson, et al., "Optimistic Cognitive Styles and Invulnerability to Depression," in *The Science of Optimism and Hope: Research Essays in Honor of Martin E. P. Seligman,* ed. J. E. Gillham (Radner, PA: Templeton Foundation Press, 2000); M. F. Scheier and C. S. Carver, "On the Power of Positive Thinking: The Benefits of Being Optimistic," *Current Directions in Psychological Science* 2, no. 1 (1993); ———, "Effects of Optimism on Psychological and Physical Well-Being: Theoretical Overview and Empirical Update," *Cognitive Therapy and Research* 16, no. 2 (1992).
79  **The researchers who direct:** For more information on the Penn Resiliency Project, go to http://www.ppc.sas.upenn.edu/prpsum.htm.
79  **Research shows that kids who:** M. E. P. Seligman, et al., *The Optimistic Child* (New York: Houghton Mifflin, 1995).
79  **Optimism is contagious:** Ibid.
79  **Pessimistic parents are more likely:** Seligman, et al., "Positive Psychology Progress: Empirical Validation of Interventions."
80  **Ten-year-olds who are taught:** D. Cicchetti and S. L. Toth, "The Development of Depression in Children and Adolescents," *American Psychologist* 53, no. 2 (1998); S. Nolen-Howksema, J. S. Girgus, and M. E. P. Seligman, "Depression in Children of Families in Turmoil," unpublished manuscript, University of Pennsylvania (1986).
80  **Famed psychologist Martin Seligman:** Seligman, *Authentic Happiness: Using the New Positive Psychology to Realize Your Potential for Lasting Fulfillment*; Abramson, et al., "Optimistic Cognitive Styles and Invulnerability to Depression"; T. R. G. Gladstone and N. J. Kaslow, "Depression and Attributions in Children and Adolescents: A Meta-Analytic Review," *Journal of Abnormal Child Psychology* 23, no. 5 (1995); P. Schulman, "Explanatory Style and Achievement in School and Work," in *Explanatory Style,* ed. G. M. Buchanan and M. E. P. Seligman (Hillsdale, NJ: Lawrence Erlbaum, 1995); C. Hammen, C. Adrian, and D. Hiroto, "A Longitudinal Test of the Attributional Vulnerability Model in Children at Risk for Depression," *British Journal of Clinical Psychology* 27 (1988); C. Peterson, M. E. P. Seligman, and G. E. Vaillant, "Pessimistic Explanatory Style Is a Risk Factor for Physical Illness: A Thirty-Five-Year Longitudinal Study," *Journal of Personality and Social Psychology* 55, no. 3 (1988); D. Rettew and K. Reivich, "Sports and Explanatory Style," in *Explanatory Style,* ed. G. M. Buchanan and M. E. P. Seligman (Hillsdale, NJ: Lawrence Erlbaum, 1995).
81  **Not surprisingly, people who:** T. E. Joiner and K. D. Wagner, "Attributional Style and Depression in Children and Adolescents: A Meta-Analytic Review," *Clinical Psychology Review* 15, no. 8 (1995); C. J. Robins and A. M. Hayes, "The Role of Causal Attributions in the Prediction of Depression," in *Explanatory Style,* eds. G. M. Buchanan and M. E. P. Seligman (Hillsdale, NJ: Lawrence Erlbaum, 1995).
82  **But genetics aren't everything:** Seligman, et al., *The Optimistic Child.*
82  **If you've got a determined pessimist:** Ibid.

STEP 5: RAISE THEIR EMOTIONAL INTELLIGENCE

84  **Psychologist John Gottman's research:** J. M. Gottman, *Raising an Emotionally Intelligent Child* (New York: Simon & Schuster, 1997).
84  **When parents and caregivers:** Ibid.
85  **Healthier:** J. A. Feeney, "Implication of Attachment Style for Patterns of Health and Illness," *Child: Care, Health and Development* 26, no. 4 (2000).
85  **More confident in their explorations:** M. E. Lamb, "Attachments, Social Networks, and Developmental Contexts," *Human Development* 48 (2005).
85  **Better liked by their teachers:** B. Pierrehumbert, R. J. Iannoti, E. M. Cummings,

and C. Zahn-Waxler, "Social Functioning with Mother and Peers at 2 and 5 Years: The Influence of Attachment," *International Journal of Behavioral Development* 12, no. 1 (1989).

85 **Less likely to be bullied:** M. Troy and L. A. Sroufe, "Victimization among Preschoolers: Role of Attachment Relationship History," *Journal of American Academy of Child and Adolescent Psychiatry* 26, no. 2 (1987).

85 **Better behaved and less impulsive:** L. A. Sroufe, N. E. Fox, and V. R. Pancake, "Attachment and Dependency in Developmental Perspective," *Child Development* 54, no. 6 (1983).

85 **Kids with secure attachments to:** Ibid.

85 **Strong attachment relationships build emotional:** J. P. Shonkoff and D. Phillips, *From Neurons to Neighborhoods: The Science of Early Child Development* (Washington, DC: National Academy Press, 2000).

85 **Securely attached children have a better:** Shonkoff and Phillips, *From Neurons to Neighborhoods: The Science of Early Child Development*, pp. 226–37.

85 **Establishing secure connections has:** M. D. S. Ainsworth, et al., *Patterns of Attachment* (Hillsdale, NJ: L. Erlbaum, 1978).

86 **Consistency matters, too:** Louis W. C. Tavecchio and M. H. van Ijendoorn, *Attachment in Social Networks: Contributions to the Bowlby-Ainsworth Attachment Theory* (New York: Elsevier Science Publishers B.V., 1987), p. 37.

87 **Kids benefit the most from three:** M. H. Van Ijendoorn, A. Sagi, and M. W. E. Lambermon, "The Multiple Caretaker Paradox: Data from Holland and Israel," *New Directions for Child and Adolescent Development* 57 (1992).

87 **For example, when infants and toddlers:** T. Field, "Attachment and Separation in Young Children," *Annual Review in Psychology* 47 (1996), p. 551.

87 **Similarly, siblings can be important:** N. A. Doherty and J. A. Feeney, "The Composition of Attachment Networks Throughout the Adult Years," *Personal Relationships* 11, no. 4 (2004), see p. 470.

87 **Here's something that may not:** Gottman and DeClaire, *Raising an Emotionally Intelligent Child*; J. M. Gottman, L. F. Katz, and C. Hooven, *Meta-Emotion: How Families Communicate Emotionally* (Mahwah, NJ: Lawrence Erlbaum Associates, 1997).

87 **Just as secure attachments create:** Gottman, *Raising an Emotionally Intelligent Child*, p. 17.

88 **Gottman teaches parents:** Gottman and DeClaire, *Raising an Emotionally Intelligent Child*.

95 **Despite the fact that:** U. Dimberg, M. Thunberg, and K. Elmehed, "Unconscious Facial Reactions to Emotional Facial Expressions," *Psychological Science* 11, no. 1 (2000); U. Hess and S. Blairy, "Facial Mimicry and Emotional Contagion to Dynamic Emotional Facial Expressions and Their Influence on Decoding Accuracy," *International Journal of Psychophysiology* 40, no. 2 (2001).

95 **Similarly, hearing someone:** D. Keltner, *Born to Be Good: The Science of a Meaningful Life*.

95 **Good feelings are infectious:** S. G. Barsade, "The Ripple Effect: Emotional Contagion and Its Influence on Group Behavior," *Administrative Science Quarterly* 47, no. 4 (2002); E. Hatfield, "Emotional Contagion," *Current Directions in Psychological Science* 2, no. 3 (2008).

96 **You can even just hold:** Fritz Strack, Leonard L. Martin, and S. Stepper, "Inhibiting and Facilitating Conditions of the Human Smile: A Nonobtrusive Test of the Facial Feedback Hypothesis," *Sabine Journal of Personality and Social Psychology* 54, no. 5 (1988).

96 **It also reduces rapport:** E. A. Butler, et al., "The Social Consequences of Expressive Suppression," *Emotion* 3, no. 1 (2003).

96 **Smiling boosts our immune:** P. Ekman, R. J. Davidson, and W. V. Fiesen, "Emotional Expression and Brain Physiology," *Journal of Personality and Social Psychology* 58, no. 2 (1990); V. Surakka and J. K. Hietanen, "Facial and Emotional Reactions to Duchenne and Non-Duchenne Smiles," *International Journal of Psychophysiology* 29

(1998); L. Harker and D. Keltner, "Expressions of Positive Emotion in Women's College Yearbook Pictures and Their Relationship to Personality and Life Outcomes across Adulthood," *Journal of Personality and Social Psychology* 80, no. 1 (2001); M. H. Abel and R. Hester, "The Therapeutic Effects of Smiling," in *An Empirical Reflection on the Smile,* ed. M. H. Abel (New York: Edwin Mellen Press, 2002); G. L. Gladstone and G. B. Parker, "When You're Smiling, Does the Whole World Smile for You?" *Australasian Psychiatry* 10, no. 2 (2002); A. Papa and G. A. Bonanno, "The Face of Adversity: The Interpersonal and Intrapersonal Functions of Smiling," *Emotion* 8, no. 1 (2008).

96  **This is at least in part:** Fredrickson, et al., "The Undoing Effect of Positive Emotions."

97  **Because to be really happy:** Fredrickson, *Positivity: Groundbreaking Research Reveals How to Embrace the Hidden Strength of Positive Emotions, Overcome Negativity, and Thrive.*

97  **Though social scientists classify:** Ibid.

98  **John Gottman has shown that:** J. M. Gottman, *What Predicts Divorce: The Relationship between Marital Processes and Marital Outcomes* (New York: Lawrence Erlbaum, 1994).

98  **Similarly, high-performance teams:** M. Losada and E. Heaphy, "The Role of Positivity and Connectivity in the Performance of Business Teams: A Nonlinear Dynamics Model," *American Behavioral Scientist* 47, no. 6 (2004); M. Losada, "The Complex Dynamics of High Performance Teams," *Mathematical and Computer Modeling* 30, no. 9-10 (1999).

98  **Specifically, a ratio above:** Fredrickson, *Positivity: Groundbreaking Research Reveals How to Embrace the Hidden Strength of Positive Emotions, Overcome Negativity, and Thrive.*

98  **Now neuroscientists have shown:** M. Suda, et al., "Emotional Responses to Music: Towards Scientific Perspectives on Music Therapy," *Neuroreport: For Rapid Communication of Neuroscience Research* 19, no. 1 (2008); P. Hills and M. Argyle, "Positive Moods Derived from Leisure and Their Relationship to Happiness and Personality," *Personality and Individual Differences* 25, no. 3 (1998).

99  **Physical activity is even:** Ratey and Hagerman, *Spark.*

99  **Exercise prepares our brains to learn:** Hills and Argyle, "Positive Moods Derived from Leisure and Their Relationship to Happiness and Personality"; Suda, et al., "Emotional Responses to Music: Towards Scientific Perspectives on Music Therapy."

99  **People generally rate:** W. T Ross and I. Simonson, "Evaluation of Pairs of Experiences: A Preferred Happy Ending," *Journal of Behavioral Decision Making* 4 (1991).

99  **This is what Barbara:** B. L. Fredrickson, "Extracting Meaning from Past Affective Experiences: The Importance of Peaks, Ends, and Specific Emotions," *Cognition and Emotion* 14, no. 4 (2000); D. Ariely and Z. Carmon, "Gestalt Characteristics of Experiences:The Defining Features of Summarized Events," *Journal of Behavioral Decision Making* 13, no. 2 (2000); D. Kahneman, et al., "When More Pain Is Preferred to Less: Adding a Better End," *Psychological Science* 4, no. 6 (1993).

99  **Here is what I think:** Fredrickson, "Extracting Meaning from Past Affective Experiences: The Importance of Peaks, Ends, and Specific Emotions."

STEP 6: FORM HAPPINESS HABITS

103  **As Jonathan Haidt artfully describes:** J. Haidt, *The Happiness Hypothesis: Finding Modern Truth in Ancient Wisdom* (New York: Basic Books, 2006).

104  **Haidt uses the metaphor:** Ibid., p. 18.

105  **Punished by Rewards?:** I'm drawing on Alphie Kohn's best-known book here: A. Kohn, *Punished by Rewards: The Trouble with Gold Stars, Incentive Plans, A's, Praise, and Other Bribes* (Boston: Houghton Mufflin, 1993).

106  **Self-motivated kids achieve more:** A. Gottfried, "Academic Intrinsic Motivation

in Young Elementary School Children," *Journal of Educational Psychology* 82, no. 3 (1990).

106 **Extrinsically motivated kids are more:** A. K. Boggiano and M. Barrett, "Gender Differences in Depression in Children as a Function of Motivational Orientation," *Sex Roles* 26, no. 1–2 (1992).

106 **Orienting kids toward external rewards:** Mireille Joussemet, Richard Koestner, Natasha Lekes, and Nathalie Houlfort, "Introducing Uninteresting Tasks to Children: A Comparison of the Effects of Rewards and Autonomy Support," *Journal of Personality* 72, no. 1 (2004). Also from this: R. M. Ryan and E. L. Deci, "When Rewards Compete with Nature: The Undermining of Intrinsic Motivation and Self-Regulation," in *Intrinsic and Extrinsic Motivation: The Search for Optimal Motivation and Performance*, ed. C. Sansone and J. Jarackiewicz (New York: Academic Press, 2000); also: E. L. Deci, R. Koestner, and R. M. Ryan, "A Meta-Analytic Review of Experiments Examining the Effects of Extrinsic Rewards on Intrinsic Motivation," *Psychological Bulletin* 125 (1999).

107 **A specific encouragement:** Joussemet, "Introducing Uninteresting Tasks to Children: A Comparison of the Effects of Rewards and Autonomy Support."

109 **Here is a plus:** Ibid.

109 **Psychologists James Prochaska and Carlo DiClemente:** J. Prochaska, and C. DiClemente, *Changing for Good* (New York: Collins, 2006); also J. Prochaska, C. DiClemente, J. C. Norcross, "In Search of How People Change," *American Psychologist* 47, no. 9 (1992).

111 **Another key part of the preparation:** R. Byrne, *The Secret* (New York/Hillsboro, OR: Atria Books/Beyond Words, 2006).

111 **Just believing that you are capable:** J. Norcross, M. Mrykalo, and M. Blagys, "Auld Lang Syne: Success Predictors, Change Processes, and Self-Reported Outcomes of New Year's Resolvers and Nonresolvers," *Journal of Clinical Psychology* 58 (2002).

111 **You can use:** G. J. Fitzsimons, "Asking Questions Can Change Choice Behavior: Does It Do So Automatically or Effortfully?" *Journal of Experimental Psychology* 6, no. 3 (2000).

112 **The key, according to Beck:** M. Beck, *The Four Day Win* (New York: Rodale Inc., 2007), p. 15.

114 **Another way to up the odds:** Prochaska, "In Search of How People Change."

115 **People who have social support:** J. Norcross and D. Vangarelli, "The Resolution Solution: Longitudinal Examination of New Year's Change Attempts," *Journal of Substance Abuse* 1 (1989).

115 **Research shows that:** R. F. Baumeister, M. Gailliot, and C. N. DeWall, "Self-Regulation and Personality: How Interventions Increase Regulatory Success, and How Depletion Moderates the Effects of Traits on Behavior," *Journal of Personality* 74, no. 6 (2006).

115 **Kids are more likely:** G. P. Latham and E. A. Locke, "Self-Regulation through Goal Setting," *Organizational Behavior and Human Decision Processes* 50 (1991).

115 **The turtle steps outlined above:** J. Szente, "Empowering Young Children for Success in School and in Life," *Early Childhood Education Journal* 34, no. 6 (2007).

116 **One of the best things you can do:** Baumeister, "Self-Regulation and Personality: How Interventions Increase Regulatory Success, and How Depletion Moderates the Effects of Traits on Behavior."

116 **For example, researchers at Case Western University:** M. Muraven, R. F. Baumeister, and D. M. Tice, "Longitudinal Improvement of Self-Regulation through Practice: Building Self-Control Strength through Repeated Exercise," *Journal of Social Psychology* 139, no. 4 (1999).

117 **New behaviors are often strongly:** D. T. Neal, W. Wood, and J. M. Quinn, "Habits—a Repeat Performance," *Current Directions in Psychological Sciences* 15, no. 4 (2006). Also W. Wood, L. Tam, and M. G. Witt, "Changing Circumstances, Disrupting Habits," *Journal of Personality and Social Psychology* 88, no. 6 (2005).

117  **Preliminary research suggests:** Wood, "Changing Circumstances, Disrupting Habits."

## STEP 7: TEACH SELF-DISCIPLINE

119  **Years ago, a researcher named Walter Mischel:** W. Mischel, "Delay of Gratification, Need for Achievement, and Acquiescence in Another Culture," *Journal of Abnormal and Social Psychology* 62, no. 3 (1961); W. Mischel and C. Gilligan, "Delay of Gratification, Motivation for the Prohibited Gratification, and Responses to Temptation," *Journal of Abnormal Social Psychology* 69, no. 4 (1964).

119  **Researchers have replicated studies:** E. O. Smirnova and O. V. Gudareva, "Igra I Proizvol'nost' U Sovremennyh Doshkol'nikov" [Play and Intentionality in Today's Preschoolers], *Voprosy psihologii* 1 (2004); E. O. Smirnova, "Development of Will and Intentionality in Toddlers and Preschool-Age Children," *Modek* (1998); Z. V. Manuilenko, "The Development of Voluntary Behavior in Preschool-Age Children," *Soviet Psychology* 13 (1948/1975). Russian journal articles translated via personal email.

120  **This is at least in part:** M. Pressley, et al., *Cognitive Strategy Training and Children's Self-Control. Cognitive Strategy Research: Psychological Foundations,* ed. M. Pressley and J. R. Levin (New York: Springer-Verlag, 1983); W. Mischel and R. Metzner, "Preference for Delayed Reward as a Function of Age, Intelligence, and Length of Delay Interval," *Journal of Abnormal Social Psychology* 64, no. 6 (1962); Mischel and Gilligan, "Delay of Gratification, Motivation for the Prohibited Gratification, and Responses to Temptation"; J. S. Stumphauzer, "Increased Delay of Gratification in Young Prison Inmates through Imitation of High-Delay Peer Models," *Journal of Personality and Social Psychology* 21, no. 1 (1972); Mischel, "Delay of Gratification, Need for Achievement, and Acquiescence in Another Culture," p. 543.

120  **In addition, self-disciplined kids cope better:** W. Mischel, Y. Shoda, and M. L. Rodriguez, "Delay of Gratification in Children," *Science* 244, no. 4907 (1989).

120  **On the other hand, kids:** G. J. Madden, et al., "Impulsive and Self-Control Choices in Opioid-Dependent Patients and Non-Drug-Using Control Patients: Drug and Monetary Rewards," *Experimental and Clinical Psychopharmacology* 5, no. 3 (1997); Roy F. Baumeister, et al., "Losing Control: How & Why People Fail at Self-Regulation and Handbook of Self-Regulation," *Journal of Psychiatry and Law* 30, no. 2 (2002); Don R. Cherek, et al., "Studies of Violent and Nonviolent Male Parolees: II. Laboratory and Psychometric Measurements of Impulsivity," *Biological Psychiatry* 41, no. 5 (1997); R. F. Baumeister and T. F. Heatherton, "Self-Regulation Failure: An Overview," *Psychological Inquiry* 7 (1996); Edelgard Wulfert, et al., "Cognitive, Behavioral, and Personality Correlates of HIV-Positive Persons' Unsafe Sexual Behavior," *Journal of Applied Social Psychology* 29, no. 2 (1999).

120  **Researchers talk about two systems:** J. Metcalfe and W. Mischel, "A Hot/Cool-System Analysis of Delay of Gratification: Dynamics of Willpower," *Psychological Review* 106, no. 1 (1999).

121  **This increases the stimuli activating:** Ibid.

121  **Stress is another factor that:** Ibid.

121  **The same researchers behind the:** Mischel, Shoda, and Rodriguez, "Delay of Gratification in Children."

122  **Parents today are saying "no":** Daniel J. Kindlon, *Too Much of a Good Thing: Raising Children of Character in an Indulgent Age* (New York: Hyperion, 2003).

122  **Four decades of research have:** Johannes Keller, "On the Development of Regulatory Focus: The Role of Parenting Styles," *European Journal of Social Psychology* 38, no. 2 (2008).

123  **Probably as a result, their kids:** Elizabeth Lecuyer and Gail M. Houck, "Maternal Limit-Setting in Toddlerhood: Socialization Strategies for the Development of Self-Regulation," *Infant Mental Health Journal* 27, no. 4 (2006); Gail M. Houckand and Elizabeth A. Lecuyer-Maus, "Maternal Limit Setting During Toddlerhood, Delay of

Gratification, and Behavioral Problems at Age Five," *Infant Mental Health Journal,* 25, no. 1 (2004).

123 **For example, in one study, children:** Although it follows that children with more self-control might elicit greater warmth from their caregivers (and kids with poor impulse control might elicit more punitive parenting practices), the study controlled for this effect over the long term and still found that parental warmth fosters self-discipline. Rebecca A. Colman, et al., "Early Predictors of Self-Regulation in Middle Childhood," *Infant and Child Development* 15, no. 4 (2006).

123 **Another study found that six-year-olds:** Jacobsen, Huss, Fendrich, Kruesi, and Ziegenhahn, from Lecuyer, "Maternal Limit-Setting in Toddlerhood: Socialization Strategies for the Development of Self-Regulation."

123 **In one study, mothers who engaged:** Holden from George W. Holden and Meredith J. West, "Proximate Regulation by Mothers: A Demonstration of How Differing Styles Affect Young Children's Behavior," *Child Development* 60, no. 1 (1989).

124 **Parents who habitually focus:** Promotion-focused parents are more likely to praise kids for positive behavior, whereas prevention-focused parents are more likely to criticize or yell at kids for bad behavior. Keller, "On the Development of Regulatory Focus: The Role of Parenting Styles."

124 **To be promotion focused, emphasize:** Nanmathi Manian, Alison A. Papadakis, Timothy J. Strauman, and Marilyn J. Essex, "The Development of Children's Ideal and Ought Self-Guides: Parenting, Temperament, and Individual Differences in Guide Strength," *Journal of Personality* 74, no. 6 (2006).

125 **Kids exercise their self-control:** Metcalfe and Mischel, "A Hot/Cool-System Analysis of Delay of Gratification: Dynamics of Willpower."

125 **They learn self-control by talking:** Ibid.

125 **This is a willpower technique that:** Elliot Aronson, "Review: Back to the Future: Retrospective Review of Leon Festinger's 'A Theory of Cognitive Dissonance,' " *American Journal of Psychology* 110, no. 1 (1997); J. Cooper and R. H. Fazio, "A New Look at Dissonance Theory," *Advances in Experimental Social Psychology* 17 (1984); Leon Festinger, *A Theory of Cognitive Dissonance* (Evanston, IL: Row Peterson, 1957); T. R. Shultz and M. R. Lepper, "Cognitive Dissonance Reduction as Constraint Satisfaction," *Psychological Review* 103, no. 2 (1996); Y. Trope and A. Fishbach, "Counteractive Self-Control in Overcoming Temptation," *Journal of Personality and Social Psychology* 79, no. 4 (2000); Troy and Sroufe, "Victimization among Preschoolers: Role of Attachment Relationship History."

125 **When a reward is covered up:** Walter Mischel and Ebbe B. Ebbesen, "Attention in Delay of Gratification," *Journal of Personality and Social Psychology* 16, no. 2 (1970).

125 **The key thing about this effective:** Lecuyer, "Maternal Limit-Setting in Toddlerhood: Socialization Strategies for the Development of Self-Regulation."

126 **In one study, researchers told kids:** Metcalfe and Mischel, "A Hot/Cool-System Analysis of Delay of Gratification: Dynamics of Willpower."

126 **Research shows that living in high-stress:** M. Rutter, "Psychosocial Resilience and Protective Mechanisms," *American Journal of Orthopsychiatry* 57 (1987).

126 **Turn off the boob tube:** V. C. Strasburger, "Children and TV Advertising: Nowhere to Run, Nowhere to Hide," *Journal of Developmental and Behavioral Pediatrics* 22, no. 3 (2001); Committee on Communications, "Children, Adolescents, and Advertising: Organizational Principles to Guide and Define the Child Health Care System and/or Improve the Health of All Children," *Pediatrics* 118, no. 6 (2006); A. M. Aachei-Mejia, et al., "Children with a TV in Their Bedroom at Higher Risk for Being Overweight," *International Journal of Obesity* 31, no. 4 (2007); Elizabeth Vanderwater, E. Beickham, and D. Lee, "Time Well Spent? Relating Television Use to Children's Free-Time Activities," *Pediatrics* 117, no. 2 (2008); F. J. Zimmerman, D. A. Christakis, and A. N. Meltzoff, "Television and DVD/Video Viewing in Children Younger Than 2 Years," *Archives of Pediatrics & Adolescent Medicine* 161, no. 5 (2007); D. A. Christakis, et al., "Television, Video, and Computer Game Usage in

Children under 11 Years of Age," *The Journal of Pediatrics* 145, no. 5 (2004); D. A. Christakis, et al., "Early Television Exposure and Subsequent Attentional Problems in Children," *Pediatrics* 113, no. 4 (2004); National Institute on Media and the Family, "Fact Sheet Children and Advertising" (2002), http://www.mediafamily.org/facts/facts_childadv.shtml; W. Gantz, et al., "Food for Thought: Television Food Advertising to Children in the United States" (2007), http://www.kff.org/entmedia/upload/7618.pdf.

127  **Self-regulation develops rapidly with:** Mischel, Shoda, and Rodriguez, "Delay of Gratification in Children"; Metcalfe and Mischel, "A Hot/Cool-System Analysis of Delay of Gratification: Dynamics of Willpower"; J. Altman and S. A. Bayer, *Development of the Cerebellar System: In Relation to Its Evolution, Structure, and Function* (Boca Raton, FL: CRC Press, 1997); Mischel, Shoda, and Rodriguez, "Delay of Gratification in Children"; Metcalfe and Mischel, "A Hot/Cool-System Analysis of Delay of Gratification: Dynamics of Willpower."

128  **Although the spare-the-rod-spoil-the-child generation:** Colman, et al., "Early Predictors of Self-Regulation in Middle Childhood."

128  **Lots of studies have found associations:** Ibid.

129  **Alphie Kohn, king of:** Alfie Kohn, *Punished by Rewards: The Trouble with Gold Stars, Incentive Plans, A's, Praise, and Other Bribes* (Boston: Houghton Mifflin Company, 1999).

129  **As Kohn says: "Don't move:** Kohn, *Punished by Rewards: The Trouble with Gold Stars, Incentive Plans, A's, Praise, and Other Bribes*, p. 230.

129  **When kids don't do what:** M. L. Hoffman, "Power Assertion by the Parent and Its Impact on the Child," *Child Development* 31 (1960).

STEP 8: ENJOY THE PRESENT MOMENT

133  **It also hurts students' school:** M. Napoli, P. R. Krech and L. C. Holley, "Mindfulness Training for Elementary School Students: The Attention Academy," *Journal of Applied School Psychology* 21, no. 1 (2005).

133  **Because emotional stress can:** John Medina, *Brain Rules: 12 Principles for Surviving and Thriving at Work, Home and School* (Seattle, WA: Pear Press, 2009).

133  **Mindful people tend to be:** K. W. Brown and R. M. Ryan, "The Benefits of Being Present: Mindfulness and Its Role in Psychological Well-Being," *Journal of Personality and Social Psychology* 84, no. 4 (2003); p. 832; S. L. Shapiro, G. E. Schwartz and G. Bonner, "Effects of Mindfulness-Based Stress Reduction on Medical and Premedical Students," *Journal of Behavioral Medicine* 21, no. 6 (1998), p. 592.

133  **More intense and frequent pleasant:** Brown, "The Benefits of Being Present: Mindfulness and Its Role in Psychological Well-Being."

134  **Kids who learn to be:** E. J. Langer, "A Mindful Education," *Educational Psychologist* 28, no. 1 (1993); Napoli, "Mindfulness Training for Elementary School Students: The Attention Academy," p. 101.

134  **One study showed that kids:** Napoli, "Mindfulness Training for Elementary School Students: The Attention Academy."

134  **Mindfulness cultivates:** D. J. Siegel, *The Mindful Brain: Reflection and Attunement in the Cultivation of Well-Being* (New York: W. W. Norton & Co., 2007).

134  **Jon Kabat-Zinn, the scientist:** J. Kabat-Zinn, "Mindfulness-Based Interventions in Context: Past, Present and Future," *Clinical Psychology: Science and Practice* 10 (2003), p. 145, as cited in K. E. Hooker and I. E. Fodor, "Teaching Mindfulness to Children," *Gestalt Review* 12, no. 1 (2008).

136  **Give each of your kids three raisins:** Adapted from J. Kabat-Zinn, *Full Catastrophe Living: Using the Wisdom of Your Body and Mind to Face Stress, Pain and Illness* (New York: Delacorte, 1990), p. 27.

137  **Sit in a chair:** Adapted from M. J. Ott, "Mindfulness Meditation in Pediatric Clinical Practice," *Pediatric Nursing* 28, no. 5 (2000), p. 489; Hooker, "Teaching Mindfulness to Children."

138  **A group of social workers:** N. N. Singh, G. E. Lanconi, A. S. W. Winton, J. Singh,

W. J. Curtis, R. G. Wahler, and K. M. McAleavey, "Mindful Parenting Decreases Aggression and Increases Social Behavior in Children with Developmental Disabilities," *Behavior Modification* 31, no. 6 (2007).

139 **If you want to become:** M. Kabat-Zinn and J. Kabat-Zinn, *Everyday Blessings: The Inner Work of Mindful Parenting* (New York: Hyperion, 1998).

140 **All told, over the last two:** Sandra L. Hofferth and John F. Sandberg, "Changes in American Children's Time 1981–1997," *Advances in Life Course Research* (2000).

140 **In the study where today's:** Smirnova and Gudareva, "Igra I Proizvol'nost' U Sovremennyh Doshkol'nikov" [Play and Intentionality in Today's Preschoolers].

140 **Researchers believe that this dramatic:** Manuilenko, "The Development of Voluntary Behavior in Preschool-Age Children"; Smirnova and Gudareva, "Igra I Proizvol'nost' U Sovremennyh Doshkol'nikov" [Play and Intentionality in Today's Preschoolers]; Smirnova, "Development of Will and Intentionality in Toddlers and Preschool-Aged Children."

140 **In addition to helping kids:** H. L. Burdette and R. C. Whitaker, "Resurrecting Free Play in Young Children: Looking Beyond Fitness and Fatness to Attention, Affiliation, and Affect," *Archives of Pediatrics and Adolescent Medicine* 159 (2005).

141 **"Neuroscientists, developmental biologists:** Stuart Brown and Christopher Vaughan, *Play: How It Shapes the Brain, Opens the Imagination, and Invigorates the Soul* (New York: Avery, 2009), p. 5.

141 **In one study, children attending:** Susanna Loeb, et al., "How Much Is Too Much? The Influence of Preschool Centers on Children's Social and Cognitive Development," *Economics of Education Review* 26, no. 1 (2007).

143 **Carol Dweck shows that kids:** Dweck, *Mindset: The New Psychology of Success.*

143 **In one study, when researchers first:** Samuel T. Hunter, Katrina E. Bedell, and Michael D. Mumford, "Climate for Creativity: A Quantitative Review," *Creativity Research Journal* 19, no. 1 (2007).

143 **Studies by children's health researcher:** Dimitri A. Christakis, "The Effects of Infant Media Usage: What Do We Know and What Should We Learn?" *Acta Paediatrica* 98, no. 1 (2008).

144 **Studies by Dutch researcher:** T. H. A. Van der Voort, *Television Violence: A Child's-Eye View* (New York: Elsevier, 1986).

144 **A study led by child development researcher:** M. N. Groves, J. K. Sawyers, and J. D. Moran, "Reward and Ideation Fluency in Preschool Children," *Early Childhood Research Quarterly,* no. 2 (1987).

145 **Savoring the present moment:** M. M. Tugade and B. L. Fredrickson, "Regulation of Positive Emotions: Emotion Regulation Strategies That Promote Resilience," *Journal of Happiness Studies* 8 (2007).

145 **Being in the habit:** Brown, "The Benefits of Being Present: Mindfulness and Its Role in Psychological Well-Being."

146 **Imagine that a specific event:** F. B. Bryant and J. Veroff, *Savoring: A New Model of Positive Experience* (Mahwah, NJ: Erlbaum, 2007).

146 **Practice being grateful:** J. K. Boehm and S. Lyubomirsky, "The Promise of Sustainable Happiness," in *Handbook of Positive Psychology,* 2nd ed., ed. S. J. Lopez (Oxford: Oxford University Press, in press), p. 16.

146 **Avoid multitasking:** M. Friedman and D. Ulmer, *Treating Type A Behavior and Your Heart* (New York: Ballantine Books, 1985), as cited in Bryant, *Savoring: A New Model of Positive Experience.*

146 **Practice labeling positive feelings:** Bryant, *Savoring: A New Model of Positive Experience,* p. 209.

146 **(One reason why women:** C. L. Gohm, "Mood Regulation and Emotional Intelligence: Individual Differences," *Journal of Personality and Social Psychology* 84 (2003), as cited in Bryant, *Savoring: A New Model of Positive Experience.*

147 **Share your positive feelings:** S. L. Gable, H. T. Reis, and A. J. Elliot, "Behavioral Activation and Inhibition in Everyday Life," *Journal of Personality and Social Psychology* 78, no. 6 (2000); C. A. Langston, "Capitalizing on and Coping with Daily-

Life Events: Expressive Responses to Positive Events," *Journal of Personality and Social Psychology* 67, no. 6 (1994).

147  **While savoring might also:** E. Diener, E. Sandvik, and W. Pavot, "Happiness Is the Frequency, Not the Intensity, of Positive Versus Negative Affect," in *Subjective Well-Being: An Interdisciplinary Perspective,* ed. F. Strack, M. Argyle, and N. Schwarz (Elmsford, NY: Pergamon Press, 1991).

147  **[A] person in flow is completely:** M. Csikszentmihalyi, *Finding Flow: The Psychology of Engagement with Everyday Life* (New York: Basic Books, 1997), pp. 31, 32; M. Csikszentmihalyi, K. Rathunde, and S. Whalen, *Talented Teenagers: The Roots of Success and Failure* (New York: Cambridge University Press, 1993).

148  **Flow is a form of mindfulness:** A. J. Elliott and C. S. Dweck, eds. *Handbook of Competence and Motivation* (New York: Guilford Press, 2005), p. 600.

148  **That's a key aspect:** J. Nakamura and M. Csikszentmihalyi, "The Concept of Flow," in *Handbook of Positive Psychology,* eds. C. R. Snyder and S. J. Lopez (London: Oxford University Press, 2002).

148  **kids learn to achieve flow:** M. Csikszentmihalyi, *Creativity: Flow and the Psychology of Discovery and Invention* (New York: Harper/Collins, 1996), p. 111.

148  **Frequent flow experiences:** S. P. Whalen, "Flow and the Engagement of Talent: Implications for Secondary Schooling," *NASSP Bulletin* 82, no. 595 (1998), p. 25.

148  **flow helps kids take pleasure:** Ibid.

148  **When challenges begin to exceed:** Nakamura, "The Concept of Flow," p. 90.

149  **As kids gain mastery:** Elliott, ed., *Handbook of Competence and Motivation*, p. 604.

149  **Kids need to be self-disciplined:** Whalen, "Flow and the Engagement of Talent: Implications for Secondary Schooling."

149  **Parenting style can also foster flow:** M. Csikszentmihalyi and B. Schneider, "Conditions for Optimal Development in Adolescence: An Experiential Approach," *Applied Developmental Science* 5, no. 3 (2001), p. 123.

## STEP 9: RIG THEIR ENVIRONMENT FOR HAPPINESS

151  **My favorite metaphor for:** Barry L. Alexander, et al., "Effect of Early and Later Colony Housing on Oral Ingestion of Morphine in Rats," *Pharmacology, Biochemistry & Behavior* 15 (1981); Robert Hercz, "Rat Trap: Why Canada's Drug Policy Won't Check Addiction," www.walrusmagazine.com/print/2007.12-health-rat-trap/.

152  **Studies with human subjects also:** For example, of the legions of people who get addicted to morphine during hospital stays, few remain addicted once discharged from the hospital. Once people aren't in pain anymore, most are happy to be off the drugs. Similarly, of the thousands of men who became addicted to heroin during the Vietnam War, 88 percent of them stopped using the drug without treatment once they were out of the war zone. Hercz, "Rat Trap: Why Canada's Drug Policy Won't Check Addiction."

154  **Jay Belsky, a British psychologist:** J. Belsky, "Quality, Quantity and Type of Child Care: Effects on Child Development in the USA," http://pro-kopf.de/fileadmin/Downloads/OC_37-Belsky-Effects_on_Child_Development.pdf.

155  **By the time kids are:** Ibid.

155  **Infants are more likely to develop:** NICHD Early Child Care Research Network, "The Effects of Infant Child Care on Infant-Mother Attachment Security: Results of the NICHD Study of Early Child Care," *Child Development* 68, no. 5 (1997); Belsky, "Quality, Quantity and Type of Child Care: Effects on Child Development in the USA."

155  **More harmonious interactions and:** NICHD Early Child Care Research Network, "Child Care and Mother-Child Interaction in the First Three Years of Life," *Developmental Psychology* 35, no. 6 (1999).

157  **And like center-based child care, the:** J. Belsky, "Quantity Counts: Amount of Child Care and Children's Socioemotional Development," *Journal of Developmental and Behavioral Pediatrics* 23, no. 3 (2002).

157  **Aggressive: more likely to:** NICHD Early Child Care Research Network, "Does

Amount of Time Spent in Child Care Predict Socioemotional Adjustment During the Transition to Kindergarten?" *Child Development* 74 (2003).

158   **When possible, reduce:** Yvonne M. Caldera and Sybil Hart, "Exposure to Child Care, Parenting Style and Attachment Security," *Infant and Child Development* 13, no. 1 (2004).

158   **It is better to focus on:** J. Belsky, "Quantity of Nonmaternal Care and Boys' Problem Behavior/Adjustment at Ages 3 and 5: Exploring the Mediating Role of Parenting," *Psychiatry: Interpersonal and Biological Processes* 62, no. 1 (1999).

161   **Play contributes in a huge way:** R. J. P. Teague, "Social Functioning in Preschool Children: Can Social Information Processing and Self-Regulation Skills Explain Sex Differences and Play a Role in Preventing Ongoing Problems?" (Brisbane, Australia, Griffith University, 2005).

161   **Child psychologists and education specialists:** N. Uren and K. Stagnitti, "Pretend Play, Social Competence and Involvement in Children Aged 5-7 Years: The Concurrent Validity of the Child-Initiated Pretend Play Assessment," *Australian Occupational Therapy Journal* 56 (2009).

161   **Children who engage in more:** E. W. Lindsey and M. J. Colwell, "Preschoolers' Emotional Competence: Links to Pretend and Physical Play," *Child Study Journal* 33, no. 1 (2003).

161   **Imaginary play helps kids embody:** M. Moore and S. Russ, "Pretend Play as a Resource for Children: Implications for Pediatricians and Health Professionals," *Journal of Developmental and Behavioral Pediatrics* 27 (2006).

161   **In addition, rough-and-tumble:** Lindsey, "Preschoolers' Emotional Competence: Links to Pretend and Physical Play."

161   **Increased emotional intelligence:** M. Bruder and L. Chen, "Measuring Social Competence in Toddlers: Play Tools for Learning," *Early Childhood Services* 1 (2007).

161   **Play increases the odds:** V. Gmitrova and J. Gmitrov, "The Impact of Teacher-Directed and Child-Directed Pretend Play on Cognitive Competence in Kindergarten Children," *Early Childhood Education Journal* 30 (2003); N. Uren and K. Stagnitti, "Pretend Play, Social Competence and Involvement in Children Aged 5-7 Years: The Concurrent Validity of the Child-Initiated Pretend Play Assessment," *Australian Occupational Therapy Journal* 56, no. 1 (2009).

162   **In addition, kids exercise logical:** J. A. Chafel, "The Play of Children: Developmental Processes and Policy Implications," *Child & Youth Care Forum* 20, no. 2 (1991).

162   **Fantasy play expands:** K. H. Rubin, "Fantasy Play: Its Role in the Development of Social Skills and Social Cognition," *New Directions for Child Development* 9 (1980); G. G. Fein, "Pretend Play in Childhood: An Integrative Review," *Child Development* 52, no. 4 (1981).

162   **When it comes to preschool:** D. Stipek, R. Feiler, D. Daniels, and S. Milburn, "Effects of Different Instructional Approaches on Young Children's Achievement and Motivation," *Child Development* 66 (1995).

163   **Avoid preschools that seem:** Ibid.

164   **Eight-year-olds recognize:** R. Banerjee and H. Dittmar, "Individual Differences in Children's Materialism: The Role of Peer Relations," *Personality and Social Psychology Bulletin* 34, no. 1 (2008).

164   **What's wrong with materialism?:** R. Banerjee and H. Dittmar, "Individual Differences in Children's Materialism: The Role of Peer Relations," *Personality and Social Psychology Bulletin* 34, no. 1 (2008); T. Kasser, "Frugality, Generosity, and Materialism in Children and Adolescents," in *What Do Children Need to Flourish?: Conceptualizing and Measuring Indicators of Positive Development*, eds. L. H. Lippman and K. A. Moore (New York: Springer Science + Business Media, 2005).

165   **Two things influence:** P. Rose and S. P. DeJesus, "A Model of Motivated Cognition to Account for the Link between Self-Monitoring and Materialism," *Psychology & Marketing* 24, no. 2 (2007); M. E. Goldberg, G. J. Gorn, L. A. Perrachio, and G. Bamossy, "Understanding Materialism among Youth," *Journal of Consumer Psychology* 13 (2003).

165  **The less obvious reason:** Rose, "A Model of Motivated Cognition to Account for the Link between Self-Monitoring and Materialism"; T. Kasser, *The High Price of Materialism* (Cambridge, MA: MIT Press, 2002).

165  **But if what kids are:** Kasser, *The High Price of Materialism*.

165  **Despite the popular belief:** A. Furnham and M. Argyle, *The Psychology of Money* (London: Routledge, 1998).

165  **Wealthier people tend to be healthier:** T. S. Langner and S. T. Michael, *Life Stress and Mental Health* (New York: Free Press, 1963); S. E. Mayer, *What Money Can't Buy: Family Income and Children's Life Chances* (Cambridge, MA: Harvard University Press, 1997).

166  **People with higher incomes experience:** J. B. Wilson, D. T. Ellwood, and J. Brooks-Gunn, "Welfare-to-Work through the Eyes of Children," in *Escape from Poverty*, ed. P. L. Chase-Lansdale and J. Brooks-Gunn (New York: Cambridge University Press, 1995); Mayer, *What Money Can't Buy: Family Income and Children's Life Chances*; D. Black, *The Behavior of Law* (New York: Academic Press, 1976).

166  **For adults, higher income is:** $50,000 is the most recent figure I've found, but it comes from a *Time* magazine poll (see Easterbrook 2005). Social scientists cite the point at which the correlations to be much lower—$15,000 annual income, or even $10,000: Ed Diener, et al., "The Relationship between Income and Subjective Well-Being: Relative or Absolute?" *Social Indicators Research* 28, no. 3 (1993); B. S. Frey and A. Stutzer, *Happiness and Economics: How the Economy and Institutions Affect Well-Being* (Princeton, NJ: Princeton University Press, 2002); G. Easterbrook, *The Progress Paradox: How Life Gets Better While People Feel Worse* (New York: Random House, 2003). This "point" is a subjective assessment of the leveling off, not a mathematical fact. Any way you look at it, the point is lower than most people would expect, though it is possibly higher than the median annual income in the United States, which in 2005 was $43,000 (Easterbrook, *The Progress Paradox: How Life Gets Better While People Feel Worse*).

166  **After our basic needs are accounted for:** Michael Argyle, "Causes and Correlates of Happiness," in *Well-Being: The Foundations of Hedonic Psychology*, eds. Daniel Kahneman, Ed Diener, and Norbert Schwarz (New York: Russell Sage Foundation, 1999); Ronald Inglehart, *Culture Shift in Advanced Industrial Society* (Princeton, NJ: Princeton University Press, 1990); David Myers, "Human Connections and the Good Life: Balancing Individuality and Community in Public Policy," in *Positive Psychology in Practice*, ed. P. Alex Linley and Stephen Joseph (Hoboken, NJ: Wiley, 2004), p. 642.

166  **Turns out that members of the Forbes 400:** E. Diener, J. Horwitz, and R. A. Emmons, "Happiness of the Very Wealthy," *Social Indicators Research* 16 (1985).

166  **Many are also sensitive to:** For example, studies show that "mass unemployment increases the incidence of physical punishment and child abuse": Jacques D. Lempers, Dania Clark-Lempers, and Ronald L. Simons, "Economic Hardship, Parenting, and Distress in Adolescence," *Child Development* 60, no. 1 (1989); Mayer, *What Money Can't Buy: Family Income and Children's Life Chances*, p. 120. However, this doesn't mean that economic hardship is causing abuse. Job loss is associated with many family changes, such as increased drug and alcohol abuse, which may actually be the cause of the abuse (——, *What Money Can't Buy: Family Income and Children's Life Chances*).

166  **My own research shows:** McLaughlin, "Buying Happiness: Family Income and Adolescent Subjective Well-Being."

167  **But then I found out:** American Academy of Pediatrics: Committee on Public Education, "Children, Adolescents, and Television," *Pediatrics* 107, no. 2 (2001).

167  **Fifty-nine percent of children:** Zimmerman, Christakis, and Meltzoff, "Television and DVD/Video Viewing in Children Younger Than 2 Years."

167  **It turns out that a large:** Vanderwater, Beickham, and Lee, "Time Well Spent? Relating Television Use to Children's Free-Time Activities"; Inge M. Ahammer and John P. Murray, "Kindness in the Kindergarten: The Relative Influence of Role Playing and Prosocial Television in Facilitating Altruism," *International Journal of Behav-*

*ioral Development* 2 (1979); Gantz et al., "Food for Thought: Television Food Advertising to Children in the United States"; Christakis, et al., "Early Television Exposure and Subsequent Attentional Problems in Children"; ———, "Television, Video, and Computer Game Usage in Children under 11 Years of Age"; "Children, Adolescents, and Advertising: Organizational Principles to Guide and Define the Child Health Care System and/or Improve the Health of All Children"; Strasburger, "Children and TV Advertising: Nowhere to Run, Nowhere to Hide"; Aachei-Mejia, et al., "Children with a TV in Their Bedroom at Higher Risk for Being Overweight"; "Fact Sheet Children and Advertising."

168  **Even videos that claim:** F. J. Zimmerman, D. A. Christakis, and A. N. Meltzoff, "Television and DVD/Video Viewing in Children Younger Than 2 Years," *Archives of Pediatrics & Adolescent Medicine* 161, no. 5 (2007).

168  **Boys who play sports video games:** C. Anderson and K. Dill, "Video Games and Aggressive Thoughts, Feelings, and Behavior in the Laboratory and in Life," *Journal of Personality and Social Psychology* 78, no. 4 (2000); K. Dill and C. Dill, "Video Game Violence: A Review of the Empirical Literature," *Aggression and Violent Behavior* 3, no. 4 (1998); J. Smith, "Playing the Blame Game," *Greater Good* 4, no. 4 (2008); Rene Weber, Ute Ritterfeld, and Klaus Mathiak, "Does Playing Violent Video Games Induce Aggression? Empirical Evidence of a Functional Magnetic Resonance Imaging Study," *Media Psychology* 8, no. 1 (2006).

168  **Watching a lot of television:** G. P. Moschis and G. A. Churchill, "Consumer Socialization: A Theoretical and Empirical Analysis," *Journal of Marketing Research* 15 (1978); G. P. Moschis and R. L. Moorse, "A Longitudinal Study of Television Advertising Effects," *Journal of Consumer Research* 9 (1982).

168  **Television viewing frequency:** Moschis, "Consumer Socialization: A Theoretical and Empirical Analysis."

170  **In fact, research demonstrates a strong:** John P. Robinson and Steven Martin, "What Do Happy People Do?" *Social Indicators Research* 89 (2008).

170  **In my own research:** McLaughlin, "Buying Happiness: Family Income and Adolescent Subjective Well-Being."

171  **Ironically (from the viewpoint of:** Jean M. Twenge, Liqing Zhang, and Charles Im, "It's Beyond My Control: A Cross-Temporal Meta-Analysis of Increasing Externality in Locus of Control, 1960–2002," *Personality and Social Psychology Review* 8, no. 3 (2004).

171  **We might be preventing pain:** S. Kobasa, "The Hardy Personality: Toward a Social Psychology of Stress in Health," in *Social Psychology of Health and Illness (Environment and Health)*, eds. G. G. Sanders and J. Suls (Hillsdale, NH: Lawrence Erlbaum Associates, 1982).

171  **It turns out that grit:** Angela Duckworth, et al., "Grit: Perseverance and Passion for Long-Term Goals," *Journal of Personality and Social Psychology* 92, no. 6 (2007).

171  **Grit was more important than:** Warren Warringham, "Measuring Personal Qualities in Admissions: The Context and the Purpose," *New Directions for Testing and Measurement* 17 (1983).

### STEP 10: EAT DINNER TOGETHER

173  **The benefits of family mealtimes:** Joseph A. Califano, "The Importance of Family Dinners III," *The National Center on Addiction and Substance Abuse at Columbia University* (2006).

173  **Studies show that kids who eat:** Marla E. Eisenberg, Rachel E. Olson, and Dianne Neumark-Sztainer, "Correlations between Family Meals and Psychosocial Well-Being among Adolescents," *Archives of Pediatrics & Adolescent Medicine* 158, no. 8 (2004); Lisa W. Foderaro, "Families with Full Plates, Sitting Down to Dinner," in the *New York Times* (nytimes.com, 2006); N. J. Summit, "Family Dinner Linked to Better Grades for Teens: Survey Finds Regular Meal Time Yields Additional Benefits," in *ABC News* (2005); Sally Squires, "To Eat Better, Eat Together" (*Washington Post*, 2005).

173   **And these associations hold:** M. Weinstein, *The Surprising Power of Family Meals: How Eating Together Makes Us Smarter, Stronger, Healthier, and Happier* (Hanover, NH: Steerforth Press, 2005).

174   **And so many social skills:** Lisa Ann Boyum and Ross D. Parke, "The Role of Family Emotional Expressiveness in the Development of Children's Social Competence," *Journal of Marriage and the Family* 57, no. 3 (1995).

174   **The research shows compelling:** Diane E. Beals and Patton O. Tabors, "Arboretum, Bureaucratic, and Carbohydrates: Preschoolers' Exposure to Rare Vocabulary at Home," in *Biennial Meeting of the Society for Research in Child Development* (New Orleans, LA: 1995).

174   **For example, a team at:** The Home-School Study of Language and Literacy Development was a longitudinal study led by Diane Beals and Patton Tabors that began with eighty-one low-income families with preschoolers. Dialogue between family members was observed and recorded over several years. This work was later replicated and extended by Zahava Weizman and Catherine Snow, and then by Rosalind Davidson in middle-class families. For an academic overview of many dinnertime studies, see Barbara Pan, Rivka Perlmann, and Catherine Snow, "Food for Thought: Dinner Table as a Context for Observing Parent-Child Discourse," in *Methods for Studying Language Production*, ed. Lise Menn and Nan Bernstein Ratner (Lawrence Erlbaum Associates, 2000). For more information about dinnertime written for a general audience, see Weinstein, *The Surprising Power of Family Meals: How Eating Together Makes Us Smarter, Stronger, Healthier, and Happier.* The original studies are Beals and Tabors, "Arboretum, Bureaucratic, and Carbohydrates: Preschoolers' Exposure to Rare Vocabulary at Home"; R. Davidson and C. Snow, "The Linguistic Environment of Early Readers," *Journal of Research in Childhood Education* 10, no. 1 (1995); Zahava O. Weizman and Catherine E. Snow, "Lexical Input as Related to Children's Vocabulary Acquisition: Effect of Sophisticated Exposure and Support for Meaning," *Developmental Psychology* 37, no. 2 (2001).

175   **Paul Rozin, an anthropologist:** P. Rozin and T. A. Vollmecke, "Food Likes and Dislikes," *Annual Review of Nutrition* 6 (1986).

176   **Nutritionist and psychologist Ellyn:** Ellyn Satter, "The Feeding Relationship," *Zero to Three Journal* 12, no. 5 (1992); ———, "Feeding Dynamics: Helping Children to Eat Well," *Journal of Pediatric Health Care* 9 (1995).

176   **Rituals, or any kind of:** Barbara H. Fiese, et al., "A Review of 50 Years of Research on Naturally Occurring Family Routines and Rituals: Cause for Celebration?" *Journal of Family Psychology* 16, no. 4 (2002); Eisenberg, Olson, and Neumark-Sztainer, "Correlations between Family Meals and Psychosocial Well-Being among Adolescents."

179   **You don't even have:** Robyn Fivush, et al., "Family Narratives and the Development of Children's Emotional Well-Being," in *Family Stories and the Lifecourse: Across Time and Generations,* eds. M. W. Pratt and B. E. Fiese (2003).

# BIBLIOGRAPHY

■ ■ ■ ■ ■ ■

Aachei-Mejia, A. M., M. R. Longacre, J. J. Gibson, M. L. Beach, L. T. Titus-Ernstoff, and M. A. Dalton. "Children with a TV in Their Bedroom at Higher Risk for Being Overweight." *International Journal of Obesity* 31, no. 4 (2007): 644–51.

Abel, M. H., and R. Hester. "The Therapeutic Effects of Smiling." In *An Empirical Reflection on the Smile,* edited by M. H. Abel. New York: Edwin Mellen Press, 2002, 217–53.

Abramson, L. Y., L. B. Alloy, B. L. Hankin, C. M. Clements, L. Zhu, M. E. Hogan, and W. G. Whitehouse. "Optimistic Cognitive Styles and Invulnerability to Depression." In *The Science of Optimism and Hope: Research Essays in Honor of Martin E. P. Seligman,* edited by J. E. Gillham. Radner, PA: Templeton Foundation Press, 2000.

Ahammer, Inge M., and John P. Murray. "Kindness in the Kindergarten: The Relative Influence of Role Playing and Prosocial Television in Facilitating Altruism." *International Journal of Behavioral Development* 2 (1979): 133–57.

Ainsworth, M. D. S., M. C. Blehar, E. Waters, and S. Wahl. *Patterns of Attachment.* Hillsdale, NJ: L. Erlbaum, 1978.

Alexander, Barry L., Patricia F. Beyerstein, Bruce K. Hadaway, and Robert B. Coambs. "Effect of Early and Later Colony Housing on Oral Ingestion of Morphine in Rats." *Pharmacology, Biochemistry & Behavior* 15 (1981): 571–76.

Allen, Joseph P., Susan Philliber, Scott Herrling, and Gabriel P. Kupermine. "Preventing Teen Pregnancy and Academic Failure: Experimental Evaluation of a Developmentally Based Approach." *Child Development* 64, no. 4 (1997): 729–42.

Allen, S., and K. Daly. "The Effects of Father Involvement: An Updated Research Summary of the Evidence." In *Report by Centre for Families, Work & Well-Being.* University of Guelph, 2007, 1–53.

Altman, J., and S. A. Bayer. *Development of the Cerebellar System: In Relation to Its Evolution, Structure, and Function.* Boca Raton, FL: CRC Press, 1997.

Amato, Paul R., Laura Spencer Loomis, and Alan Booth Source. "Parental Divorce, Marital Conflict, and Offspring Well-Being During Early Adulthood." *Social Forces* 73, no. 3 (1995): 895–915.

American Academy of Pediatrics: Committee on Public Education. "Children, Adolescents, and Television." *Pediatrics* 107, no. 2 (2001): 423–26.

Anderson, A. M. "Factors Influencing the Father-Infant Relationship." *Journal of Family Nursing* 2, no. 3 (1996): 306–24.

Anderson, C., and K. Dill. "Video Games and Aggressive Thoughts, Feelings, and Behavior in the Laboratory and in Life." *Journal of Personality and Social Psychology* 78, no. 4 (2000): 772–90.

Anderson, C., D. Keltner, and O. P. John. "Emotional Convergence between People over Time." *Journal of Personality and Social Psychology* 84, no. 5 (2003): 1054–68.

Argyle, Michael. "Causes and Correlates of Happiness." In *Well-Being: The Foundations of Hedonic Psychology,* edited by Daniel Kahneman, Ed Diener, and Norbert Schwarz. New York: Russell Sage Foundation, 1999: 353–73.

Ariely, D., and Z. Carmon. "Gestalt Characteristics of Experiences: The Defining Features of Summarized Events." *Journal of Behavioral Decision Making* 13, no. 2 (2000): 191–201.

Aronson, Elliot. "Review: Back to the Future: Retrospective Review of Leon Festinger's 'A Theory of Cognitive Dissonance.'" *American Journal of Psychology* 110, no. 1 (1997): 127–37.

Bandura, A., C. Barbaranelli, G. V. Caprara, and C. Pastorelli. "Self-Efficacy Beliefs as Shapers of Children's Aspirations and Career Trajectories." *Child Development* 72, no. 1 (2001): 187–206.

Bandura, A., and D. H. Schunk. "Cultivating Competence, Self-Efficacy, and Intrinsic Interest through Proximal Self-Motivation." *Journal of Personality and Social Psychology* 41, no. 3 (1981): 586–98.

Bandura, A., and R. Wood. "Impact of Conceptions of Ability on Self-Regulatory Mechanisms and Complex Decision Making." *Journal of Personality and Social Psychology* 56, no. 3 (1989): 407–15.

Banerjee, R., and H. Dittmar. "Individual Differences in Children's Materialism: The Role of Peer Relations." *Personality and Social Psychology Bulletin* 34, no. 1 (2008): 15.

Barsade, S. G. "The Ripple Effect: Emotional Contagion and Its Influence on Group Behavior." *Administrative Science Quarterly* 47, no. 4 (2002): 644–75.

Baumeister, R. F., M. Gailliot, and C. N. DeWall. "Self-Regulation and Personality: How Interventions Increase Regulatory Success, and How Depletion Moderates the Effects of Traits on Behavior." *Journal of Personality* 74, no. 6 (2006): 30.

Baumeister, R. F., and T. F. Heatherton. "Self-Regulation Failure: An Overview." *Psychological Inquiry* 7 (1996): 1–15.

Baumeister, Roy F., Todd F. Heatherton, Dianne M. Tice, Monique Boekaerts, Paul R. Pintrich, and Moshe Zeidner. "Losing Control: How & Why People Fail at Self-Regulation and Handbook of Self-Regulation." *Journal of Psychiatry and Law* 30, no. 2 (2002): 283–84.

Beals, Diane E., and Patton O. Tabors. "Arboretum, Bureaucratic, and Carbohydrates: Preschoolers' Exposure to Rare Vocabulary at Home." In *Biennial Meeting of the Society for Research in Child Development*. New Orleans, LA: 1995, 57–76.

Beck, M. *The Four-Day Win.* New York: Rodale Inc., 2007.

Begley, Sharon. *Train Your Mind, Change Your Brain.* New York: Random House, 2007.

Belsky, J. "Quality, Quantity and Type of Child Care: Effects on Child Development in the USA." http://pro-kopf.de/fileadmin/Downloads/OC_37-Belsky-Effects_on_Child_Development.pdf.

———. "Quantity Counts: Amount of Child Care and Children's Socioemotional Development." *Journal of Developmental and Behavioral Pediatrics* 23, no. 3 (2002): 167–70.

———. "Quantity of Nonmaternal Care and Boys' Problem Behavior/Adjustment at Ages 3 and 5: Exploring the Mediating Role of Parenting." *Psychiatry: Interpersonal and Biological Processes* 62, no. 1 (1999): 1–20.

Benson, Peter L., E. Gil Clary, and Peter C. Scales. "Altruism and Health: Is There a Link During Adolescence." In *Altruism and Health: Perspectives from Empirical Research*, edited by Stephen G. Post. New York: Oxford University Press, 2007.

Berman, M. G., J. Jonides, and S. Kaplan. "The Cognitive Benefits of Interacting with Nature." *Psychological Science* 19, no. 12 (2008): 1207–12.

Bernieri, F. J. "Coordinated Movement and Rapport in Teacher-Student Interactions." *Journal of Nonverbal Behavior* 12, no. 2 (1988): 120–38.

———. "Interpersonal Sensitivity in Teacher-Student Interactions." *Personality and Social Psychology Bulletin* 17, no. 1 (1991): 98–103.

Bianchi, Suzanne, John P. Robinson, and Melissa A. Milkie. *Changing Rhythms of American Family Life.* New York: Russell Sage Foundation, 2007.

Black, D. *The Behavior of Law.* New York: Academic Press, 1976.

Boehm, J. K., and S. Lyubomirsky. "The Promise of Sustainable Happiness." In *Handbook of Positive Psychology*, 2nd ed. Edited by S. J. Lopez. Oxford: Oxford University Press, in press.

Boggiano, A. K., and M. Barrett. "Gender Differences in Depression in Children as a Function of Motivational Orientation." *Sex Roles* 26, no. 1-2 (1992): 7.

Bonari, L., H. Bennett, A. Einarson, and G. Koren. "Risks of Untreated Depression During Pregnancy." *Canadian Family Physician* 50 (Jan 2004): 37–39.

Bono, G., M. E. McCullough, and L. M. Root. "Forgiveness, Feeling Connected to Others, and Well-Being: Two Longitudinal Studies." *Personality and Social Psychology Bulletin* 34, no. 2 (2008): 182–95.

Bowhm, Julia K., and Sonja Lyubomirsky. "Does Happiness Promote Career Success?" *Journal of Career Assessment* 16, no. 1 (2008): 101–16.

Boyum, Lisa Ann, and Ross D. Parke. "The Role of Family Emotional Expressiveness in the Development of Children's Social Competence." *Journal of Marriage and the Family* 57, no. 3 (1995): 593–608.

Branje, S. J. T., W. H. J. Meeus, and M. D. Van Doorn. "Longitudinal Transmission of Conflict Resolution Styles from Marital Relationships to Adolescent-Parent Relationships." *Journal of Family Psychology* 21, no. 3 (2007): 426–34.

Brody, G. H., S. R. H. Beach, R. A. Philibert, Y. Chen, M. Lei, and V. M. Murry. "Parenting Moderates a Genetic Vulnerability Factor in Longitudinal Increases in Youths' Substance Use." *Journal of Consulting and Clinical Psychology* 77, no. 1 (Feb 2009): 1–11.

Brown, K. W., and R. M. Ryan. "The Benefits of Being Present: Mindfulness and Its Role in Psychological Well-Being." *Journal of Personality and Social Psychology* 84, no. 4 (2003): 27.

Brown, Stuart, and Christopher Vaughan. *Play: How It Shapes the Brain, Opens the Imagination, and Invigorates the Soul*. New York: Avery, 2009.

Bruder, M., and L. Chen. "Measuring Social Competence in Toddlers: Play Tools for Learning." *Early Childhood Services* 1 (2007): 22.

Bryant, F. B., and J. Veroff. *Savoring: A New Model of Positive Experience*. Mahwah, NJ: Erlbaum, 2007.

Buckley, Norman, Linda S. Siegel, and Steven Ness. "Egocentrism, Empathy and Altruistic Behavior in Young Children." *Developmental Psychology* 5, no. 3 (1979): 329–31.

Burdette, H. L., and R. C. Whitaker. "Resurrecting Free Play in Young Children: Looking Beyond Fitness and Fatness to Attention, Affiliation, and Affect." *Archives of Pediatrics and Adolescent Medicine* 159 (2005): 5.

Butler, E. A., B. Egloff, F. H. Wilhelm, N. C. Smith, E. A. Erickson, and J. J. Gross. "The Social Consequences of Expressive Suppression." *Emotion* 3, no. 1 (2003): 48–67.

Byrne, R. *The Secret*. New York/Hillsboro, OR: Atria Books/Beyond Words, 2006.

Caldera, Yvonne M., and Sybil Hart. "Exposure to Child Care, Parenting Style and Attachment Security." *Infant and Child Development* 13, no. 1 (2004): 21–33.

Califano, Joseph A. "The Importance of Family Dinners III." *The National Center on Addiction and Substance Abuse at Columbia University* (2006): 1–17.

Call, Vaughn, Susan Sprecher, and Pepper Schwartz. "The Incidence and Frequency of Marital Sex in a National Sample." *Journal of Marriage and the Family* 57, no. 3 (1995): 639–52.

Campbell, S. B., P. Matestic, C. von Stauffenberg, R. Mohan, and T. Kirchner. "Trajectories of Maternal Depressive Symptoms, Maternal Sensitivity, and Children's Functioning at School Entry." *Developmental Psychology* 43, no. 5 (2007): 1202–15.

Carlo, Gustavo, Meredith McGinley, Rachel Hayes, Candice Batenhorst, and Jamie Wilkinson. "Parenting Styles or Practices? Parenting, Sympathy, and Prosocial Behaviors among Adolescents." *Journal of Genetic Psychology* 168, no. 2 (2007): 147–76.

Casas, Ferran, Germa Coenders, Robert Cummins, Monica Gonzalez, Cristina Figuer, and Sara Malo. "Does Subjective Well-Being Show a Relationship between Parents and Their Children?" *Journal of Happiness Studies* 9, no. 2 (2008): 197–205.

Chafel, J. A. "The Play of Children: Developmental Processes and Policy Implications." *Child & Youth Care Forum* 20, no. 2 (1991): 18.

Chen, D. "Preventing Violence by Promoting the Development of Competent Conflict Resolution Skills: Exploring Roles and Responsibilities." *Early Childhood Education Journal* 30, no. 4 (2003): 203–8.

Cherek, Don R., F. Gerard Moeller, Donald M. Dougherty, and Howard Rhoades. "Studies of Violent and Nonviolent Male Parolees: II. Laboratory and Psychometric Measurements of Impulsivity." *Biological Psychiatry* 41, no. 5 (1997): 523–29.

Christakis, D. A., F. Ebel, F. Rivara, and F. J. Zimmerman. "Television, Video, and Computer Game Usage in Children under 11 Years of Age." *Journal of Pediatrics* 145, no. 5 (2004): 652–56.

Christakis, D. A., F. J. Zimmerman, D. L. DiGiuseppe, and C. A. McCarthy. "Early Television Exposure and Subsequent Attentional Problems in Children." *Pediatrics* 113, no. 4 (2004): 708–13.

Christakis, Dimitri A. "The Effects of Infant Media Usage: What Do We Know and What Should We Learn?" *Acta Paediatrica* 98, no. 1 (2008): 8–16.

Cicchetti, D., and S. L. Toth. "The Development of Depression in Children and Adolescents." *American Psychologist* 53, no. 2 (1998): 221–42.

Colman, Rebecca A., Sam A. Hardy, Myesha Albert, Marcela Raffaelli, and Lisa Crocket. "Early Predictors of Self-Regulation in Middle Childhood." *Infant and Child Development* 15, no. 4 (2006): 421–37.

Colvin, Geoffrey. "What It Takes to Be Great." CNNMoney.com, http://money.cnn.com/magazines/fortune/fortune_archive/2006/10/30/8391794/index.htm.

Committee on Communications. "Children, Adolescents, and Advertising: Organizational Principles to Guide and Define the Child Health Care System and/or Improve the Health of All Children." *Pediatrics* 118, no. 6 (2006): 2563–69.

Cooper, J., and R. H. Fazio. "A New Look at Dissonance Theory." *Advances in Experimental Social Psychology* 17 (1984): 229–66.

Coussons-Read, M. E., M. L. Okun, and C. D. Nettles. "Psychosocial Stress Increases Inflammatory Markers and Alters Cytokine Production across Pregnancy." *Brain, Behavior, and Immunity* 21, no. 3 (Mar 2007): 343–50.

Cowan, C. P., and P. A. Cowan. *When Partners Become Parents: The Big Life Change for Couples.* Mahwah, NJ: Lawrence Erlbaum Associates, 2000.

Cowan, C. P., P. A. Cowan, M. K. Pruett, and K. Pruett. "An Approach to Preventing Coparenting Conflict and Divorce in Low-Income Families: Strengthening Couple Relationships and Fostering Fathers' Involvement." *Family Process* 46, no. 1 (2006): 109–21.

Cowan, P. A., and C. P. Cowan. "Strengthening Couples to Improve Children's Well-Being: What We Know Now." *Poverty Research News* 6, no. 3 (2002): 18–21.

Csikszentmikalyi, M. *Creativity: Flow and the Psychology of Discovery and Invention.* New York: Harper/Collins, 1996.

Csikszentmihalyi, M., K. Rathunde, and S. Whalen. *Talented Teenagers: The Roots of Success and Failure.* New York: Cambridge University Press, 1993.

Csikszentmihalyi, M. *Finding Flow: The Psychology of Engagement with Everyday Life.* New York: Basic Books, 1997.

Csikszentmikalyi, M., and B. Schneider. "Conditions for Optimal Development in Adolescence: An Experiential Approach." *Applied Developmental Science* 5, no. 3 (2001): 3.

Cummings, E. M., K. S. Simpson, and A. Wilson. "Children's Responses to Interadult Anger as a Function of Information About Resolution." *Developmental Psychology* 29, no. 6 (1993): 978–85.

Cummings, E. M., D. Vogel, J. S. Cummings, and M. el-Sheikh. "Children's Responses to Different Forms of Expression of Anger between Adults." *Child Development* 60, no. 6 (1989): 1392–404.

Davidson, R., and C. Snow. "The Linguistic Environment of Early Readers." *Journal of Research in Childhood Education* 10, no. 1 (1995): 5–21.

Davis, E. P., C. Hobel, C. A. Sandman, L. M. Glynn, and P. D. Wadhwa, eds. *Prenatal Stress and Stress Physiology Influence Human Fetal and Infant Development, Placenta and Brain, Birth and Behavior, Health and Disease.* Cambridge University Press, 2006.

Deci, E. L., R. Koestner, and R. M. Ryan. "A Meta-Analytic Review of Experiments Examining the Effects of Extrinsic Rewards on Intrinsic Motivation." *Psychological Bulletin* 125 (1999): 42.

de la Garza-Mercer, Felicia, Andrew Christensen, and Brian Doss. "Sex and Affection in

Heterosexual and Homosexual Couples: An Evolutionary Perspective." *Electronic Journal of Human Sexuality* (2006), http://www.ejhs.org/volume9/Garza.htm.

Diener, E., J. Horwitz, and R. A. Emmons. "Happiness of the Very Wealthy." *Social Indicators Research* 16 (1985): 263–74.

Diener, E., E. Sandvik, and W. Pavot. "Happiness Is the Frequency, Not the Intensity, of Positive Versus Negative Affect." In *Subjective Well-Being: An Interdisciplinary Perspective.* Edited by F. Strack, M. Argyle, and N. Schwarz. Elmsford, NY: Pergamon Press, 1991.

Diener, E., and M. E. P. Seligman. "Very Happy People." *Psychological Science* 13, no. 1 (2002): 81–84.

Diener, Ed, and Robert Biswas-Diener. *Happiness: Unlocking the Mysteries of Psychological Wealth.* Malden, MA: Blackwell Publishing, 2008.

Diener, Ed, Ed Sandvik, Larry Seidlitz, and Marissa Diener. "The Relationship between Income and Subjective Well-Being: Relative or Absolute?" *Social Indicators Research* 28, no. 3 (1993): 195–223.

Dill, K., and C. Dill. "Video Game Violence: A Review of the Empirical Literature." *Aggression and Violent Behavior* 3, no. 4 (1998): 407–28.

Dimberg, U., M. Thunberg, and K. Elmehed. "Unconscious Facial Reactions to Emotional Facial Expressions." *Psychological Science* 11, no. 1 (2000): 86–89.

Dixon, M., N. Booth, and R. Powell. "Sex and Relationships Following Childbirth: A First Report from General Practice of 131 Couples." *British Journal of General Practice* 50, no. 452 (2000): 223–24.

Doherty, N. A., and J. A. Feeney. "The Composition of Attachment Networks Throughout the Adult Years." *Personal Relationships* 11, no. 4 (2004): 469–88.

Duckworth, Angela, Christopher Peterson, Michael Matthews, and Dennis Kelly. "Grit: Perseverance and Passion for Long-Term Goals." *Journal of Personality and Social Psychology* 92, no. 6 (2007): 1087–101.

———. *Mindset: The New Psychology of Success.* New York: Random House, 2006.

Dweck, C. S., and M. L. Kamins. "Person Versus Process Praises and Criticism: Implications for Contingent Self-Worth and Coping." *Developmental Psychology* 35, no. 3 (1999): 835–47.

Dweck, C. S. "Caution—Praise Can Be Dangerous." In *Educational Psychology in Context: Readings for Future Teachers.* Edited by Bruce A. Marlowe and Alan S. Canestrari. SAGE, 2005.

Easterbrook, G. *The Progress Paradox: How Life Gets Better While People Feel Worse.* New York: Random House, 2003.

Eisenberg, Marla E., Rachel E. Olson, and Dianne Neumark-Sztainer. "Correlations between Family Meals and Psychosocial Well-Being among Adolescents." *Archives of Pediatrics & Adolescent Medicine* 158, no. 8 (2004): 792–96.

Eisenberg-Berg, Nancy, and Elizabeth Geisheker. "Content of Preachings and Power of the Model/Preacher: The Effect on Children Generosity." *Developmental Psychology* 15, no. 2 (1979): 168–85.

Ekman, P., R. J. Davidson, and W. V. Fiesen. "Emotional Expression and Brain Physiology: II." *Journal of Personality and Social Psychology* 58, no. 2 (1990): 342–53.

Elliott, A. J., and C. S. Dweck, eds. *Handbook of Competence and Motivation.* New York: Guilford Press, 2005.

Emmons, Robert A. "Pay It Forward." *Greater Good* (2007).

———. *The Psychology of Gratitude.* New York: Oxford University Press, 2004.

Emmons, Robert A., and Michael E. McCullough. "Counting Blessings Versus Burdens: An Experimental Investigation of Gratitude and Subjective Well-Being in Daily Life." *Journal of Personality and Social Psychology* 84, no. 2 (2003): 377–83.

Ericsson, K. A., R. T. Krampe, and C. Tesch-Romer. "The Role of Deliberate Practice in the Acquisition of Expert Performance." *Psychological Review* 100, no. 3 (1993): 363–406.

Feeney, J. A. "Implication of Attachment Style for Patterns of Health and Illness." *Child: Care, Health and Development* 26, no. 4 (2000): 277–288.

Fein, G. G. "Pretend Play in Childhood: An Integrative Review." *Child Development* 52, no. 4 (1981): 24.

Feng, Xin, Daniel S. Shaw, and Jennifer S. Silk. "Developmental Trajectories of Anxiety Symptoms among Boys across Early and Middle Childhood." *Journal of Abnormal Psychology* 117, no. 1 (2008): 32–47.

Feng, Xin, Daniel S. Shaw, Emily M. Skuban, and Tonya Lane. "Emotional Exchange in Mother-Child Dyads: Stability, Mutual Influence, and Associations with Maternal Depression and Child Problem Behavior." *Journal of Family Psychology* 21, no. 4 (2007): 714–25.

Festinger, Leon. *A Theory of Cognitive Dissonance*. Evanston, IL: Row Peterson, 1957.

Field, T. "Attachment and Separation in Young Children." *Annual Review in Psychology* 47 (1996): 541–61.

Fiese, Barbara H., Thomas J. Tomcho, Michael Douglas, Kimberly Josephs, Scott Poltrock, and Tim Baker. "A Review of 50 Years of Research on Naturally Occurring Family Routines and Rituals: Cause for Celebration?" *Journal of Family Psychology* 16, no. 4 (2002): 381–90.

Fischman, Susan H., Elizabeth A. Rankin, Elaren L. Soeken, and Elizabeth R. Lenz. "Changes in Sexual Relationships in Postpartum Couples." *Journal of Obstetric, Gynecologic, & Neonatal Nursing* 15, no. 1 (1986): 58–63.

Fitzsimons, G. J. "Asking Questions Can Change Choice Behavior: Does It Do So Automatically or Effortfully?" *Journal of Experimental Psychology* 6, no. 3 (2000): 12.

Fivush, Robyn, Jennifer Bohanek, Rachel Robertson, and Marshall Duke. "Family Narratives and the Development of Children's Emotional Well-Being." In *Family Stories and the Lifecourse: Across Time and Generations*. Edited by M. W. Pratt and B. E. Fiese (2003).

Flouri, E. "Fathering and Adolescents' Psychological Adjustment: The Role of Fathers' Involvement, Residence and Biology Status." *Child: Care, Health, and Development* 34, no. 2 (2007): 152–61.

Foderaro, Lisa W. "Families with Full Plates, Sitting Down to Dinner." In the *New York Times*: nytimes.com, 2006.

Fowler, J. H., and N. A. Christakis. "Dynamic Spread of Happiness in a Large Social Network: Longitudinal Analysis over 20 Years in the Framingham Heart Study." *British Medical Journal* 337, no. a2338 (2008).

Franck, Karen L., and Cheryl Beuehler. "A Family Process Model of Marital Hostility, Parental Depressive Affect, and Early Adolescent Problem Behavior: The Roles of Triangulation and Parental Warmth." *Journal of Family Psychology* 21, no. 4 (2007): 614–25.

Fredrickson, B. L. "Extracting Meaning from Past Affective Experiences: The Importance of Peaks, Ends, and Specific Emotions." *Cognition and Emotion* 14, no. 4 (2000): 577–606.

———. "Why Positive Emotions Matter in Organizations: Lessons from the Broaden-and-Build Model." *Psychologist-Manager Journal* 4, no. 2 (2000): 131–42.

Fredrickson, B. L., R. A. Mancuso, C. Branigan, and M. M. Tugade. "The Undoing Effect of Positive Emotions." *Motivation and Emotion* 24, no. 4 (2000): 237–58.

Fredrickson, Barbara L. *Positivity: Groundbreaking Research Reveals How to Embrace the Hidden Strength of Positive Emotions, Overcome Negativity, and Thrive*. New York: Crown Publishers, 2009.

Frey, B. S., and A. Stutzer. *Happiness and Economics: How the Economy and Institutions Affect Well-Being*. Princeton, NJ: Princeton University Press, 2002.

Friedman, M., and D. Ulmer. *Treating Type A Behavior and Your Heart*. New York: Ballantine Books, 1985.

Frost, Randy O., and Patricia A. Marten. "Perfectionism and Evaluative Threat." *Cognitive Therapy and Research* 14, no. 6 (1990): 559–72.

Frost, Randy O., Theresa A. Turcotte, Richard G. Heimberg, Jill I. Mattia, Craig S. Holt, and Debra A. Hope. "Reactions to Mistakes among Subjects High and Low in Perfectionistic Concern over Mistakes." *Cognitive Therapy and Research* 19, no. 2 (1995): 195–205.

Fujita, Frank, and Ed Diener. "Life Satisfaction Set Point: Stability and Change." *Journal of Personality and Social Psychology* 88, no. 1 (2005): 158–64.

Furnham, A., and M. Argyle. *The Psychology of Money.* London: Routledge, 1998.

Gable, S. L., H. T. Reis, and A. J. Elliot. "Behavioral Activation and Inhibition in Everyday Life." *Journal of Personality and Social Psychology* 78, no. 6 (2000): 15.

Gantz, W., N. Schwartz, J. Angelini, and V. Rideout. "Food for Thought: Television Food Advertising to Children in the United States." (2007), http://www.kff.org/entmedia/upload/7618.pdf.

Geoeke-Morey, Marcie C., E. Mark Cummings, and Lauren M. Papp. "Children and Marital Conflict Resolution: Implications for Emotional Security and Adjustment." *Journal of Family Psychology* 21, no. 4 (2007): 744–53.

Gladstone, G. L., and G. B. Parker. "When You're Smiling, Does the Whole World Smile for You?" *Australasian Psychiatry* 10, no. 2 (2002): 144–46.

Gladstone, T. R. G., and N. J. Kaslow. "Depression and Attributions in Children and Adolescents: A Meta-Analytic Review." *Journal of Abnormal Child Psychology* 23, no. 5 (1995): 597–606.

Gmitrova, V., and J. Gmitrov. "The Impact of Teacher-Directed and Child-Directed Pretend Play on Cognitive Competence in Kindergarten Children." *Early Childhood Education Journal* 30 (2003): 6.

Gohm, C. L. "Mood Regulation and Emotional Intelligence: Individual Differences." *Journal of Personality and Social Psychology* 84 (2003): 13.

Goldberg, M. E., G. J. Gorn, L. A. Perrachio, and G. Bamossy. "Understanding Materialism among Youth." *Journal of Consumer Psychology* 13 (2003): 11.

Goleman, Daniel. *Social Intelligence: The New Science of Human Relationships.* New York: Bantam Dell, 2006.

Gottfried, A. "Academic Intrinsic Motivation in Young Elementary School Children." *Journal of Educational Psychology* 82, no. 3 (1990): 14.

Gottman, J. M., L. F. Katz, and C. Hooven. *Meta-Emotion: How Families Communicate Emotionally.* Mahwah, NJ: Lawerence Erlbaum Associates, 1997.

Gottman, J. M., and Nan Silver. *The Seven Principles for Making Marriage Work.* New York: Crown Publishers, 1999.

Gottman, John, and Joan DeClaire. *Raising an Emotionally Intelligent Child.* New York: Simon & Schuster Paperbacks, 1997.

———. *What Predicts Divorce: The Relationship between Marital Processes and Marital Outcomes.* New York: Lawrence Erlbaum, 1994.

Groves, M. N., J. K. Sawyers, and J. D. Moran. "Reward and Ideation Fluency in Preschool Children." *Early Childhood Research Quarterly* no. 2 (1987): 332–40.

Haidt, J. *The Happiness Hypothesis: Finding Modern Truth in Ancient Wisdom.* New York: Basic Books, 2006.

Hammen, C., C. Adrian, and D. Hiroto. "A Longitudinal Test of the Attributional Vulnerability Model in Children at Risk for Depression." *British Journal of Clinical Psychology* 27 (1988): 37–46.

Harker, L., and D. Keltner. "Expressions of Positive Emotion in Women's College Yearbook Pictures and Their Relationship to Personality and Life Outcomes across Adulthood." *Journal of Personality and Social Psychology* 80, no. 1 (2001): 112–24.

Harlow, H. F., and M. A. Novak. "Psychopathological Perspectives." *Perspectives in Biology and Medicine* 16, no. 3 (1973): 461–78.

Harold, G. T., J. J. Aitken, and K. H. Shelton. "Inter-Parental Conflict and Children's Academic Attainment: A Longitudinal Analysis." *Journal of Child Psychology and Psychiatry* 48, no. 12 (2007): 1223–32.

Hatfield, E. "Emotional Contagion." *Current Directions in Psychological Science* 2, no. 3 (2008): 96–100.

Healy, Eileen D. *EQ and Your Child: 8 Proven Skills to Increase Your Child's Emotional Intelligence.* San Carlos, CA: Familypedia Publishing, 2005.

Hercz, Robert. "Rat Trap: Why Canada's Drug Policy Won't Check Addiction." www.walrusmagazine.com/print/2007.12-health-rat-trap/.

Hess, U., and S. Blairy. "Facial Mimicry and Emotional Contagion to Dynamic Emotional

Facial Expressions and Their Influence on Decoding Accuracy." *International Journal of Psychophysiology* 40, no. 2 (2001): 129–41.

Hills, P., and M. Argyle. "Positive Moods Derived from Leisure and Their Relationship to Happiness and Personality." *Personality and Individual Differences* 25, no. 3 (1998): 523–35.

Hofferth, Sandra L., and John F. Sandberg. "Changes in American Children's Time 1981–1997." *Advances in Life Course Research* (2000): 1–49.

Hoffman, M. L. "Power Assertion by the Parent and Its Impact on the Child." *Child Development* 31 (1960): 129–43.

Hoffman, Martin L. "Altruistic Behavior and the Parent-Child Relationship." *Journal of Personality and Social Psychology* 31, no. 5 (1975): 937–43.

Holden, George W., and Meredith J. West. "Proximate Regulation by Mothers: A Demonstration of How Differing Styles Affect Young Children's Behavior." *Child Development* 60, no. 1 (1989): 64–69.

Hooker, K. E., and I. E. Fodor. "Teaching Mindfulness to Children." *Gestalt Review* 12, no. 1 (2008): 17.

Houck, Gail M., and Elizabeth A. Lecuyer-Maus. "Maternal Limit Setting During Toddlerhood, Delay of Gratification, and Behavioral Problems at Age Five." *Infant Mental Health Journal* 25, no. 1 (2004): 28–46.

Howe, Michael J. A., Jane W. Davidson, and John A. Sloboda. "Innate Talents: Reality or Myth?" *Behavioral and Brain Sciences* 21 (1998): 399–442.

Huang, Julie Y., and John A. Bargh. "Peak of Desire: Activating the Mating Goal Changes Life-Stage Preferences across Living Kinds." *Psychological Science* 19, no. 6 (2008): 573–78.

Hunter, Samuel T., Katrina E. Bedell, and Michael D. Mumford. "Climate for Creativity: A Quantitative Review." *Creativity Research Journal* 19, no. 1 (2007): 69–90.

Inglehart, Ronald. *Culture Shift in Advanced Industrial Society.* Princeton, NJ: Princeton University Press, 1990.

Johnson, D. W., R. Johnson, B. Dudley, and K. Acikgoz. "Effects of Conflict Resolution Training on Elementary School Students." *Journal of Social Psychology* 134, no. 6 (2001): 803–17.

Johnson, David P., David L. Penn, Barbara L. Fredrickson, Piper S. Meyer, Ann M. Kring, and Mary Brantley. "Loving-Kindness Meditation to Enhance Recovery from Negative Symptoms of Schizophrenia." *Journal of Clinical Psychology* 65, no. 5 (2009): 499–509.

Joiner, T. E., and K. D. Wagner. "Attributional Style and Depression in Children and Adolescents: A Meta-Analytic Review." *Clinical Psychology Review* 15, no. 8 (1995): 777–98.

Jorge, Moll, Frank Krueger, Roland Zahn, Matteo Pardini, Ricardo de Oliveira-Souza, and Jordan Grafman. "Human Fronto-Mesolimbic Networks Guide Decisions About Charitable Donation." *Proceedings of the National Academy of Sciences of the United States of America* 103, no. 42 (2006): 15623–28.

Joussemet, Mireille, Richard Koestner, Natasha Lekes, and Nathalie Houlfort. "Introducing Uninteresting Tasks to Children: A Comparison of the Effects of Rewards and Autonomy Support." *Journal of Personality* 72, no. 1 (2004): 139–66.

Kabat-Zinn, J. *Full Catastrophe Living: Using the Wisdom of Your Body and Mind to Face Stress, Pain and Illness.* New York: Delacorte, 1990.

———. "Mindfulness-Based Interventions in Context: Past, Present and Future." *Clinical Psychology: Science and Practice* 10 (2003): 13.

Kabat-Zinn, M., and J. Kabat-Zinn. *Everyday Blessings: The Inner Work of Mindful Parenting.* New York: Hyperion, 1998.

Kahneman, D., B. L. Fredrickson, C. A. Schreiber, and D. A. Redelmeier. "When More Pain Is Preferred to Less: Adding a Better End." *Psychological Science* 4, no. 6 (1993): 401–5.

Kasser, T. "Frugality, Generosity, and Materialism in Children and Adolescents." In *What Do Children Need to Flourish? Conceptualizing and Measuring Indicators of Positive*

*Development*. Edited by K. A. Moore and L. H. Lippman. New York: Springer Science + Business Media, 2005.

———. *The High Price of Materialism*. Cambridge, MA: MIT Press, 2002.

Kawamura, Kathleen Y., Sandra L. Hunt, Randy O. Frost, and Patricia Marten DiBartolo. "Perfectionism, Anxiety, and Depression: Are the Relationships Independent?" *Cognitive Therapy and Research* 25, no. 3 (2001): 291–301.

Keller, Johannes. "On the Development of Regulatory Focus: The Role of Parenting Styles." *European Journal of Social Psychology* 38, no. 2 (2008): 354–64.

Keltner, Dacher. *Born to Be Good: The Science of a Meaningful Life*. New York: W. W. Norton & Company, 2009.

Kindlon, Daniel J. *Too Much of a Good Thing: Raising Children of Character in an Indulgent Age*. New York: Hyperion, 2003.

Knafo, Ariel, and Robert Plomin. "Parental Discipline and Affection and Children's Prosocial Behavior: Genetic and Environmental Links." *Journal of Personality and Social Psychology* 90, no. 1 (2006): 147–64.

———. "Prosocial Behavior from Early to Middle Childhood: Genetic and Environmental Influences on Stability and Change." *Developmental Psychology* 42, no. 5 (2006): 771–786.

Kobasa, S. "The Hardy Personality: Toward a Social Psychology of Stress in Health." In *Social Psychology of Health and Illness (Environment and Health)*. Edited by G. G. Sanders and J. Suls. Hillsdale, NJ: Lawrence Erlbaum Associates, 1982.

Kohn, Alfie. *Punished by Rewards: The Trouble with Gold Stars, Incentive Plans, A's, Praise, and Other Bribes*. Boston: Houghton Mifflin Company, 1999.

Koutsos, P., E. H. Wertheim, and J. Kornblum. "Paths to Interpersonal Forgiveness: The Roles of Personality, Disposition to Forgive and Contextual Factors in Predicting Forgiveness." *Personality and Individual Differences* 44, no. 2 (2008): 337–48.

Krause, Neal. "Church-Based Social Support and Mortality." *Journal of Gerontology* 61B, no. 3 (2006): S140-S146.

Krause, Neal, Christopher G. Ellison, and Keith M. Wuff. "Church-Based Emotional Support, Negative Interaction, and Psychological Well-Being: Findings from a National Sample of Presbyterians." *Journal for the Scientific Study of Religion* 37, no. 4 (1998): 725–41.

Lamb, M. E. "Attachments, Social Networks, and Developmental Contexts." *Human Development* 48 (2005): 108–12.

Langer, E. J. "A Mindful Education." *Educational Psychologist* 28, no. 1 (1993): 8.

Langner, T. S., and S. T. Michael. *Life Stress and Mental Health*. New York: Free Press, 1963.

Langston, C. A. "Capitalizing on and Coping with Daily-Life Events: Expressive Responses to Positive Events." *Journal of Personality and Social Psychology* 67, no. 6 (1994): 14.

Latham, G. P., and E. A. Locke. "Self-Regulation through Goal Setting." *Organizational Behavior and Human Decision Processes* 50 (1991): 36.

Lazare, Aaron. "Making Peace through Apology." *Greater Good* (2004): 16–19.

———. *On Apology*. New York: Oxford University Press, 2005.

Lecuyer, Elizabeth, and Gail M. Houck. "Maternal Limit-Setting in Toddlerhood: Socialization Strategies for the Development of Self-Regulation." *Infant Mental Health Journal* 27, no. 4 (2006): 344–70.

Lempers, Jacques D., Dania Clark-Lempers, and Ronald L. Simons. "Economic Hardship, Parenting, and Distress in Adolescence." *Child Development* 60, no. 1 (1989): 25–39.

Lewis, Jone Johnson. "Diane Ackerman Quotes." http://womenshistory.about.com/od/quotes/a/ackerman.htm.

Lindsey, E. W., and M. J. Colwell. "Preschoolers' Emotional Competence: Links to Pretend and Physical Play." *Child Study Journal* 33, no. 1 (2003): 14.

Loeb, Susanna, Margaret Bridges, Daphna Bassok, Brue Fuller, and Russell W. Rumberger. "How Much Is Too Much? The Influence of Preschool Centers on Children's Social and Cognitive Development." *Economics of Education Review* 26, no. 1 (2007): 52–66.

Loehr, J., and T. Schwartz. *The Power of Full Engagement*. New York: Free Press, 2003.

Losada, M. "The Complex Dynamics of High Performance Teams." *Mathematical and Computer Modeling* 30, no. 9–10 (1999): 179–92.

Losada, M., and E. Heaphy. "The Role of Positivity and Connectivity in the Performance of Business Teams: A Nonlinear Dynamics Model." *American Behavioral Scientist* 47, no. 6 (2004): 740–65.

Luks, Allan. "Doing Good: Helper's High." *Psychology Today* 22, no. 10 (1988).

Luskin, Frederic. "The Choice to Forgive." *Greater Good* (2004): 13–15.

———. *Forgive for Good*. New York: HarperCollins, 2003.

Luthar, Suniya S. "The Culture of Affluence: Psychological Costs of Material Wealth." *Child Development* 74, no. 6 (2003): 1581–93.

Luthar, Suniya S., and Bronwyn E. Becker. "Privileged but Pressured? A Study of Affluent Youth." *Child Development* 73, no. 5 (2002): 1593–610.

Luthar, Suniya S., and K. D'Avanzo. "Contextual Factors in Substance Use: A Study of Suburban and Inner-City Adolescents." *Development and Psychopathology* 11 (1999): 845–67.

Luthar, Suniya S., and S. Latendresse. "Children of the Affluent: Challenges to Well-Being." *American Psychological Society* 14, no. 1 (2005): 49–53.

Luthar, Suniya S., and C. C. Sexton. "The High Price of Affluence." In *Advances in Child Development and Behavior*. Edited by R. Kail. San Diego, CA: Academic Press, 2005.

Lyubomirsky, S., L. A. King, and E. Diener. "The Benefits of Frequent Positive Affect: Does Happiness Lead to Success?" *Psychological Bulletin* 131 (2005): 803–55.

———. "Pursuing Happiness: The Architecture of Sustainable Change." *Review of General Psychology* 9, no. 2 (2005): 111–31.

Lyubomirsky, Sonja. *The How of Happiness: A Scientific Approach to Getting the Life You Want*. New York: Penguin Press, 2007.

Madden, G. J., N. M. Petry, G. J. Badger, and Warren K. Bickel. "Impulsive and Self-Control Choices in Opioid-Dependent Patients and Non-Drug-Using Control Patients: Drug and Monetary Rewards." *Experimental and Clinical Psychopharmacology* 5, no. 3 (1997): 256–62.

Magen, Zipora. "Commitment Beyond Self and Adolescence." *Social Indicators Research* 37 (1996): 235–67.

Manian, Nanmathi, Alison A. Papadakis, Timothy J. Strauman, and Marilyn J. Essex. "The Development of Children's Ideal and Ought Self-Guides: Parenting, Temperament, and Individual Differences in Guide Strength." *Journal of Personality* 74, no. 6 (2006): 619–645.

Manuilenko, Z. V. "The Development of Voluntary Behavior in Preschool-Age Children." *Soviet Psychology* 13 (1948/1975).

Marano, Hara Estroff. "Pitfalls of Perfectionism." *Psychology Today* (2008).

Maruyama, Geoffrey, Scott C. Fraser, and Norman Miller. "Personal Responsibility and Altruism in Children." *Journal of Personality and Social Psychology* 42, no. 4 (1982): 658–64.

Mayer, S. E. *What Money Can't Buy: Family Income and Children's Life Chances*. Cambridge, MA: Harvard University Press, 1997.

McClelland, D. C., and C. Kirshnit. "The Effect of Motivational Arousal through Films on Salivary Immunoglobulin A." *Psychology & Health* 2, no. 1 (1988): 31–52.

McCullough, M. E., G. Bono, and L. M. Root. "Rumination, Emotion, and Forgiveness: Three Longitudinal Studies." *Journal of Personality and Social Psychology* 92, no. 3 (2007): 490–505.

McCullough, M. E., E. L. Worthington, and K. C. Rachal. "Interpersonal Forgiving in Close Relationships." *Journal of Personality and Social Psychology* 73, no. 2 (1997): 321–36.

McCullough, Michael E. "Forgiveness: Who Does It and How Do They Do It?" *Current Directions in Psychological Science* 10, no. 6 (2002): 194–97.

McCullough, Michael E., and Robert A. Emmons. "The Grateful Disposition: A Conceptual and Empirical Topography." *Journal of Personality and Social Psychology* 82, no. 1 (2002): 112–27.

McCullough, Michael E., and Charlotte van Oyen Witvliet. "The Psychology of Forgiveness." In *Handbook of Positive Psychology.* Edited by C. R. Snyder and S. J. Lopez. New York: Oxford University Press, 2002.

McGurk, Harry, Marlene Caplan, Elilis Hennessy, and Peter Moss. "Controversy, Theory and Social Context in Contemporary Day Care Research." *Journal of Child Psychology and Psychiatry* 34, no. 1 (1993): 3–23.

McLaughlin, Christine Carter. "Buying Happiness: Family Income and Adolescent Subjective Well-Being." Berkeley: University of California, Berkeley, 2007.

Medina, John. *Brain Rules: 12 Principles for Surviving and Thriving at Work, Home and School.* Seattle, WA: Pear Press, 2009.

Meltzoff, A. N. "Imitation and Other Minds: The 'Like Me' Hypothesis." In *Perspectives on Imitation: From Cognitive Neuroscience to Social Science.* Edited by S. Hurley and N. Chater. Cambridge, MA: MIT Press, 2005, 55–77.

Metcalfe, J., and W. Mischel. "A Hot/Cool-System Analysis of Delay of Gratification: Dynamics of Willpower." *Psychological Review* 106, no. 1 (1999): 3–19.

Mikulincer, Mario, Phillip R. Shaver, and Dana Pereg. "Attachment Theory and Affect Regulation: The Dynamics, Development, and Cognitive Consequences of Attachment-Related Strategies." *Motivation and Emotion* 27, no. 2 (2003): 77–102.

Miller, C. "Teaching the Skills of Peace: More Elementary and Preschools Are Going Beyond 'Conflict Resolution' to Teach Positive Social Behavior." *Children's Advocate* (2001), http://www.4children.org/news/501teach.htm.

Miller, Gregory E., and Carsten Wrosch. "You've Gotta Know When to Fold 'em: Goal Disengagement and Systemic Inflammation in Adolescence." *Psychological Science* 19, no. 9 (2007): 773.

Mischel, W. "Delay of Gratification, Need for Achievement, and Acquiescence in Another Culture." *Journal of Abnormal and Social Psychology* 62, no. 3 (1961): 543–52.

Mischel, W., and C. Gilligan. "Delay of Gratification, Motivation for the Prohibited Gratification, and Responses to Temptation." *Journal of Abnormal Social Psychology* 69, no. 4 (1964): 411–17.

Mischel, W., and R. Metzner. "Preference for Delayed Reward as a Function of Age, Intelligence, and Length of Delay Interval." *Journal of Abnormal Social Psychology* 64, no. 6 (1962): 425–31.

Mischel, W., Y. Shoda, and M. L. Rodriguez. "Delay of Gratification in Children." *Science* 244, no. 4907 (1989): 933–38.

Mischel, Walter, and Ebbe B. Ebbesen. "Attention in Delay of Gratification." *Journal of Personality and Social Psychology* 16, no. 2 (1970): 329–37.

Moore, K. A., E. C. Hair, S. Vandivere, C. B. McPhee, M. McNamara, and T. Ling. "Depression among Moms: Prevalence, Predictors, and Acting Out among Third-Grade Children." Washington, DC: Child Trends, 2006.

Moore, M., and S. Russ. "Pretend Play as a Resource for Children: Implications for Pediatricians and Health Professionals." *Journal of Developmental and Behavioral Pediatrics* 27 (2006): 12.

Morrison, Donna Ruane, and Mary Jo Coiro. "Parental Conflict and Marital Disruption: Do Children Benefit When High Conflict Marriages Are Dissolved?" *Journal of Marriage and the Family* 61, no. 3 (1999): 626–37.

Moschis, G. P., and G. A. Churchill. "Consumer Socialization: A Theoretical and Empirical Analysis." *Journal of Marketing Research* 15 (1978): 11.

Moschis, G. P., and R. L. Moorse. "A Longitudinal Study of Television Advertising Effects." *Journal of Consumer Research* 9 (1982): 8.

Mueller, C. M., and C. S. Dweck. "Praise for Intelligence Can Undermine Children's Motivation and Performance." *Journal of Personality and Social Psychology* 75, no. 1 (1998): 33–52.

Muraven, M., R. F. Baumeister, and D. M. Tice. "Longitudinal Improvement of Self-Regulation through Practice: Building Self-Control Strength through Repeated Exercise." *Journal of Social Psychology* 139, no. 4 (1999): 12.

Musick, Marc A., and John Wilson. "Volunteering and Depression: The Role of Psychological and Social Resources in Different Age Groups." *Social Science & Medicine* 56
(2003): 259–69.

Myers, D. G. *The American Paradox: Spiritual Hunger in an Age of Plenty.* New Haven, CT:
Yale University Press, 2000.

Myers, David. "Human Connections and the Good Life: Balancing Individuality and Community in Public Policy." In *Positive Psychology in Practice.* Edited by P. Alex Linley
and Stephen Joseph. Hoboken, NJ: Wiley, 2004, 641–57.

Nakamura, J., and M. Csikszentmihalyi. "The Concept of Flow." In *Handbook of Positive
Psychology.* Edited by C. R. Snyder and S. J. Lopez. London: Oxford University Press,
2002, 89–105.

Napoli, M., P. R. Krech, and L. C. Holley. "Mindfulness Training for Elementary School
Students: The Attention Academy." *Journal of Applied School Psychology* 21, no. 1
(2005): 27.

National Institute on Media and the Family. "Fact Sheet Children and Advertising" (2002),
http://www.mediafamily.org/facts/facts_childadv.shtml.

Neal, D. T., W. Wood, and J. M. Quinn. "Habits—a Repeat Performance." *Current Directions in Psychological Sciences* 15, no. 4 (2006): 5.

NICHD. "Does Amount of Time Spent in Child Care Predict Socioemotional Adjustment
During the Transition to Kindergarten?" *Child Development* 74 (2003): 976–1005.

———. Early Child Care Research Network. "Child Care and Mother-Child Interaction
in the First Three Years of Life." *Developmental Psychology* 35, no. 6 (1999): 1399–
413.

———. "The Effects of Infant Child Care on Infant-Mother Attachment Security: Results
of the NICHD Study of Early Child Care." *Child Development* 68, no. 5 (1997): 860–
79.

Nolen-Howksema, S., J. S. Girgus, and M. E. P. Seligman. "Depression in Children of
Families in Turmoil." Unpublished manuscript, University of Pennsylvania (1986).

Norcross, J., M. Mrykalo, and M. Blagys. "Auld Lang Syne: Success Predictors, Change
Processes, and Self-Reported Outcomes of New Year's Resolvers and Nonresolvers."
*Journal of Clinical Psychology* 58 (2002): 9.

Norcross, J., and D. Vangarelli. "The Resolution Solution: Longitudinal Examination of
New Year's Change Attempts." *Journal of Substance Abuse* 1 (1989): 8.

Oishi, Shigehiro, Ed Diener, and Richard E. Lucas. "The Optimum Level of Well-Being:
Can People Be Too Happy?" *Perspectives on Psychological Science* 2, no. 4 (2007):
346–60.

Oman, Doug, Carl E. Thoresen, and Kay McMahon. "Volunteerism and Mortality among
the Community-Dwelling Elderly." *Journal of Health Psychology* 4, no. 3 (1999): 301–
16.

Ott, M. J. "Mindfulness Meditation in Pediatric Clinical Practice." *Pediatric Nursing* 28,
no. 5 (2000): 4.

Palkovitz, R. "Reconstructing 'Involvement': Expanding Conceptualizations of Men's Caring in Contemporary Families." In *Generative Fathering: Beyond Deficit Perspectives.*
Edited by A. J. Hawkins and D. C. Dollahite. Thousand Oaks, CA: Sage, 1997, 200–
16.

Pamuk, E., D. Makuc, K. Heck, C. Reuben, and K. Lochner. *Socioeconomic Status and
Health Chartbook: Health, United States, 1998.* Hyattsville, MD: National Center for
Health Statistics, 1998.

Pan, Barbara, Rivka Perlmann, and Catherine Snow. "Food for Thought: Dinner Table as a
Context for Observing Parent-Child Discourse." In *Methods for Studying Language
Production.* Edited by Lise Menn and Nan Bernstein Ratner. Hillsdale, NJ: Lawrence
Erlbaum Associates, 2000, 205–24.

Papa, A., and G. A. Bonanno. "The Face of Adversity: The Interpersonal and Intrapersonal
Functions of Smiling." *Emotion* 8, no. 1 (2008): 1–12.

Parker-Pope, Tara. "Is It Love or Mental Illness? They're Closer Than You Think." *Wall
Street Journal* (February 13, 2007): D1.

Pearlman, C. "Finding the 'Win-Win': Nonviolent Communication Skills Help Kids—and

Adults—Resolve Conflicts in Ways That Work for Everybody." *Children's Advocate* (2007), www.4children.org/news/1107hcone.htm.

Peterson, Bill E. "Generativity and Successful Parenting: An Analysis of Young Adult Outcomes." *Journal of Personality* 74, no. 3 (2006): 847–69.

Peterson, C., M. E. P. Seligman, and G. E. Vaillant. "Pessimistic Explanatory Style Is a Risk Factor for Physical Illness: A Thirty-Five-Year Longitudinal Study." *Journal of Personality and Social Psychology* 55, no. 3 (1988): 23–27.

Pierrehumbert, B., R. J. Iannoti, E. M. Cummings, and C. Zahn-Waxler. "Social Functioning with Mother and Peers at 2 and 5 Years: The Influence of Attachment." *International Journal of Behavioral Development* 12, no. 1 (1989): 85–100.

Polak, Emily L., and Michael E. McCullough. "Is Gratitude an Alternative to Materialism?" *Journal of Happiness Studies* 7, no. 3 (2006): 343–60.

Post, Stephen G. "Altruism, Happiness, and Health: It's Good to Be Good." *International Journal of Behavioral Medicine* 12, no. 2 (2005): 66–77.

Post, Stephen, and Jill Neimark. *Why Good Things Happen to Good People*. New York: Broadway Books, 2007.

Pressley, M., W. M. Reynolds, K. D. Stark, and M. Gettinger. "Cognitive Strategy Training and Children's Self-Control." *Cognitive Strategy Research: Psychological Foundations*. Edited by M. Pressley and J. R. Levin. New York: Springer-Verlag, 1983.

Prochaska, J., and C. DiClemente. *Changing for Good*. New York: Collins, 2006.

Prochaska, J., C. DiClemente, and J. C. Norcross. "In Search of How People Change." *American Psychologist* 47, no. 9 (1992): 13.

Putnam, Robert D. *Bowling Alone: The Collapse and Revival of American Community*. New York: Simon & Schuster, 2001.

Ratey, John J., and Eric Hagerman. *Spark*. New York: Little, Brown and Company, 2008.

Rettew, D., and K. Reivich. "Sports and Explanatory Style." In *Explanatory Style*. Edited by G. M. Buchanan and M. E. P. Seligman. Hillsdale, NJ: Lawrence Erlbaum, 1995, 173–86.

Rinaldi, Christina M., and Nina Howe. "Perceptions of Constructive and Destructive Conflict within and across Family Subsystems." *Infant and Child Development* 12 (2003): 441–89.

Riscn, Clay. "Quitting Can Be Good for You." *New York Times* (December 19, 2007).

Robins, C. J., and A. M. Hayes. "The Role of Causal Attributions in the Prediction of Depression." In *Explanatory Style*. Edited by G. M. Buchanan and M. E. P. Seligman. Hillsdale, NJ: Lawrence Erlbaum, 1995, 71–98.

Robinson, John P., and Steven Martin. "What Do Happy People Do?" *Social Indicators Research* 89 (2008): 565–71.

Rose, P., and S. P. DeJesus. "A Model of Motivated Cognition to Account for the Link between Self-Monitoring and Materialism." *Psychology & Marketing* 24, no. 2 (2007): 23.

Ross, W. T., and I. Simonson. "Evaluation of Pairs of Experiences: A Preferred Happy Ending." *Journal of Behavioral Decision Making* 4 (1991): 273–82.

Rozin, P., and T. A. Vollmecke. "Food Likes and Dislikes." *Annual Review of Nutrition* 6 (1986): 433–56.

Rubin, K. H. "Fantasy Play: Its Role in the Development of Social Skills and Social Cognition." *New Directions for Child Development* 9 (1980): 16.

Rubin, K. H., W. Bukowski, et al. *Peer Interactions, Relationships, and Groups. Handbook of Child Psychology*. 5th ed., Vol. 3: *Social, Emotional, and Personality Development*. Edited by W. Damon. New York: John Wiley & Sons, 1998.

Rutter, M. "Psychosocial Resilience and Protective Mechanisms." *American Journal of Orthopsychiatry* 57 (1987): 316–31.

Ryan, R. M., and E. L. Deci. "When Rewards Compete with Nature: The Undermining of Intrinsic Motivation and Self-Regulation." In *Intrinsic and Extrinsic Motivation: The Search for Optimal Motivation and Performance*. Edited by C. Sansone and J. Jarackiewicz. New York: Academic Press, 2000, 13–54.

Satter, Ellyn. "Feeding Dynamics: Helping Children to Eat Well." *Journal of Pediatric Health Care* 9 (1995): 178–84.

————. "The Feeding Relationship." *Zero to Three Journal* 12, no. 5 (1992): 1–9.

Sayer, Liana C., Suzanne M. Bianchi, and John P. Robinson. "Are Parents Investing Less in Children? Trends in Mothers' and Fathers' Time with Children." *American Journal of Sociology* 110, no. 1 (2004): 1–43.

————. "On the Power of Positive Thinking: The Benefits of Being Optimistic." *Current Directions in Psychological Science* 2, no. 1 (1993): 26–30.

Scheier, M. F., and C. S. Carver. "Effects of Optimism on Psychological and Physical Well-Being: Theoretical Overview and Empirical Update." *Cognitive Therapy and Research* 16, no. 2 (1992): 201–28.

Scheier, M. F., C. S. Carver, and M. W. Bridges. "Distinguishing Optimism from Neuroticism (and Trait Anxiety, Self-Mastery, and Self-Esteem): A Re-Evaluation of the Life Orientation Test." *Journal of Personality and Social Psychology* 67, no. 6 (1994): 1063–78.

Scherwitz, Larry, Robert McKelvain, Carol Laman, John Patterson, Laverne Dutton, Solomon Yusim, Jerry Lester, Irvin Kraft, Donald Rochelle, and Robert Leachman. "Type A Behavior, Self Involvement, and Coronary Atherosclerosis." *Psychosomatic Medicine* 45, no. 1 (1983): 47–57.

Schmitt, David P., Todd K. Shackelford, Joshua Duntley, William Tooke, David M. Buss, Maryanne L. Fisher, Marguerite Lavallee, and Paul Vasey. "Is There an Early-30s Peak in Female Sexual Desire? Cross-Sectional Evidence from the United States and Canada." *Canadian Journal of Human Sexuality* 11 (2002): 1–18.

Schoppe-Sullivan, Sarah, G. L. Brown, E. A. Cannon, S. C. Mangelsdorf, and M. Szewczyk Sokolowski. "Maternal Gatekeeping, Coparenting Quality, and Fathering Behavior in Families with Infants." *Journal of Family Psychology* 22, no. 3 (2008): 389–98.

Schor, Juliet. *Born to Buy: The Commercialized Child and the New Consumer Culture.* New York: Simon & Schuster, 2004.

Schulman, P. "Explanatory Style and Achievement in School and Work." In *Explanatory Style.* Edited by G. M. Buchanan and M. E. P. Seligman. Hillsdale, NJ: Lawrence Erlbaum, 1995, 159–71.

Schwartz, Barry. *The Paradox of Choice: Why More Is Less.* New York: HarperCollins Publishers Inc., 2004.

Schwartz, Carolyn E., Janice Bell Meisenhelder, Yunsheng Ma, and George Reed. "Altruistic Social Interest Behaviors Are Associated with Better Mental Health." *Psychosomatic Medicine* 65 (2003): 778–85.

Schwartz, Carolyn E., and Rabbi Meir Sendor. "Helping Others Helps Oneself: Response Shift Effects in Peer Support." *Social Science & Medicine* 48, no. 11 (1999): 1563–75.

Seligman, M. E. P., K. J. Reivich, L. H. Jaycox, and J. Gillham. *The Optimistic Child.* New York: Houghton Mifflin, 1995.

Seligman, Martin E. P. *Authentic Happiness: Using the New Positive Psychology to Realize Your Potential for Lasting Fulfillment.* New York: Simon & Schuster, 2002.

Seligman, Martin E. P., Tracy A. Steen, Nansook Park, and Christopher Peterson. "Positive Psychology Progress: Empirical Validation of Interventions." *American Psychologist* 60, no. 5 (2005): 410–21.

Shapiro, Alyson, John Gottman, and Sybil Carrere. "The Baby and the Marriage: Identifying Factors That Buffer against Decline in Marital Satisfaction after the First Baby Arrives." *Journal of Family Psychology* 14, no. 1 (2000): 59–70.

Shapiro, S. L., G. E. Schwartz, and G. Bonner. "Effects of Mindfulness-Based Stress Reduction on Medical and Premedical Students." *Journal of Behavioral Medicine* 21, no. 6 (1998): 19.

Sheldon, K. M., and S. Lyubomirsky. "Achieving Sustainable Gains in Happiness: Change Your Actions, Not Your Circumstances." *Journal of Happiness Studies* 7 (2006): 55–86.

Shelton, K. H., and G. T. Harold. "Marital Conflict and Children's Adjustment: The Mediating and Moderating Role of Children's Coping Strategies." *Social Development* 16, no. 3 (2007): 497–512.

Shonkoff, J. P., and D. Phillips. *From Neurons to Neighborhoods: The Science of Early Child Development.* Washington, DC: National Academy Press, 2000.

Shultz, T. R., and M. R. Lepper. "Cognitive Dissonance Reduction as Constraint Satisfaction." *Psychological Review* 103, no. 2 (1996): 219–40.

Siegel, D. J. *The Mindful Brain: Reflection and Attunement in the Cultivation of Well-Being.* New York: W. W. Norton & Co., 2007.

Singh, N. N., G. E. Lanconi, A. S. W. Winton, J. Singh, W. J. Curtis, R. G. Wahler, and K. M. McAleavey. "Mindful Parenting Decreases Aggression and Increases Social Behavior in Children with Developmental Disabilities." *Behavior Modification* 31, no. 6 (2007): 23.

Smirnova, E. O. "Development of Will and Intentionality in Toddlers and Preschool-Aged Children." *Modek* (1998).

Smirnova, E. O., and O. V. Gudareva. "Igra I Proizvol'nost' U Sovremennyh Doshkol'nikov" [Play and Intentionality in Today's Preschoolers]. *Voprosy psihologii* 1 (2004): 91–103.

Smith, J. "Playing the Blame Game." *Greater Good* 4, no. 4 (2008): 24–27.

Squires, Sally. "To Eat Better, Eat Together." *Washington Post*, 2005.

Sroufe, L. A., N. E. Fox, and V. R. Pancake. "Attachment and Dependency in Developmental Perspective." *Child Development* 54, no. 6 (1983): 1615–27.

Stipek, D., R. Feiler, D. Daniels, and S. Milburn. "Effects of Different Instructional Approaches on Young Children's Achievement and Motivation." *Child Development* 66 (1995): 15.

Strack, Fritz, Leonard L. Martin, and S. Stepper. "Inhibiting and Facilitating Conditions of the Human Smile: A Nonobtrusive Test of the Facial Feedback Hypothesis." *Sabine Journal of Personality and Social Psychology* 54, no. 5 (1988): 768–77.

Strasburger, V. C. "Children and TV Advertising: Nowhere to Run, Nowhere to Hide." *Journal of Developmental and Behavioral Pediatrics* 22, no. 3 (2001): 185–87.

Stumphauzer, J. S. "Increased Delay of Gratification in Young Prison Inmates through Imitation of High-Delay Peer Models." *Journal of Personality and Social Psychology* 21, no. 1 (1972): 10–17.

Suda, M., K. Morimoto, A. Obata, H. Koizumi, and A. Maki. "Emotional Responses to Music: Towards Scientific Perspectives on Music Therapy." *Neuroreport: For Rapid Communication of Neuroscience Research* 19, no. 1 (2008): 75–78.

Sullivan, Oriel, and Scott Coltrane. "Men's Changing Contribution to Housework and Child Care: A Discussion Paper on Changing Family Roles." In *11th Annual Conference of the Council on Contemporary Families.* Chicago: University of Illinois, 2008.

Summit, N. J. "Family Dinner Linked to Better Grades for Teens: Survey Finds Regular Meal Time Yields Additional Benefits." In *ABC News,* 2005.

Suomi, Stephen J., and Harry F. Harlow. "Social Rehabilitation of Isolate-Reared Monkeys." *Developmental Psychology* 6, no. 3 (1972): 487–96.

Surakka, V., and J. K. Hietanen. "Facial and Emotional Reactions to Duchenne and Non-Duchenne Smiles." *International Journal of Psychophysiology* 29 (1998): 23–33.

Szente, J. "Empowering Young Children for Success in School and in Life." *Early Childhood Education Journal* 34, no. 6 (2007): 5.

Tavecchio, Louis W. C., and M. H. van Ijendoorn. *Attachment in Social Networks: Contributions to the Bowlby-Ainsworth Attachment Theory.* New York: Elsevier Science Publishers B.V., 1987.

Teague, R. J. P. "Social Functioning in Preschool Children: Can Social Information Processing and Self-Regulation Skills Explain Sex Differences and Play a Role in Preventing Ongoing Problems?" Brisbane, Australia, Griffith University, 2005.

Tickle-Degnen, Linda, and Robert Rosenthal. "The Nature of Rapport and Its Nonverbal Correlates." *Psychological Inquiry* 1, no. 4 (1990): 324–29.

Tkach, C., and S. Lyubomirsky. "How Do People Pursue Happiness?: Relating Personality, Happiness-Increasing Strategies, and Well-Being." *Journal of Happiness Studies* 7, (2006): 183–225.

Tronick, E. Z., S. Winn, and G. A. Morelli. "Multiple Caretaking in the Context of Human Evolution: Why Don't the Efe Know the Western Prescription to Child Care?" In *The Psychobiology of Attachment and Separation.* Edited by M. Reite and T. Field. New York: Academic Press, 1985, 293–321.

Trope, Y., and A. Fishbach. "Counteractive Self-Control in Overcoming Temptation." *Journal of Personality and Social Psychology* 79, no. 4 (2000): 493–506.

Troy, M., and L. A. Sroufe. "Victimization among Preschoolers: Role of Attachment Relationship History." *Journal of American Academy of Child and Adolescent Psychiatry* 26, no. 2 (1987): 166–72.

Tugade, M. M., and B. L. Fredrickson. "Regulation of Positive Emotions: Emotion Regulation Strategies That Promote Resilience." *Journal of Happiness Studies* 8 (2007): 23.

Twenge, Jean M., Liqing Zhang, and Charles Im. "It's Beyond My Control: A Cross-Temporal Meta-Analysis of Increasing Externality in Locus of Control, 1960–2002." *Personality and Social Psychology Review* 8, no. 3 (2004): 308–19.

Uren, N., and K. Stagnitti. "Pretend Play, Social Competence and Involvement in Children Aged 5–7 Years: The Concurrent Validity of the Child-Initiated Pretend Play Assessment." *Australian Occupational Therapy Journal* 56, no. 1 (2009).

Van der Voort, T. H. A. *Television Violence: A Child's-Eye View.* New York: Elsevier, 1986.

Vanderwater, E. Beickham, and D. Lee. "Time Well Spent? Relating Television Use to Children's Free-Time Activities." *Pediatrics* 117, no. 2 (2008): 181–91.

Van Ijendoorn, M. H., A. Sagi, and M. W. E. Lambermon. "The Multiple Caretaker Paradox: Data from Holland and Israel." *New Directions for Child and Adolescent Development* 57 (1992): 5–24.

Wallerstein, Judith S. *The Unexpected Legacy of Divorce: The 25 Year Landmark Study.* New York: Hyperion, 2001.

Warneken, Felix, and Michael Tomasello. "Extrinsic Rewards Undermine Altruistic Tendencies in 20-Month-Olds." *Developmental Psychology* 44, no. 6 (2008): 1785–88.

Warringham, Warren. "Measuring Personal Qualities in Admissions: The Context and the Purpose." *New Directions for Testing and Measurement* 17 (1983): 45–54.

Weber, Rene, Ute Ritterfeld, and Klaus Mathiak. "Does Playing Violent Video Games Induce Aggression? Empirical Evidence of a Functional Magnetic Resonance Imaging Study." *Media Psychology* 8, no. 1 (2006): 39–60.

Weinstein, M. *The Surprising Power of Family Meals: How Eating Together Makes Us Smarter, Stronger, Healthier, and Happier.* Hanover, NH: Steerforth Press, 2005.

Weizman, Zahava O., and Catherine E. Snow. "Lexical Input as Related to Children's Vocabulary Acquisition: Effect of Sophisticated Exposure and Support for Meaning." *Developmental Psychology* 37, no. 2 (2001): 265–79.

Whalen, S. P. "Flow and the Engagement of Talent: Implications for Secondary Schooling." *NASSP Bulletin* 82, no. 595 (1998): 16.

Wilson, J. B., D. T. Ellwood, and J. Brooks-Gunn. "Welfare-to-Work through the Eyes of Children." In *Escape from Poverty.* Edited by P. L. Chase-Lansdale and J. Brooks-Gunn. New York: Cambridge University Press, 1995.

Wink, Paul, and Michele Dilon. "Religiousness, Spirituality, and Psychological Functioning in Late Adulthood: Findings from a Longitudinal Study." *Psychology of Religion and Spirituality* 5, no. 1 (2008): 916–24.

Wirtz, Petra H., Sigrid Elssenbruch, Luljeta Emini, Katharina Rudisuli, Sara Groessbauer, and Ulrike Ehlert. "Perfectionism and the Cortical Response to Psychosocial Stress in Men." *Psychosomatic Medicine* 69 (2007): 249–55.

Witvliet, C. V. O., T. E. Ludwig, and K. L. Vander Laan. "Granting Forgiveness or Harboring Grudges: Implications for Emotion, Physiology, and Health." *Psychological Science* 12, no. 2 (2001): 117–23.

Wood, W., L. Tam, and M. G. Witt. "Changing Circumstances, Disrupting Habits." *Journal of Personality and Social Psychology* 88, no. 6 (2005): 16.

Worthington, Everett L. "The New Science of Forgiveness." *Greater Good* (2004): 6–9.

Wulfert, Edelgard, Steven A. Safren, Irving Brown, and Choi K. Wan. "Cognitive, Behavioral, and Personality Correlates of HIV-Positive Persons' Unsafe Sexual Behavior." *Journal of Applied Social Psychology* 29, no. 2 (1999): 223–44.

Yarrow, Marian Radke, Phyllis M. Scott, and Carolyn Zahn Waxler. "Learning Concern for Others." *Developmental Psychology* 8, no. 2 (1973): 240–60.

Zimmerman, F. J., D. A. Christakis, and A. N. Meltzoff. "Television and DVD/Video Viewing in Children Younger Than 2 Years." *Archives of Pediatrics & Adolescent Medicine* 161, no. 5 (2007): 473–79.

Zimmerman, Rachel. "Researchers Target Toll Kids Take on Parents' Sex Lives." *Wall Street Journal* (April 24, 2007).

# INDEX

■ ■ ■ ■ ■ ■

CHRISTINE CARTER, PH.D., is a sociologist and happiness expert at UC-Berkeley's Greater Good Science Center, an interdisciplinary research center that "translates" the study of happiness, resilience, and emotional intelligence for the public. Best known for her science-based parenting advice, Dr. Carter blogs regularly for Greater Good, The Huffington Post, and Psychology Today. Her favorite work is teaching her online parenting class, which she does for a global audience.

Carter has been quoted in dozens of national online and print publications, including the magazines *Working Mother*, *American Baby*, *Parents*, and *Parenting*, and *The Boston Globe* and *The New York Times*. She has appeared on *The Oprah Winfrey Show*, the *Rachael Ray* morning show, and NPR. Carter speaks regularly to parents, grandparents, and teachers; she has been a keynote speaker at Harvard and numerous other schools and professional groups. She has two children and lives with her family near San Francisco.

## ABOUT THE TYPE

This book was set in Fairfield, the first typeface from the hand of the distinguished American artist and engraver Rudolph Ruzicka (1883–1978). In its structure Fairfield displays the sober and sane qualities of the master craftsman whose talent has long been dedicated to clarity. It is this trait that accounts for the trim grace and vigor, the spirited design and sensitive balance, of this original typeface.

Rudolph Ruzicka was born in Bohemia and came to America in 1894. He set up his own shop, devoted to wood engraving and printing, in New York in 1913 after a varied career working as a wood engraver, in photoengraving and banknote printing plants, and as an art director and freelance artist. He designed and illustrated many books, and was the creator of a considerable list of individual prints—wood engravings, line engravings on copper, and aquatints.